Congo Solo

Congo Solo
Misadventures Two Degrees North

E M I L Y   H A H N

Edited and with an Introduction
by Ken Cuthbértson
Foreword by Anneke Van Woudenberg

McGill-Queen's University Press   Montreal & Kingston • London • Ithaca

© McGill-Queen's University Press 2011

ISBN 978-0-7735-3904-4

Legal deposit third quarter 2011
Bibliothèque nationale du Québec

Printed in Canada on acid-free paper that is 100% ancient forest free
(100% post-consumer recycled), processed chlorine free

McGill-Queen's University Press acknowledges the support of the Canada Council
for the Arts for our publishing program. We also acknowledge the financial support
of the Government of Canada through the Canada Book Fund for our publishing
activities.

Unless otherwise indicated, all photos are published courtesy of the Hahn Estate.

Library and Archives Canada Cataloguing in Publication

Hahn, Emily, 1905–1997
Congo solo : misadventures two degrees north / Emily Hahn ; edited and with
an introduction by Ken Cuthbertson.

Includes bibliographical references.
ISBN 978-0-7735-3904-4

1. Hahn, Emily, 1905–1997—Travel—Congo (Democratic Republic).
2. Congo (Democratic Republic)—Description and travel. 3. Congo
(Democratic Republic)—Social life and customs. 4. Congo, Belgian.
5. Women travelers—United States—Biography. 6. Authors, American—
20th century—Biography. I. Cuthbertson, Ken II. Title.

PS3515.A2422Z465 2011   967.51'024092   C2011-901881-0

Designed and typeset by studio oneonone in Janson 10/14

CONTENTS

FOREWORD

When I first read *Congo Solo*, I knew I had met a kindred spirit in Emily Hahn, its author. Here was a woman who, like me, had gone to Congo for escape and adventure but left deeply changed by what she experienced. Hahn jumped out from the pages as gutsy, adventurous, and impulsive, with a "devil-may-care" attitude. She was interested in the Congolese people, got to know them, and heard their stories. The injustices the Congolese people suffered, so evident to Hahn in 1931, touched her. Through her curiosity, her eyes were opened. She witnessed the cruelty firsthand and began to question those responsible. I liked her.

Hahn's adventure in the Belgian Congo began in a way surprisingly similar to my own. I have worked in the Democratic Republic of Congo, as it is called today, for twelve years: first for Oxfam Great Britain and currently for Human Rights Watch. It seemed Hahn and I had both gone to Congo for all the wrong reasons. On a whim, Hahn set out for Congo in 1931 seeking adventure, following a romantic notion, and looking to escape the drudgery of the Great Depression. Some sixty-eight years later, I too set out for Congo on a whim. When I complained of being miserable in my job in the financial industry in London, a close friend dared me to take a humanitarian job in war-torn Congo. Rarely one to turn down a dare, following a fight with my boyfriend I decided a Congo adventure was just what I needed. In the summer of 1999, I packed my bags, said my good-byes, and thought little about what I might encounter.

Like Hahn, I arrived in Congo to be met with the intimidating, and in hindsight amusing, arrivals ritual. Recognizing that I was new to the country, a Congolese immigration official immediately took me aside, methodically examined my documents, and then proceeded to explain, in a very authoritative manner, that they were not in order. I was told I would need to apply for the "correct" visa if I wished to leave the airport that evening. And, of course, the "correct" visa would cost more money. I was amused to learn that in 1931 Hahn had encountered a similar routine when she arrived by boat at the port town of Boma. It seems the attempt to scam money off unsuspecting foreigners has a long history. In each of our cases, we were saved by the kindness of a stranger and entered the country with a huge sigh of relief.

In *Congo Solo*, Hahn describes her marvelous adventure crossing the country. The journey is an extraordinary feat, especially for a single woman in the 1930s. Her descriptions of what she encounters make for fascinating reading. She vividly details her journey from the port of Boma to Kinshasa in the west, then on to Penge in the north-east by rail, boat, car, and pirogue (a wooden dug-out canoe) to reach the village where her humanitarian friend is managing a Red Cross medical centre. Months later she continues her journey, trekking on foot further eastward through the Ituri forest and over the green hills of what is today North Kivu province to reach east Africa.

Reading it, I was envious of her journey. How I wish it was possible to do a similar trek. But that is one of the stark differences in the Congo that Hahn describes and the Congo of today. In the years that have passed between Hahn's arrival and my own, the Congo has regressed rather than progressed. Congo is now less developed than it was in the 1930s. Most of the trains and boats no longer run, the roads are dilapidated and often impassible, and the countryside is overrun by dozens of marauding armed groups who prey on civilians.

Hahn's journey, difficult as it was at the time, would be nearly impossible today.

There has been regression in other important areas as well, most notably in the daily lives of Congolese civilians. Hahn describes the suffering she witnessed in the 1930s, including mass forced labor and the starvation that followed. Hahn's description of how thousands of Congolese were forced to construct roads by the Belgian colonial authorities shows she was far from blind to the horrors the policy caused.

In her own way, Hahn tells the story of these earlier times. It is not a book about these abuses – she was not a human rights activist but a literary travel writer – but the absurdity and abusive nature of the colonial authorities is blindingly apparent. Hahn is genuinely open to getting to know Congolese people and, when she does, she becomes increasingly aware of the cruelty and unfair treatment they suffer. What she witnessed made her question her own preconceptions about Africans and about her fellow whites. Her anger at the abuse, and her courage to begin to take steps against it, is an important part of her experience in Congo. It also places her firmly in the tradition of other eminent literary travelers who bore witness to the sufferings of people in central Africa and beyond, such as Joseph Conrad, Graham Green, V.S. Naipaul, and André Gide.

Sadly, the suffering in Congo continues. Today Congo carries the tragic label of the site of the deadliest war in the world. An estimated five million people have died since 1998, some directly from the violence, many others due to hunger and the lack of medical care. Over 200,000 women and girls have been raped. The recent violence is at the hands of predatory Congolese and foreign rebel groups, armies from neighboring countries attracted by Congo's vast mineral wealth, and the country's own soldiers, who prey on civilians rather than defending them. But, as we see from Hahn's writing and that of others, this story of tragedy is not new. Congo has suffered horribly throughout its history at the hands of foreigners and its own officials. Powerful outside interests have often been directly to blame but the victims are always the same: ordinary Congolese people.

In early 2010 I was in Tapili, a village in north-eastern Congo not far from Penge, where Hahn was based for eight months. I was following up on reports about a massacre by the Lord's Resistance Army (LRA), a Ugandan rebel group based in northern Congo who are notorious for their brutal killings and abduction of children. A colleague and I had been dropped off by a small plane on a nearby dirt airstrip, the only way to cover significant distances these days. From there we took motorcycles to reach the affected area, crossing makeshift log bridges and following a path that in colonial days had been a road. We found devastation and a population traumatized by what had happened. In the days that followed, we documented how the LRA had killed more than 321 civilians and abducted more than 250 others in a well-planned four-day attack. The vast majority of those killed were adult men, who were tied up before LRA combatants hacked them to death with machetes or crushed their skulls with heavy wooden sticks.

This incident is only one of the recent attacks in which Congolese people have suffered at the hands of brutal armed groups. I mention it because the victims of this massacre were from the Mangbetu tribe, the same ethnic group amongst whom Hahn lived for eight months in 1931. She describes the Mangbetu in detail in *Congo Solo*, marveling at their elongated heads and decorative facial scars. She also describes their suffering.

For me, the visit to Tapili and the surrounding area was the first time I had met the Mangbetu people. Like Hahn, I too stared at their beautiful and striking elongated heads (formed after birth when a baby's head is wrapped in cloth to mold it into a conical shape). I was also deeply struck by their suffering. One afternoon, I sat across from an elderly Mangbetu chief as he described in detail how the LRA had killed his son and abducted his grandchildren while he watched helplessly. He was stunned that his government and the international community had not heard about the events or come to help his people. "We have been forgotten. It's as if we don't exist." he said to me as tears streamed down his scarred cheeks. "I beg of you, please talk to others about what has happened to us."

We have done that, and, in her own way, Hahn did too. That is why, for me, this uncensored version of *Congo Solo* is so precious. Not only does it tell the tale of a gutsy young woman who travels across central Africa but it is also a story about the Congolese people she encounters and what they have suffered. From the pages of her book, we can see that Congo changed Hahn, as Congo changed me.

Anneke Van Woudenberg
Berkeley, California
April 2011

INTRODUCTION

You hold in your hands a new edition of Emily Hahn's long-lost 1933 travel narrative *Congo Solo*. This remarkable book, published here for the first time as Hahn wanted, is the work of a writer with insatiable curiosity and an unbridled passion for life. Not only is it a lost treasure of women's travel literature, it is one of the most compelling eyewitness accounts we have about the harsh realities of everyday life in colonial Africa.

Congo Solo could – and arguably should – have been as celebrated and popular a book as *Out of Africa*, the 1937 classic bestseller by Baroness Karen Dinesen Blixen, a.k.a. Isak Dinesen. Hahn's book would certainly have been far more widely read and influential than it was had it not been published in an censured version at the nadir of the Great Depression. In the world of letters, as in life, timing is everything.

For the past seventy-seven years *Congo Solo* has been all but unavailable, except as rare copies of the original to be found in libraries and used book shops – where it sells for as much as two hundred dollars – or in bootleg e-book editions posted on the Internet. This is unfortunate, for Emily Hahn's account of her "misadventures two degrees north" is a revealing, insightful read for armchair travelers and scholars alike. It also offers invaluable insights into the history of a land that suffered horribly under the rule of one of colonial Africa's most ruthless administrations. Hahn reminds us of the roots of this turmoil and suffering, the end of which is nowhere in sight even today.

The Congo, so quintessentially African, is a land rich in natural resources. This has been both a blessing and its curse. The developed world's insatiable hunger for gold, diamonds, and now for a precious mineral known as coltan – the source of tantalum, a vital element in the electronic circuitry of cell phones and similar devices – has sent commodity prices soaring. This trend can only continue at a time when the emerging economies of China, India, and other develop- ing nations with voracious appetites for raw materials drive the markets. "It is the temptations of this wealth – more than ethnic rival- ries, the legacy of colonialism, or anything else – that has turned Congo into the horrific battleground it has been in recent years," American journalist Adam Hochschild has written[1] about the world's largest failed state, one ruled by the gun. Murder, mass rape, and intimidation are the stock-and-trade of the soldiers of the warlord armies that now rule the Democratic Republic of Congo, as it is now known.[2] The echoes of the Congo's tortured colonial past reverberate to this day. Fear, suffering, and exploitation are the realities of every- day life for the sixty-three million residents of Africa's third largest country.

This new edition of *Congo Solo* is a literary time capsule packed with first-hand observations and insights and as such it helps explain how and why this came to be. Here at long last is the book that Hahn wanted the world to read. Reconstructing it was a time-consuming and at times frustrating task, which has been accomplished by recon- ciling the original edition of *Congo Solo* with Hahn's later writings, her letters home from Africa, information she provided in interviews I did

1 Hochschild, Adam, "Rape of the Congo," *The New York Review of Books*, August 13, 2009.
2 Belgium granted the Congo its independence in 1960. The country was re- named Zaire in 1971 following a military coup led by Joseph Mobutu; he in turn was ousted in May 1997 by the army of Laurent Kabila. Kabila changed the name of the country to Democratic Republic of the Congo.

with her while I was writing my 1998 Hahn biography, *Nobody Said Not to Go*, and details gleaned from other sources. The end product of these efforts is a restored version of *Congo Solo* as it read originally, before the enforced 1933 revisions that created puzzling gaps in the narrative and gutted it of its thematic soul.

This work of non-fiction, in quasi-diary format, reads like a well-written novel. It is the creation of a remarkable woman who dared to live life on her own terms – to deliberately tread what she called "the uncertain paths in life."

Emily Hahn was one of the most peripatetic, unconventional, and prolific American writers of the twentieth century. She was the author of fifty-three books and hundreds of articles, essays, short stories, and poems. At least three of her books are still in print, and most of the others can be found in university libraries. Yet surprisingly few readers are familiar with Hahn's literary legacy. The sheer range of her interests was as much a handicap as her gender. The British writer Rebecca West, Hahn's friend and mentor, put her finger on it when she lamented that if she and Hahn had been born male, they would have enjoyed "a far higher reputation."[3]

Hahn lived life on her own terms and had a flair for the dramatic. Never was that more apparent than on that cold day in December 1929 when she quit her job, threw her meagre belongings into a suitcase, and headed off for the Belgian Congo in search of adventure. As a twenty-four-year-old single woman and a fledgling writer, with the world slipping ever deeper into the economic morass that became the Great Depression, she felt she had many reasons to go, few to stay.

In the wake of a failed romance and broken engagement, Hahn's emotions were as spent as her bank account. She was among the millions of ordinary people whose lives were changed forever by the events of 29 October 1929, the infamous "Black Tuesday" when the giddy prosperity of a roaring decade fueled by excess and greed came

---

3 Ken Cuthbertson, *Nobody Said Not to Go: The Life, Loves, and Adventures of Emily Hahn* (New York: Faber and Faber, 1998), 1.

to an abrupt, inglorious end. Many of those whose dreams were shattered and who saw their life savings wiped out had no idea what had hit them. "I hardly knew anything about the great crash on Wall Street," Hahn would recall, "and if I hadn't been told the connection later, I would never have known that it caused the scarcity of jobs that gave me and my friends so much leisure. Stock market panics happened to the sort of people I had no contact with."[4]

When Hahn reached Africa she spent eight months living and working at a Croix Rouge medical-aid station in the Belgian Congo. The fact that she had dared to travel there on her own was in itself astounding – so much so that her six-hundred-kilometre hike through the wilds of East Africa on the way home seems almost an afterthought.

By the time Hahn returned to New York in early 1933 the world's economic woes had deepened. The lines of hungry, desperate people outside soup kitchens in cities across North America were growing ever longer. In the United States, more than eleven million workers were unemployed. However, Hahn managed to find a job to tide her over until she could finish work on the book that she hoped would secure her literary reputation. There was no question she had an extraordinary tale to tell.

Her African adventure had been a wild, improbable affair, almost too incredible to be believed. Hahn proceeded to recount her experiences in a way that was so frank, so uninhibited, that it unnerved some readers, particularly men. At the time, respectable ladies were not supposed to have "attitude," but Emily Hahn did. And she revelled in it. Like her writer friends Rebecca West and Dorothy Parker, Hahn was a feminist – even if she shunned the label – before the word ever entered the popular lexicon. This was just one of the distinguishing characteristics that set her apart and made her writing as distinctive as her personality. At the same time, it caused her no end of grief. That was certainly the case in 1933.

4 Emily Hahn, *Times and Places* (New York: Thomas Y. Crowell, 1970), 113.

Under pressure from her publisher and from the family of the man who had been her host in Africa, she was forced to expurgate her manuscript for legal reasons and in the name of propriety. Clumsy editing by her publisher did not help. The adulterated version of *Congo Solo* that appeared in June 1933 was not the book that Hahn wanted to write, nor was it the book she *had written*. But, desperate for the advance money her publisher had promised and impatient to make her name as a writer, she knuckled under. Such practicality came naturally to Hahn.

Born January 14, 1905, in St. Louis, Missouri, she was the sixth of the seven children of Isaac and Hannah (*née* Schoen) Hahn. From an early age, Emily was encouraged to think and to do things for herself. Her father, a hardware salesman by vocation, was a sceptic by avocation. He was also an atheist who, with an almost messianic zeal, would read aloud passages of the scriptures to his children while pointing out the illogic and inconsistencies.

Hahn's mother, a free-spirited suffragette, wore bloomers while riding her bicycle and dared to work outside the home even *after* she got married. It was Hannah Hahn who nicknamed her daughter "Mickey" owing to the girl's facial resemblance to a popular cartoon strip character of the day: a gregarious Irish saloonkeeper named Mickey Dooley. The Hahns were of German-Jewish heritage with nary a drop of Irish blood in their veins but Emily Hahn was a tomboy to whom the matey moniker stuck.

Reading, writing, music, and the arts were central to life in the Hahn household, and Mickey Hahn and her siblings grew up with a love of words and books. Writing became Hahn's emotional outlet, whether in the form of letters, poems, or the journal she began keeping soon after her family's 1920 move to Chicago. It was a natural progression when Hahn announced two years later that she intended to study English literature at the University of Wisconsin. She would have done so, too, had she not changed her plans abruptly on the day a male professor advised her that the female mind was "incapable of grasping mechanics or higher mathematics." Intent on proving him wrong, Hahn took up the challenge. Successfully. In the spring of 1926 she became the first woman to graduate from the university's mining engineering program.

Hahn defied the odds once again when she found a job in the oil industry. However, no amount of bluster or bravado could overcome the systemic misogyny she encountered, and so she quit in disgust. She never forgot the exact moment she resolved to do so. It was the evening of May 22, 1927, the day after Charles Lindbergh became the first person to fly solo across the Atlantic. Inspired by the aviator's daredevil exploits, Hahn swore that never again would she be "ordinary."

Much to the dismay of her family, she followed through on that vow, taking a summer job as a horseback trail guide in New Mexico. However, patience not being one of Hahn's virtues, the novelty of escorting tourists on wilderness outings soon waned. Next she settled into a life of solitude, taking up residence in an adobe hut in the desert near the art colony of Taos and scratching out a living as a writer of greeting card verses.

In the autumn of 1928 Hahn acceded to her parents' pleas to "make something of herself," enrolling in graduate studies in geology at Columbia University in New York. The strain of her return to big-city life was eased somewhat by the presence in the Big Apple of one of her sisters, Helen, whose husband was Herbert Asbury, a prominent newspaperman and the author of several best-selling books; among them *The Gangs of New York*, the inspiration for director Martin Scorsese's 2002 film of the same name. When Asbury began introducing his sister-in-law around town, she embraced the bohemian lifestyle, resolving to make her living as a writer.

The first articles for which Emily Hahn was paid appeared in the pages of *The New Yorker*, which at the time was emerging as America's pre-eminent literary magazine. Hahn's initial editorial contributions were versions of personal letters she had mailed home to Chicago. In them she offered her impressions on the vacuous lifestyle of the smart set who idled away the time in Manhattan's trendy cafés and night-

spots. Unbeknownst to Hahn, her brother-in-law removed the salu-
tations on her letters and sent them to *The New Yorker* as freelance
editorial submissions. Reading these pieces today is akin to perusing
an on-line blog. The articles are informal, witty, and mischievously
irreverent. They are also pregnant with literary promise. Harold Ross,
the magazine's legendary founding editor, was so delighted by what he
read that he summoned Hahn to his office. "Young woman, you've got
a great talent," he advised her. "You can be cattier than anyone I know,
except maybe Rebecca West. Keep it up!"[5]

For one of the few times in her life, Hahn did as she was told. And
in doing so, she emerged as one of the most enduring and prolific
talents among the stable of writers whose work graced the pages of
The New Yorker during its "golden era" and well beyond. Hahn wrote
for four *New Yorker* editors: her first by-lined article appeared in the
magazine in 1929, her last in 1996. At the beginning of this astounding sixty-seven-year run Hahn was more aspiring than accomplished
as a writer. She made ends meet by working as a telephone recep-
tionist and a part-time geology teacher, hardly the stuff of dreams for
a feisty young woman who had vowed never to be "ordinary." With
the global economic crisis deepening, Hahn's mood spiralled down-
ward until the day she took a near-fatal dose of sleeping pills. She later
blamed the incident on "a depressive gene" that she claimed to have
inherited from her father's side of the family.

That unhappy experience proved to be an epiphany of a sort. Out
of it Hahn gained fresh perspective and resolved to find new purpose
in life. What that might be, she had no idea. She chanced upon a
possibility one night at a party when she met Patrick Tracy Lowell
Putnam, a flamboyant twenty-six-year-old anthropologist and "gentleman scholar."

On his father's side, Putnam was descended from two of New
England's most illustrious families: the Putnams and the Lowells.
His father, Charles, was a prominent New York ear, nose, and throat

5 Ibid., 72.

surgeon, his mother, Angelica, a socialite. Patrick was the couple's only biological child (the Putnams adopted a half-dozen New York street waifs). According to Patrick Putnam's biographer, Joan Mark, it was said that all the members of the Putnam family were either "touched with genius or [were] a little mad."[6] That description certainly fit Patrick Putnam.

While he studied at Harvard and showed occasional flashes of charm and intellectual brilliance, he was too undisciplined to be a real scholar. He was spoiled, imperious, and self-indulgent to the point of being irresponsible. As a child, he had announced that his career goal was to be "King of the World." When Hahn met him, Putnam still had not claimed his crown, although he was intent on doing so.

His professors and classmates at Harvard certainly took note of his eccentricities. How could they *not*? Putnam's physical appearance – he was scarecrow lean with flaming red hair and beard – and his quirky behaviour made him hard to ignore. For instance, he ate ants and was sometimes seen devouring those he scooped up on the front steps of the Peabody Museum. At times his antics went beyond bizarre to foolhardy and dangerous. Joan Mark recounts one occasion when Putnam and a friend climbed out a sixth-floor window of the Peabody. Then, like gambolling squirrels, they chased each other around on a two-foot-wide sloped ledge, stopping from time-to-time to engage in a wrestling match.[7] Onlookers on the street below watched in horror as the bizarre scene played itself out.

Putnam's intellectual interests were no less dramatic. While earning a Bachelor of Arts degree in anthropology – just barely – he developed a fascination with equatorial Africa and its pygmy tribes. In the fall of 1927 he traveled to the Belgian Congo on a Harvard-sponsored academic expedition.[8] While hunting on the last day of the trip, he and his native guide were attacked by a bull elephant. Putnam

6 Joan Mark, *The King of the World in the Land of the Pygmies* (Lincoln: University of Nebraska Press, 1995), 23.
7 Ibid., 33.

was badly gored and during his ten-month convalescence, he was nursed back to health by a young local woman named Abanzima, the daughter of a Mangbetu village chief. "That was when the trouble started," Putnam later told Hahn. "If Abanzima had been white, we'd have got married. She could have come home with me ... I may marry her yet, but even so, I certainly won't be able to bring her home. I realize that now ... I've found that out by trying to talk over [the situation] sensibly with [my parents]."9

Putnam returned to New York just long enough to make arrangements for a return to the Congo, ostensibly to continue his anthropological field studies. To pay his way he signed on for a two-year stint at a Belgian Red Cross medical-aid clinic located near Abanzima's home village in the Ituri Forest, an area in the remote northeast corner of the colony. The agency, the Croix Rouge du Congo, employed American and European volunteers, giving them basic medical training before assigning them to its network of remote outposts.

In Hahn's mind, Putnam's love story had all the hallmarks of a grand romantic tragedy. "I saw Abanzima in my imagination – a combination of Undine and Madame Butterfly, wild and graceful, and prey to fears that I could hardly understand as she wondered if her alien lover would ever return," Hahn would write.10 When Putnam suggested that she visit him in the Congo and meet Abanzima, Hahn agreed. As crazy and improbable as such a trip may have sounded, it was exactly the kind of adventure she had been seeking. Like Putnam, Hahn was drawn to Africa. What is more, she delighted in the kind of impulsive behaviour that attracted attention and shocked people, and in her mind, a trip to the Belgian Congo was an attention-getter of the first rank. However, money was a problem.

8 In 1928 American journalist Grace Flandrau (1889–1971) traveled to the Belgian Congo, where she encountered Patrick Putnam. (For her account of that meeting, see Appendix 1.) The St. Paul, Minnesota, native wrote six books, four of which were turned into feature films. While she enjoyed a solid literary reputation in the 1920s, her writings are all but forgotten today.
9 Emily Hahn, "Stewart," *The New Yorker*, October 22, 1966, 207–10.
10 Ibid.

Patrick Putman's 1933 passport photo
Courtesy of the Houghton Library, Harvard University

Hahn got only as far as London on the first leg of her trip. She spent nine months there building up her bank account by working as a researcher at the British Museum. During this time, she rejoiced at the news that her first book had been published back home in the States. *Seductio Ad Absurdum: The Principles and Practice of Seduction, a Beginner's Handbook*[11] was a satirical look at gender relations. It was panned by the critics, mostly men who failed to see the humour in poking fun at the male ego.[12] Despite this, the appearance of Hahn's first book further whetted her appetite for literary fame. It also erased any lingering self-doubts that she really *could* succeed as a writer.

11 *Seductio Ad Absurdum: The Principles and Practice of Seduction, a Beginner's Handbook* (New York: Brewster and Warren, 1930).
12 One of the exceptions was an April 2, 1930, *Chicago Daily News* review of the book by poet Carl Sandburg, a Hahn family friend. Sandburg recommended *Seductio Ad Absurdum* "with no hesitations," concluding that "At first, we thought [Miss Hahn] was just one smart kid who enjoyed being smart, but she is a lot more than that."

Meanwhile, Putnam was busy taking his Croix Rouge basic medical training in Brussels. He took up his posting in the Congo in December 1930 and promptly recounted his impressions – likely at Hahn's urging – in the article "Report from the Field," published in the February 28, 1931, edition of *The New Yorker.*

Inspired by Putnam's resolve and by his success in finding such a ready store of exotic literary fodder, Hahn forged ahead with her own travel plans. Her family, ever dismayed by her footloose ways, were aghast when she announced her plan to save money by traveling to Africa on a third-class ticket aboard a French troop ship. At the time, no "respectable white woman" would have dared do such a thing. Even more alarming was the fact that in 1931 much of Africa was still uncharted wilderness. In the popular imagination, fired by images drawn from the pages of Edgar Rice Burroughs' popular *Tarzan* novels and from countless Hollywood films, Equatorial Africa was a primal land of fierce beasts, headhunting cannibals, hideous diseases, and dark, steamy jungles where death lurked at every turn.

Six European powers claimed sovereignty over areas of the African continent at the time: France, Germany, Great Britain, Italy, Portugal, and Belgium. The Belgian monarch, King Leopold II (who was not actually Belgian, but German), ruled the Congo with an iron fist, not in an official capacity but as his own personal fiefdom. His claim to "a slice of [the] magnificent African cake," cut out for him by the celebrated African explorer and mercenary Sir Henry Stanley, was for all intents and purposes sanctioned at a historic 1885 international conference in Berlin. Leopold had set up a private holding company to exploit the region's vast stores of natural resources – rubber, ivory, diamonds, copper, and gold – which had been discovered in 1903. The Congo Free State became history's largest and most opulent private domain.[13]

---

13 For the full story of King Leopold II's brutal plundering of the Congo, see American journalist Adam Hochschild's bestselling book *King Leopold's Ghost* (Boston: Houghton Mifflin Harcourt, 1998).

The atrocities that Leopold's henchmen committed in his name during a twenty-three-year reign of terror were among the most heinous in the long history of white exploitation of Africa: the people of the Belgian Congo fell victim to crimes against humanity that rank as being among the worst – and least known – in history. The carnage was on a mass scale. As many as ten million people were murdered, mutilated, raped, enslaved, or died from starvation because they were conscripted to work at forced labour rather than being allowed to grow and harvest crops. The colony's resource-based economy was almost entirely dependent on forced labour and local chiefs were compelled to supply men to work in the rubber and mining industries. Those who resisted were killed and had their villages burned. The abuse of the Congo's indigenous population was so brutal, so egregious, so unrestrained, that in 1908 Leopold was shamed into relinquishing his hold on the colony, which then came under the control of the Belgian government. The country's parliament appointed a governor general to oversee the administration of the colony's four provinces, each of which was divided into districts, each district was subdivided into territories, and each territory into chiefdoms, or *chef-feries*. While the worst of the atrocities now ceased, the new colonial administration continued using forced labour in the resource industries and to build infrastructure projects such as roads and railways.

The Congo remained largely undeveloped in the early 1930s and still faced daunting problems for which there were no solutions, even if there had been the will to look for answers. The colony's 9.5 million inhabitants belonged to more than two hundred tribes and spoke a bewildering polyglot of languages – at least thirty-eight, by one count. All of this underscored the reality that national boundaries were a European concept, one utterly foreign to Africa's tribal societies.

There were just seventeen thousand whites in the Belgian Congo at the time; nevertheless, colonial officials continued to maintain tight control over all aspects of life. It was assumed that any unmarried, unescorted white women who were brazen enough to travel there were prostitutes, and so the usual practice was so to deny them entry to the colony. At the same time, the dearth of white women prompted many of the European men stationed there – single and married alike – to take native mistresses.[14] Understandably, these harem-like relationships and the mixed-race children they produced caused no end of woe for all involved.[15]

When Hahn stepped off the ship at the port of Boma on January 19, 1931, after the three-week voyage from France, she gained entry to the colony only after considerable effort and intrigue. Once admitted, she hurriedly made her way inland to Matidi, as far up the Congo River as ocean-going vessels could travel. After that, for the next four hundred kilometres, rapids made the river impassable to anything but small boats and canoes.

Hahn's journey continued with a fourteen-hour train ride to Léopoldville (now known as Kinshasha). There in the wilting heat she awaited the arrival of a riverboat that would carry her on the one-week voyage upriver to Stanleyville (now Kisangani). Next it was on by truck to the town of Avakubi, before she completed the last leg of her trip in a native dugout canoe, a pirogue. Her ultimate destination was Putnam's medical-aid outpost, located at Penge, a dot on the map of the Ituri Forest.[16] Once there, with little money and nowhere else to go, she settled in. When a couple of packing crates containing a set of

14 The French called this arrangement a *ménagère*, a vague, rather derogatory term that described the harem-like situation when a white man in Africa lived with multiple local women, concubines who looked after his house, cooked his meals, and shared his bed.

15 An interesting footnote to Putnam's involvement with African women is that in 1960, when photos of Patrice Lumumba – the leader of the Congo's fight for independence from Belgium and the man who would become the new nation's first prime minister – appeared in western newspapers, some people who had known Putnam wondered if the facial similarities between Putnam and Lumumba were more than coincidence. There was speculation that Putnam was Lumumba's father. However, Putnam biographer Joan Mark concludes that was not the case. Her rationale was simple and irrefutable: Lumumba was born in 1925, two years before Putnam's first visit to the Belgian Congo.

16 The settlement had been a regional trading post and colonial administrative centre earlier in the century, but the Belgian authorities had abandoned it.

the *Encyclopaedia Britannica*, ordered by Putnam, arrived at his door, Hahn set about an ambitious program of self-education. "I've always preferred reading to work," she would later quip.[17]

Hahn lived at Penge for eight months, reading, writing, exploring, assisting Putnam in his work, and learning to speak Kingwana, a regional dialect of Swahili. She might well have stayed at Penge even longer if the extent of her host's eccentricities – or was it madness? – had not became so frighteningly evident.

Putnam's duties with the Croix Rouge included compiling census and health-care data and running a medical-aid clinic. He treated wounds, gave injections for various diseases such as yaws, leprosy, and syphilis, and even performed "textbook" surgeries for which he had no real training. Putnam did not take direction well, and he often delved into political issues. This proved problematic, for it routinely brought him into conflict with colonial officials. Like the Kurtz character in writer Joseph Conrad's 1902 classic novella, *Heart of Darkness*, the longer Putnam stayed in the Congo, the more unpredictable, domineering, and threatening his behaviour became. The would-be King of the World "went native," as Hahn would recall many years later. In addition to Abanzima, Putnam took a half-dozen other native wives and acted as a law unto himself. It was after a particularly shocking incident in November 1931, in which he beat and publicly humiliated Abanzima, that Hahn, in "a fit of white-hot anger," re-solved to leave Penge as soon as possible.

Inspired by an *Encyclopaedia Britannica* article on the travels of Alexandrine Tinné, an intrepid Dutch woman who had explored parts of East Africa in the 1860s,[18] Hahn left Penge on foot. Accompanied only by some local porters, she trekked the six hundred kilometres to

17 Sarah Anderson, "Obituary: Emily Hahn," *The Independent*, May 17, 1997.
18 Dutch-born Alexandrine Pieternella Françoise Tinné (1835–1869) explored the Congo region in the early 1860s as well as the area in which the headwaters of the Nile River originate. She was intent on becoming the first woman to walk across the Sahara Desert when in 1869 she was robbed and murdered by her guides.

Kigoma, a Tanzanian town on the shores of Lake Tanganyika. From there, she took the train to the Indian Ocean port of Dar es Salaam. It was an extraordinary feat for anyone to hike that far across East Africa – especially a young woman equipped only with her wits and a gritty determination to survive. For most people, an eight-month stay in the Congo and a great march across half of the African continent would have been *the* grand adventure of a lifetime; for Hahn it was just one more incident in a life that bubbled with remarkable, improbable, and extraordinary adventures.

Upon her return to New York in late 1932, she set about converting her diary into a book about her Congo adventures. The idea seemed like a good one. There was considerable interest in all things African at the time, and some well-known writers who had visited Equatorial Africa recently had reported on their experiences. Most notable among them was the French author-playwright André Gide, whose 1927 writings about the injustices of life in his own country's colonies influenced public opinion and helped spur changes in French colonial policies.[19] Not long afterward, American journalist Grace Flandrau visited the Belgian Congo with a group of academics and in 1930 wrote *Then I Saw the Congo*, a conventional travel narrative that enjoyed a brief popularity with readers. Both Gide and Flandrau, like so many of the European, British, and American writers who have written about the Congo, were mere visitors to the region. Hahn had actually *lived* there, and she was intent on relating her experiences and on writing a different kind of book. There is no real evidence that she had any intention of trying to change public attitudes toward Africa, as Gide had done, but it seems likely that that may have been what she had in mind. Regardless, her approach proved problematic.

19 André Gide (1869–1951) had traveled to Africa as a special envoy of the French colonial ministry in 1925–26 and wrote two books describing conditions in his country's African colonies. So influential were *Voyage au Congo* (1927) and *Retour du Tchad* (1927) that they swayed public opinion and helped bring about reforms in French colonial policies. The two books were published together in English as *Travels in the Congo* (1929).

Despite their differences when they parted, Putnam had assured Hahn she was free to write whatever she wanted – including the unsavoury details of his life at Penge. Nonetheless, Hahn's publisher was concerned about a possible libel suit, and so Hahn was compelled to obtain Putnam's written permission before her book could go to press. To expedite matters, Putnam sent a letter authorizing his parents in New York to act as his agents.

The Putnams were shocked when they read the *Congo Solo* manuscript, so much so that Charles Putnam insisted if the book was published as written, his life would no longer be worth living; he threatened to kill himself to escape the shame. His blood, he warned, would be on Hahn's hands. It is unclear if the elder Putnam's threat was real or hyperbole. What was certain is that the Putnams were ready to sue Hahn and her publisher.

In the face of this pressure and desperate for the promised advance from her publisher, Hahn agreed to make changes. She removed some of the revealing details in the manuscript and obscured both the younger Putnam's identity and the nature of his relationship with the African women who shared his house and his bed. Patrick Putnam became "Den Murray." Penge became "Sanga." And Hahn attributed some of Putnam's most shocking behaviour to a fictional "Englishman from South Africa." The result, as Joan Mark observed, "was a published book that was in places nearly incomprehensible."[20]

Nevertheless, *Congo Solo* still earned some favourable reviews. For example, Walter White of the National Association for the Advancement of Colored People wrote in the journal *Books* that "The uniqueness of Miss Hahn's book is in Miss Hahn herself. She went to Africa and saw Africans neither as funny, nor different people … Instead, she saw them as human beings, completely identified herself with them, entered into their lives and joys and sorrows and tribulations with the same understanding objectivity with which she might have written of her own friends in the United States."[21]

20 Mark, *The King of the World in the Land of the Pygmies*, 63.
21 *Books*, July 30, 1933, 12.

White's comments can only be described as naive. While Hahn was no racist, there can be no doubt – nor any denying – that she subscribed to many of the racial stereotypes of the day. However, like many white liberals at that time, she made a curious and specious distinction between American blacks and those who lived in Africa.

Some reviewers of *Congo Solo* were dismayed by Hahn's casual approach to her subject and by the fact that she did not fit the stereotypical image of the "lady traveller" or scholar. *New York Times* reviewer E.H. Walton chided her for having "attitude,"[22] while an anonymous critic for the journal *Forum* opined that *Congo Solo* was "slightly marred" by the author's "offhand pose" and her tendency to wisecrack.[23]

Despite the media attention and Hahn's breezy literary style, sales were disappointing. The fact the Great Depression was still tightening its grip on America helps explain why Hahn's next effort also sold poorly. Having failed to have her say in *Congo Solo*, she crafted a 1934 novel that also was based on her African experiences. *With Naked Foot* is an uncompromising look at the corrosive effects of white colonialism, sexism, racism, and miscegenation. Hahn always insisted this was her best work, even if the story and the subject matter made many readers uneasy. The comments of the reviewer for the *Boston Transcript* speak volumes about the prevailing attitudes of American, British, and European readers of the day. "One may seriously doubt whether any American or European can get successfully inside the heart of a woman such as Mawa [the novel's main female character]" the reviewer stated, "any more than they can portray the feelings of a dog."

Neither *Congo Solo* nor *With Naked Foot* was the literary breakthrough Hahn had hoped for. However, but she refused to dwell on her setbacks and soon departed on another improbable adventure, one that would last nine years and take her to the farthest corners of the globe – to breathtaking adventures in China, a struggle with opium

22 *New York Times Book Review*, 30 July 1933, 4.
23 *Forum*, November 1933.

addiction, a harrowing wartime ordeal in occupied Hong Kong, and a love affair that *Life* magazine described as "one of the best-publicized romances of [World War Two]."[24]

In late 1945 Hahn married the father of the daughter she had borne in Hong Kong on the eve of World War Two. Charles Boxer was an eccentric English army officer turned professor of Portuguese colonial history. After four years in a Japanese prisoner-of-war camp, he returned to England intent on pursuing an academic career and living at Conygar, the Boxer family's estate in southwest England. Hahn and Boxer were living there in October 1948 when they had a second child, another daughter whom they named Amanda. Despite this, Hahn concluded she was not cut out for an "ordinary" life of domestic tranquility, so in 1950 she returned to New York and a job as a staff writer at *The New Yorker*. Hahn and Boxer remained husband and wife, even when they settled into separate lives. Thereafter, Hahn divided her time between two continents. The Hahn-Boxer marriage, long-distance and unorthodox though it was, endured for more than a half century, until Hahn's death in 1997.

And what became of Patrick Putnam? Not surprisinglyPutnam's erratic behaviour lost him his job with the Belgian Red Cross not long after Hahn's departure from Penge. While he continued to cultivate a scholarly reputation, his research methodology was so haphazard that he never got around to writing his long-promised anthropological study of the pygmy tribes of the Belgian Congo. He claimed to have lost most of his field notes in a pirogue accident, the academic equivalent of "the dog ate my homework."

Putnam married three times, for he needed a woman in his life. His third and last wife, whom he wed in 1945, was Anne Eisner, an artist and writer from Newark, New Jersey. The couple spent much of the next eight years in the Belgian Congo, living in a remote spot on the Epulu River where they worked to establish an African "dude ranch"

24 *Life*, December 3, 1945, 40.

– another of Putnam's fanciful schemes. Putnam fell ill and died there on December 12, 1953. He was just forty-nine years of age.

While Putnam's mother had predeceased him, his father survived until April 1962. When Emily Hahn learned of the elder Putnam's death, being an inveterate recycler of her own writings, she considered restoring and republishing *Congo Solo*. However, busy with other projects, she contented herself with revising the book's pivotal chapter, which recounted the shocking incident that had spurred her to leave Penge. Out of deference to Anne Putnam, now terminally ill with cancer, Hahn renamed the Putnam character "Stewart Cass" and for some inexplicable reason Penge became "Tange." The essence of Hahn's true experiences in the Congo was now there, but the revised account, as published in the October 22, 1966, edition of *The New Yorker* under the title "Stewart," still failed to tell the whole story.

In subsequent years, Hahn continued her frenetic pace, writing sixteen more books, – including *Africa to Me: Person to Person*, an account of her return to Africa at a time when the white man's grip on the continent was finally slipping.[25] Another was *Times and Places*, a 1970 memoir made up of autobiographical articles she had written over the years for *The New Yorker*, among them the aforementioned "Stewart." Why did Hahn not revise her account of her Congo adventures then? The answer to that question is that she had other and more pressing priorities; her need for income to support her lifestyle was constant.

Time ran out for Hahn herself on February 18, 1997. She died in New York at the age of ninety-two. In the years before and after her death, many of her books have been reissued. Sadly, *Congo Solo* is not among them; it is obvious why: the edits and changes made to the original 1933 manuscript had left puzzling gaps and inconsistencies in the narrative. It is only now, with publication of this restored edition of *Congo Solo*, that the full story of Emily Hahn's African adventures is finally told. In *Congo Solo*, the author set out to share with readers what

25 Emily Hahn, *Africa to Me: Person to Person* (Garden City: Doubleday and Company, 1964).

she saw, thought, and experienced during her eight-month stay in the Ituri forest. What she left us is an unforgettable account of her (mis)adventures "two degrees north."

As with any project of this kind, it could not have been completed without the help of others. In particular, I would like to thank Emily Hahn's elder daughter and literary executrix, Carola Vecchio, New York, for her unstinting kindness, cooperation, and encouragement, and her sister, Amanda Boxer, who has provided her goodwill and unwavering support. In addition, I have received invaluable and timely help from my colleagues at the *Queen's Alumni Review* magazine at Queen's University in Kingston, ON. They include Editor *Emerita* Cathy Perkins, Associate Editor Lindy Mechefske, and Art Director Larry Harris. In addition, I have been aided by and would like to thank freelance London, ON, writer-editor Alice Gibb; Dr. Alphonse Mutima, adjunct assistant professor, Department of African and Afro-American Studies, University of North Carolina at Chapel Hill, NC; Dorthea Sartain, curator of archives, Collections and Books at The Explorers Club, New York, NY; Steven Sheffield of Precision Colour Reproduction, Kingston, ON; and, McGill-Queen's University Press Editor Joan Harcourt; Joan McGilvray, coordinating editor, McGill-Queen's University Press; Senior Editor and Douglas Professor of Canadian and Colonial History Donald H. Akenson, and Executive Director Philip Cercone. And a special thank you to Anneke Van Woudenberg, senior researcher for the Democratic Republic of Congo (DRC) in Human Rights Watch's Africa division, who so kindly agreed to wrote the Foreword to this volume.

Illustrations, except where specified, are from the original edition of *Congo Solo* and are published courtesy of the Hahn Estate.

Ken Cuthbertson
Kingston, ON
April 2011

Congo Solo

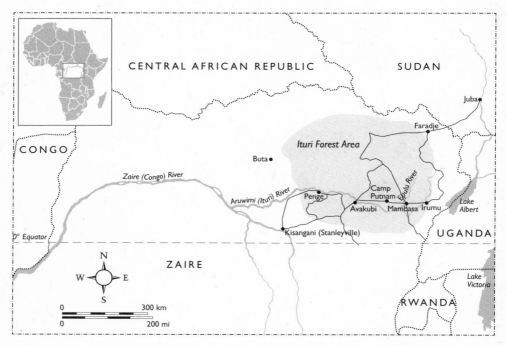

Map of the northeastern Democratic Republic of the Congo.
Created by Larry Harris.

CHAPTER 1

VOYAGE OUT

WHAT I REALLY WANTED TO DO more than anything else was to go home and cry. It would be nice, I thought – I enjoy crying, just a little, and afterward I would go out for a walk and feel sentimental because it was Christmas Eve and the fog was coming up over London, and I have never seen enough of the river at Westminster, and I was going away to Africa next day. But first I had to deliver presents to people here and there, before they had all scattered to their homes in the country.

I started at four in the afternoon, and wherever I went with a present they had something to say about good luck in Africa, and I grew more and more sentimental. The last present was for my friend Rosa at her hotel, and I didn't get there until about nine. She liked her present – a little locket – and she asked me to stay for dinner. I tried to go away, but I'm not very determined, so ten o'clock found me, as they say, sitting at table in the hotel dining room, eating veal and ham pie and listening to a young man play the piano.

There were other people there too, all eating pie and drinking champagne because it was Christmas Eve. There was an American lady in a peacock-blue hat, trying to get away to catch her last train. There was a stranger, a blond man with glasses and a supercilious expression that ill became him. There was Flossie, who is always there, and there was the Worst Man in London, who is Flossie's young man just now. Rosa said to the American lady: "Mickey's an American too, and she is going to be married when she gets back."

Then I remembered. "No, I'm not," I said. "He won't marry me. I had a letter today. He is mad at me for going to Africa."

"Do you mind?" asked Rosa.

I considered for a moment. "Yes," I said finally. "Yes, I mind very much. I must go home now to pack."

"No, no," said Rosa, who never wants anyone to go home.

"No, no," said the American lady, as much out of politeness as anything.

"No," said the blond, who was drinking.

"No," said the Worst Man in London, who is an old friend of mine, though not a warm one. "You just want to go home and cry. I know all about that."

That was the truth, so I waited a while. The boy at the piano played a lot of songs, and we sang those that we knew, and he made some up. The Worst Man was sorry for me, more sorry than he need have been, and once he patted my head. Flossie saw it and was angry. She went out for a walk with the blond and stayed away a long time, and the Worst Man pretended unsuccessfully not to care. It grew late, and Rosa went to bed.

At last I saw my chance to go, and just as I was slipping out of the lobby Edith, the secretary, came out with a package. "With compliments," she said, and I opened it and found that Rosa had given me a brown handbag. I always cry when people are nice to me, and this pleased me very much. I felt all mixed up, and ran out to get a taxi. Just as I caught one and got in, the Worst Man came running out after me.

"You mustn't go," he said. "You'll just cry and be miserable because that man jilted you. Am I right?"

"That's none of your business," I said, being near the overflow. "Close the door."

"I won't," he said. "You come on back and sing."

"I don't want to." I gave the driver the address, but the Worst Man wouldn't close the door and go away. So I told him to get in, and when he did the driver naturally started for home. That frightened the Worst Man, because now Flossie would come back and find him gone. Still, there was no help for it.

"Go ahead and cry," he said. "I'll fix things with Flossie. Cry on my shoulder, and you'll feel better."

So I did, all of a sudden: I burst into loud sobs all over his collar, and he was nice about it, just saying, "Never mind, baby, never mind. He's a bastard."

"No, he isn't," I sobbed. "It's not just him. I'm homesick."

But he wouldn't believe me, having a romantic mind, and he just held tight and said, "Go on. Cry. Pretend you love me, and go on crying. It's all right." And he went on patting my head and saying, "No man in the world is worth it. Who's feeling low? Who's mad at her boy? Never mind, baby."

It was ridiculous, but comforting. I blew my nose and invited him in when I got home, and he told the cab to wait because he was afraid of Flossie. He came in to make sure I was all right. He sat by the fire. I sat on the floor and he patted my head and talked about life in a sad monologue.

"What's it all about? Christ, you cry and you laugh, and what's it all about? Mustn't grumble. *Courage, le diable est mort* ["Courage, the devil is dead." You just hang on and hang on and make the best of it, getting drunk and getting sober, and some day – what's the end? Stuff up the window and turn on the gas. ... Go on, baby. Cry your heart out."

But I didn't want to cry any more, and I said so. He told me that there was a girl in Paris who meant everything to him, but she wouldn't look at him. Anyway, he said, Flossie was very good to him, and she was a marvellous girl really. "A lady," he said.

"How did she get this way?" I asked, because I've often wondered.

"Just for the devil of it. She doesn't give a damn, and we mustn't either. Mustn't gamble."

"All right," I said. "You can go back to her now."

"You won't cry any more? You'll go to bed?"

"Yes," I said. He kissed me good-by, and I said, "You're very nice."

"No," he said. "I'm the Worst Man in London." And with a proud swagger, he went out.

Tuesday, December 30, 1930

This is after two days of inaction. I'm writing in the dining room [of the ship], where there are eight soldiers playing cards and smoking and making the air worse than it seemed to my too sensitive nose. I'm giving thanks to God that I can write anywhere, anything, after two days of seasickness. My first experience of it. It is not so bad, in a way, as it is described. My soul took wings, that is all. I lay in a trance, now and then awaking to a horrible reality, and then slipping off again to happier places.[1]

I have a cabin alone, with four bunks, two basins (I used them both), a gray, stiff towel, and a mirror. The wall slopes in to the floor, reminding me how near I am to water down here in third-class, and there is a staircase up to the port, out of which I can see a great deal of ocean, which is composed on gray-green water, very energetic and inquisitive. It wants to get in, but it can't, except in very tiny driblets around the frame.

There is very little deck and it is an uncomfortable shape, narrow and cluttered with iron lumps. But there aren't many people about. Most of those who are seem to be soldiers dressed indiscriminately in khaki and dark blue, with ballet slippers like those the people used to wear in Carcassonne.[2] Twenty days still to go. I am happy even when seasick, whenever I remember that I am going to Africa and that everything is completely cut off. I am a stranger even to myself. I can't even talk: no one speaks English. This fact may get on my nerves

---

1 Hahn traveled by ship from London to the French port of Bordeaux on Christmas Day 1930. The ship on which she sailed to Africa, the *Brazza*, departed three days later.
2 A town in the southern French province of Aude.

before I'm through, but now it is a lovely private feeling. It's only in my dreams that I'm not a completely new person. Then I'm back in New York or London, or even in Paris, walking by the Seine in my dream, feeling sick. … No, I'm here. I'm back here, a new person, going to Africa, and there is a green dress tangled up with a blue silk shirt in my suitcase in the corner opposite, and a smell of wet wood, and a little sergeant (how ever did he get in?) is patting my head and asking me if I wouldn't like some lemonade. He actually is: when did he appear? And how nice of him, although he talks too much. Everyone is very kind. The steward just asked me if I was not afraid to travel alone, and I said, "Why? It is life." That's the way I always feel when I'm in bed: I can't help it. He waved his hand and said, "*Ah, oui. Ça va, ça va!*" ["Ah, yes. That's how it goes."] I fell to sleep feeling incredibly gallant. And when I woke up, there was the little sergeant with a bottle of aspirin. But he shouldn't sit here all the time, holding my hand, even though I am weak. I just told him.[3]

Wednesday, December 31

The little sergeant has a "phono" with a blue cover, and a blue box to carry the records. He brought it to my cabin yesterday afternoon and began to play, and immediately many people gathered outside the door, so I asked them in. They brought camp chairs and settled down for the day, a pimply youth, a young woman with a baby, a merry matron without a baby, a sad-eyed soldier. We played *Carmen* and *La Tosca* and several songs I had never heard, but which they sang with great enthusiasm. The pimply one danced about in a circle or sat on a top bunk, grimacing. The baby wailed, and the air grew foul, so foul that they noticed it and left after a while, and so did I, leaving the door open in spite of possible thieves.

---

3 Hahn shared many of the details of her voyage to Africa in the shipboard letters she sent home to her mother. What she recounted in a letter dated December 30, 1930, is essentially what she later reported in *Congo Solo*.

There are two meals a day – not counting morning coffee in pyjamas – ten-thirty a.m. and five p.m. The food is good, better than it would be in second-class on an English ship. The more time I spend here, the more indignant I am with all the English people who raised hell at my coming this way. They were so sure it would be dreadful – "appalling" was the word. How could they tell, who only first-class know? It's not even as if I were being a good sport; it's not bad enough to have to be a good sport. It's perfectly comfortable and clean.

Thursday, January 1, 1931

Most of these men are from the Pyrenees section, I think, which accounts for their small size. My sergeant is from Perpignan, and I cannot understand his French at all, but some others are easier.

What a crew they look at dinner, at the other table! I am between a large Italian, who uses a bottle of oil at every meal, and a gentle little man whose wife, Henriette, sits across the table and serves everything to her unattractive son. The little man makes polite conversation … "Does one drink much tea in the United States, Mademoiselle?"

"One prefers coffee," I answer.

"Ah," he says brightly. "Henriette, Mademoiselle has said that in the United States one prefers coffee to tea."

"Truly?" says Madame benevolently. And we all go on chewing.

I have learned how to cut bread properly – i.e., to clutch the loaf to my bosom, sawing away at one end with my knife until I've detached enough for a meal. I'm even learning to wipe everything on my napkin before using it, though it seems a dirty custom to me, the napkin is so dishevelled by this time, what with gravy and so forth. We have two funny men at our table; they keep filling my glass with wine when I'm not looking, and the funnier of the two never laughs, though he is small and round. I like him.

Hahn and some fellow passengers aboard the *Brazza*

WE DIDN'T GET UP TO THE DOCK at Dakar[4] last night until eleven-thirty. For an hour before, the ship waltzed back and forth trying to nudge up, but the wind was too strong. We leaned on the rail all that time, all dressed up and panting to go, and by the time we did get off, my feet were tired, and I was in a bad mood to feel very exhilarated. The Canary – so called because he was born on a Canary island – and the pompous sergeant came with me, and we walked furiously, feeling our feet on the ground and sniffing the air. Slowly my irritation melted, and I said to myself over and over, "I'm in Africa."

The two little men kept telling me with affection about the buildings we passed, pointing out cafés, closed now, and naming the parks

4 The capital of the West African nation of Senegal.

and post offices. The town was asleep, but taxis full of people from the ship kept charging down on us, and yet somehow we didn't want to walk on the pavement but kept to the middle of the street. White buildings and a sweetish smell, and soft warm air.

We had beer at a café and then went on to the Gay White Way, a place called the Tabarin, naturally. The dance floor was open to the sky. Lots of hostesses, mostly old, and the waiters were coal-black and wore bright berets. It was listless and tawdry, but we liked it. Then it grew late and boring. We went back to the café for coffee and sand-wiches, and to the boat at two a.m., pushing one another into the street and running and making a big noise. I suppose the sergeant went back and ended up his evening properly: I went to bed like a good *jeune fille*, but unlike the *jeune fille*, I left my door open because it was hot. Much later, I heard a loud noise and realized, tossing fret-fully on my pillow, that some of the boys were whooping it up. One of them came tripping by my door, and seeing it open, he peered in as he passed. He saw me looking at him and grinned. I grinned. He came back and shook hands with me through the door and continued on his unsteady way down the corridor, whistling.

This morning, according to arrangement, I met the Canary at seven o'clock, and we started out to see Dakar. First, we bought sun spectacles, and then we had coffee, and then we walked and talked. If the people were not so black, I should think I was in Tunis because the sweet smell is the same and the language and the white houses, but it's not a sightseen place like Tunis, and there aren't many Arabs. I saw several Moors, lovely teak color they are, with Biblical clothes, but an un-Biblical way of staring and moving. The Canary kept meeting old friends, black and white, and stopping to chat. At last he suggested a drink, and I said I would like one if he would let me pay this time. He was startled.

"If anyone should see, they would think you are a woman who ... "

"Oh, hell," I said, or words to that effect.

He shrugged. "If you don't care," he said and took my nine francs graciously. But it made him think, because he began to talk about Americans. He had always wanted to know one, he said. "And I am glad I do, because you are an original. One can discuss anything with you, like a man. Exactly like a man, to pay for your own drinks. ... Do you know, everyone on the ship, because I am walking with you, is thinking bad thoughts of us."

"Naturally," I answered. "Didn't you have a lot of bad thoughts about the other women on the ship? You told me lots of things about the married ladies; you said that all of them are sleeping with the sergeants, and you told me exactly who was sleeping with whom. You haven't any more reason for thinking so ... ."

"Pardon *me!*" he said indignantly. "What I see, I see. For why should the fat Madame be in the cabin of the aviator at three o'clock in the morning? I saw her come out."

"She might have been talking to him," I said.

He almost burst. "What I see, I see. Why not talk on deck?"

"Why not talk in the cabin, if she wants to? You have bad thoughts."

We glared at each other, and then he shrugged again. "Never shall I understand you, and never will you understand me," he decided. "But I understand these Madames, and you don't."

"I am not ingenuous," I said, growing indignant in turn. "But I get bored with all this talk of love."

"Then I should *not* make love to you?"

"I wouldn't consider it an insult if you didn't," I assured him.

As we walked back to the ship, he said, "We go on together to Matadi, but I leave hope here."

"With politeness," I assented. "Both stay here at the café."

With relief on both sides, we shook hands.

Wednesday, January 7

Just now the redhead who is slowly wading his way through *An Outcast of the Islands*[5] – he spent a year in London – chatted with me for a while, and I noticed that his hand was shaking wildly. It's the quinine; I feel shaky myself. [He] presented me with a cigarette picture of a very bare, very white, very fat lady, which I have sent off to Mother.

Last night there was a celebration at dinner because it was Napoleon's name-day, and the six Croatians had bought a big cake with lucky pieces baked in it. Afterward I went to my cabin for a short snooze and was awakened by the quite smiling sergeant who was appointed a committee of one to invite me to champagne. It was sweet champagne, but I drank two glasses and danced better than I usually do, which was fortunate because I had to dance a lot, mostly polkas. The six Corsicans have formed a club, Les Fils de Napoleon Ire, and it was their party, but I was the guest of honor and had a swell time. The tall skinny one was in fine fettle and teased me about my reading and writing ..." In the morning, Mees takes coffee at seven-thirty."

He imitated me drinking the coffee, very delicately with small bites of bread. "Afterward to the deck to read." He held his hands up close to his nose and moved his eyes back and forth over the palms. "Then, lunch. Afterward at the machine." He typed wildly on the table and stopped now and then to read, laughing heartily at the imaginary book. "After dinner, to the deck, and then to bed. You lead a good life, Mees, and you never have the blues. Tomorrow I shall tell you about the women of France here on board and how immoral they are. It is terrible! Look about you. Where are they now? Ah, where?"

And indeed, the ladies had all retired.

He jumped up and seized Ricardi and they danced, then came back to the table. "We are brothers," he said, ruffling the Canary's hair. "We were together a whole year in Marseilles. Drink your champagne, Mees, it is Napoleon's fête day."

5 An 1896 novel by Joseph Conrad.

Sunday, January 11

Everyone was light-headed last night. The people who were getting off today were excited: I was excited because I had finished a story, and I suppose the others simply caught the spirit. At ten o'clock the crew on their side of the palings set up a glad roar to greet three men who came out with instruments: a drum on a stand and two horns. They dragged out a bench and sat down solemnly to sort their music, then struck up. It was good music. All the crew began to dance; the tall man with the bass voice grabbed the little cook's assistant and the two lank sailors in berets seized each other and then all the others – shirtless, with cigarettes hanging from their mouths and the sweat glistening on their faces – began to dance: the deck was jammed with them. Now and then one of them would lose a sandal. On our side of the palings, some of us danced, but not so many. It was better to watch the others.

It grew cooler and you could see the coast, the Ivory Coast, slipping along in the darkness by the side of the ship. The band struck into *Les Artichauts* and suddenly two of the men went completely berserk: they dropped their arms and started to dance alone, a sort of glorified Charleston with a tango motif, upflung hands and quick-stepping feet. "*Aie!*" cried the little one with the moustache, jumping over his ankle, and the rest of them crowded around, clapping in time to the music and stamping to help the drum. Then the tall man with the voice took the drum-sticks and accompanied his own song, and after all that we all sang *Tous les Toits de Paris*, and then, overcome with laughing and feeling happy, I went to bed.

We were at Grand-Bassam[6] this morning when Ricardi knocked on my door to get dressed and come ashore. It was too shallow to go to the dock: we were carried ashore in batches of four, swung out over the side of the ship like so many cows being unloaded, and settled down in a big boat, then swung up to the dock the same way. I was

6 The capital city of the Ivory Coast in the years 1893–96 of the French colonial era. It remained an important seaport until the 1930s when it was eclipsed by Abidjan and became a ghost town.

afraid at first, but it was rather pleasant. Grand-Bassam is a tiny place with lots of palm trees and flowers; it smelled good. Women paraded along the street with baskets on their heads, but most of the people were in the marketplace. It was Sunday and the shops were closed, but we found a café and had a pink drink. I thought guiltily of my Hygiene Lectures, but after all one can't walk in and demand to know the antecedents of the water, in a strange place run by a Syrian. The color of everything was so clear that I almost cried – the clothes of the Negroes and the water, vivid blue, and the sand, which was actually gold. I've never seen such golden sand.

Tuesday, January 13

We had all day yesterday at Lomé.[7] This morning we were are Cotonau,[8] where the last two ladies got off. There is another lady passenger in third, however: a tall scornful negress who is fed off in a corner by herself.

I like the Catalan adjutant very much, except his habit of imitating a monkey scratching whenever he sees a Negro. A black peddler came on board this morning with slippers and mats and a lot of trash; he was very talkative and a crowd gathered around him. "What will you have, Madame? All the latest styles from Paris. I myself am a Parisian." There was a scream of laughter, and he pulled out a photograph with the signature of a Parisian photographer. "There, see?" It was of himself arm-in-arm with one of the hardest-looking white women I've ever seen. "She was a marquise," he said, "and I had to pay her twelve hundred francs."

"Ah," Susini said dubiously, "if she had been a marquise really, you wouldn't have had to pay her anything," and the rest nodded seriously.

7 The capital city and largest port in the West African country of Togo.
8 (Also spelled Cotonou) A port city in the West African nation of Benin.

☙

I'M NOT FEELING SO WELL AS I OUGHT TO BE, but then I'm not feeling so ill as I should either. Somehow in the course of yesterday afternoon, while Ricardi was cleaning my white shoes, we promised each other to get drunk in the evening. Four Pernods, I promised to drink – he insisted on Pernod, though I complained – and then he drew himself up and announced that he would drink eight. I didn't look forward to the trial with much pleasure, but after declaring my intentions at dinner I began to feel some glow of pride in the horror it caused. The black-haired man with the spectacles advised me to take two aspirin pills after the third Pernod. The little mechanic chuckled and wagged his head. The Italian told how at a wedding he had drunk eleven whiskeys and then driven his car home afterward.

We started at eight o'clock after an argument with the *maître d'hôtel*, who was shocked at first but quickly entered into the spirit of the thing. The Napoleons sat around and watched. "One!" cried Ricardi as the drink was set down. We gulped it and ordered another, chalking the score on the table. "Two!" This went slower. He was getting more excitable than ever. "Do you notice that the six Napoleons are always together?" he said. "Always, whenever they are on the boat? That's because we're Corsicans. Any of us would give his blood to save a brother." They all shouted in agreement. He grew sentimental and said over and over, "Corsica! That's the way we all are in Corsica."

"All right," said Susini. "Drink up. She's finished with hers."

"Three!" This time the *maître* said to me in English. "For you, a leetle one." At the same moment Vecchioli cried, "Hers is weak. Look at the color!" So I mixed the two together, to make them even, and we went on. Across the room, my spectacled friend shook his finger warningly, and I went out and took the aspirin. I felt fine, but I was tired of the taste of Pernod. Too sweet. "Four! America is strong."

"Not at all drunk?" asked the *maître*.

"No," I said. "I'm not drunk until I begin to cry. Please send me to bed when you see me crying."

Ricardi declared again, at the top of the crest of excitement, that I was always safe with him, drunk or sober, sober or drunk; it didn't matter. It occurred to me then that he's really an awfully little man to carry all that liquid, just in bulk. Still, when we finished the fourth he asked me if we should go on.

"Do you want to?" I asked.

"It's for you to say."

"Good. We'll go on." There was a roar of applause that almost recompensed me for that sticky-sweet taste. "Five!"

People began to come to the table just to look at us. After the fifth, the *maître* announced that the market in Pernod was closed. He sent us cocktails of his own invention – cognac, champagne, and God knows what else. Then we had another. Then Ricardi insisted that he would see me to my cabin, and I made Susini come too, and it's a good thing I did. Because the moment we got there the Canary climbed more or less nimbly to a top berth and went to sleep.

"Now what do I do?" I asked Susini.

He laughed, as always, and said, "Leave him there. He'll stay that way till morning."

"Never," I said, scandalized. Really scandalized, too. I must have been slightly tipsy. I pounded Ricardi on the back and said, "André, wake up." No answer but a tiny snore. "Well," I said, "you'll have to stay, too."

"All right," said Susini equably.

I tumbled all my books off the lower bunk for him and then went to the bathroom. When I came back, he had gone. "Deserted," I thought bitterly. Suddenly, André woke up and climbed down, looking puzzled and drunk. I packed him out without trouble, locked the door, and took off my dress contentedly. Someone knocked; it was Susini come back.

"He's gone," I said proudly.

"That's fine. Good night, Mees." He disappeared down the corridor, still laughing.

Then André came back. "I want to talk to you just a minute," he said. "Let me in."

He pushed in past me and sat down on a trunk. "I want to prove to you that you can trust me," he said. "Go to bed, and I'll keep watch."

"No, I don't want to be protected," I said. "Go on home. I trust you all right. You don't have to prove it."

"Ah!" he cried in his most Corsican and fiery manner, "you don't trust me. We're not really friends. Why, I swear to you that I could sit here all night, and you would be safe."

I looked at his tiny body and said, "I believe you, darling. Now go home."

We argued about it for a while; it was necessary to soothe his pride before he would go. But he did at last, while I pretended to be frightened.

Everyone looked at me mischievously and questioningly this morning when I appeared on deck. Mela scolded. Ricardi appeared late, haggard and frowsy in pyjamas. The Catalan adjutant invited us for an apéritif, and, damn it, I had to drink two more of those green things.

Friday, January 16

We arrived at Libreville[9] at nine this morning, and Ricardi got his orders, along with Julia, the flirtatious one, and Susini as sergeant. I've never seen such a change in anyone as there is in Susini. Now that it's settled that he is to stay here for two years, he can send for his family. He did, in fact, right away by telegraph. We had three drinks each in farewell, bought by the three men, and we all swapped addresses and handclasps and promises, and off they went. What a queer life, to be so dependent on the whims of a government! I've had a taste

9 The capital of the West African nation of Gabon.

of sudden traveling, but no one ever said to me, "Be ready in five minutes to live on the shore of Africa for the next two years in a town you've never seen before."[10]

10 In a letter to her mother dated January 20, 1930, Hahn confided that looking back on her experiences aboard the ship, "In a funny way, I enjoyed every minute of it."

CHAPTER 2

TO THE MIDDLE OF THE MAP

Tuesday, January 20, 1930

THE TROUBLE STARTED AT BOMA, the last town before Matadi at the beginning of the Congo River. An official came on board to see our papers. He looked at me and he looked at my certificates and he said brusquely, "You haven't enough money to get in."

I was appalled and looked at him, then at my directions from London. I did too have enough. Not more than enough, but enough. I tried to argue, but he just said, "Wait till you get to Matidi, and talk to the police there." Then he went away and left me in a state. It's true that if they wanted to, they could insist on me leaving ten thousand francs with them as a deposit, but the Belgian consul in London had said they wouldn't. Even at that, I had enough.

He telegraphed Matidi about it and I found a mare's nest here. The office was closed and they couldn't hear my case until after the daily train had gone the next day, with the other passengers. Even if I did get in, I thought, how was I going to smuggle my revolver as we had planned? Because the Corsicans had promised to do it for me. I argued and argued, and the *commissaire* [superintendent] was unpleasant and said I had to get off the boat because I was a third-class passenger, and the immigration man said I couldn't get off until things were settled. I lost my courage, my temper, and my control. Of course it was natural that they should think I was a whore; they're that way, and I didn't look at all prosperous – barelegged and ragged. At last the *commissaire* said I could stay on if I would pay for my lodging and breakfast.

Suddenly someone thought of the baggage. Good heavens, the baggage. It was being packed up with the trunks of the soldiers, bound for Brazzaville in the French Congo. … I asked Hayer, one of the soldiers, to come with me and interpret my French to the *chef de gar* [station master]. We had to wait a long time for him at the station, and then he only referred us back to the dock. My things were all packed under a couple of tons of other things, and the man in charge had apoplexy at the very suggestion that he unpack it. So everyone was airy about it and said, "Oh, telegraph ahead and tell them to hold it at Kinshasa." I raised hell again – I was fighting mad – and people began to be impatient with me, as was natural. It wasn't their baggage. Hayer, however, was so sympathetic, withal helpless, that I became disgustingly feminine. I nearly wept.

The Corsicans, who had been out for a walk, came back at this juncture and heard about it. Dear, dear, dear! What to do about that revolver?

They convened in my cabin, arguing about it. Giudicelli was for putting it into my pocketbook. No, said Mela, sometimes they search pocketbooks. Ceccaldi thought they might take it ahead and leave it in a little package at the hotel in Kinshasa. No, then it would be stolen. With shrill cries and loud oaths they seized it from one another and gesticulated, until I had the idea of putting it on a belt under my clothes. This was fine except that with all the cartridges stuffed into the holder I had a strangely bulky look about the middle. "I don't want Mademoiselle to go to prison," Mela said idiotically every few minutes. At last they agreed that I was to wear my green jacket over my dress all day to hide the bulge. They congratulated one another and walked out to have a drink on it.

Friday, January 23

There was a loud gong and a great shuffling. Someone banged on my door and called, "*Au 'voir*," and I heard a giggle and then lots of people walked by. I dressed and hurried out. Everything was ominously deserted. Stray members of the crew rushed about distractedly. I drank black coffee, paid twenty francs for the extra day on board, and walked off the ship into Matidi.

It was a hilly town, dazzlingly white and yet disorderly, as if the buildings had been sprinkled, together with large white boulders, indiscriminately over the steep slope. A jagged staircase led up between white houses and a new high building topped a hill: all about in a ring around the clearing were trees and vines, green, green, green. It was early and the sun was still soft and safe. I found a boy to carry my bags, and we started for the stairs. A black policeman barred the path, smiling with white teeth, and said, "*Douane, Madame.*" ["Customs, madame"]

Good heavens – I'd forgotten to fix the revolver and it was on top of everything in my hatbox. I stopped. The policeman stopped. The boy stopped. We all looked at the sky for a minute and then I said, "Wait: I've forgotten something." He implied that he was willing to wait, that he was used to waiting. I went into the ship again and in the cabin put on the whole affair: the leather belt under the dress and the coat on top. It was hot. Feeling very bulky and filled with guilt, I advanced once more into Africa.

The customs office wasn't open, but a fat man in his shirtsleeves who would be in charge when it *was* open was glad to talk to someone. I told him about my trunks and why they weren't there for inspection. He said, "*Tiens, tiens!*" ["Well, well"] and sent off a telegraph to Kinshasa. This was heartening. Someone cared; somebody was taking it for granted that I was a traveler and not simply a criminal or a prostitute. He invited me to breakfast in his rooms next to the office. I didn't dare refuse, so I went with him and drank coffee for the second time, leaning uncomfortably against the revolver, while he ate omelette and sausage and told me to take off my coat and be comfortable. I professed a violent chill, while the sweat dripped off my nose. But my spirits rose under his politeness, his indignation with the police, and the ship's company and the whole universe that tried to prevent a nice girl coming into the Congo if she were idiot enough to want to do it.

It was still too early after breakfast to open the office. I left my luggage there and climbed the hill to town, meaning to find the office of the ship's company and register a complaint – any complaint. I was burning with a general rage. The streets were confusing and each one ahead was higher than the one I was on. I immediately got lost.

I couldn't find the office. At last, in desperation, I walked into an open door where I saw a white man sitting at a desk. "Excuse me," I said, "can you tell me ..."

Then a miracle happened. The young man stood up and said, "Oh, Miss Hahn? Sit down: I tried to find you on the ship yesterday, but I couldn't. Now then ..."

It really was a miracle. He was a member of a trading company here. Someone in the same firm in Stanleyville[1] had written him, at the request of Patrick Putnam, [the man I was going to visit][2] to meet me and to do anything he could for me. Out of the whole town, I had just happened to walk into his office. Otherwise we would never have met: God knows what I'd have done without him. I found out later that the man at Boma had even wired the railway station not to sell me a ticket because I was a woman traveling alone.

The nightmare was over now. We went to the post office, and I found letters from Patrick. I had known him in America and in Belgium; he had often told me about the Congo, where he was the *Agent Sanitaire* at a medical post. A long time before I started for Africa, I told him I would come, and he laughed and said that I must surely look him up. But he's a bad correspondent, and when I tele-

---

1 Stanleyville, renamed in 1970, is now known as Kisangani.
2 Under pressure from the Putnam family in New York, Hahn disguised Patrick Putnam's identity in the *Congo Solo* manuscript, calling him "Den Murray."

graphed that I was on my way I had no reply, and so I decided that he must have gone again, or died. Then just before I sailed I got his answer, simply giving me his address, and telling me how much quinine I ought to take each day.

We went to the police and slid through this whole business as easily as it should have gone at first. Everyone apologized and we shook hands. We went to the hotel and I stood alone in my room for a few minutes, looking in a small wavy mirror and pinching myself. I washed my face and took off the gun. We got my luggage. We telegraphed again about the trunks. I almost kissed that man's feet.

Alone again in the hotel, I lay down. The room faced a veranda; it had huge doors with screens, and there was a mosquito net.

In the afternoon, my guide called and took me to a tennis game at the club. I met a lot of people and smiled foolishly at all of them. I drank beer and watched the game and wondered how anyone could play in the heat. That night, in whatever purple and fine linen I could garner from my hand baggage, I dined in state in a big house on the hill, with assorted wines to drink and music playing, and quite unexcited voices. ... It was a terrifying sensation after all this time. I sat very still and tried not to wipe the silver on my napkin.

These men were depressed. There were no other women there; most of the wives in town had been sent home for their health. The men drank a lot in celebration of – I don't know just what, but the more they drank the sadder they became, and my host, who was very nice, became the saddest of all. It was a queer rambling sort of night. We went to the Brazza for a drink in the first-class salon this time, and the *garçon* winked at me.

They wouldn't let me even talk of going to bed. My train, the daily one, left at five-thirty in the morning and I had just time to change my clothes and get ready. As it turned out, I would have had more time because the train didn't start when it should have. There was something wrong on the road higher up. So the railway manager took some of us to his house for breakfast, and after an hour and a half up there, his telephone rang. It was the *chef de gare*, who said that he would like to let the train go, so would Monsieur please send down the passenger?

Laden with plates of food and bottles of water, I climbed into the train – first-class, witness of my broken morale – and waved enthusiastically as the engine pulled us away, under a fiercely bright morning sun.

It was the strangest train I had ever seen. There were three tiny carriages, one for each class, and it was on a narrow-gauge line. We plodded rather than ran, and the other passengers kept telling me how much better it was than it had been the year before when the trip to Kinshasa took two days instead of one.

We ambled along for fourteen hours, stopping occasionally at stations that consisted of single houses. The blacks along the road, always ran with us for a way, shouting. Where the hills had been cut for the road, the rock was red. Most of the forest had been cleared. There was a lot of corn. Slowly we climbed. "Kin" is only four hundred kilometres away, but it's higher, above the rapids of the river.

Sometimes I slept. A passenger across the way poured cologne on my arms for coolness. At the stations we picked up new people and set down others; there were bursts of conversation and sporadic snoring. At midday we pulled down the shades. At sunset we pulled them up again. The soot, unhampered, blackened my dress in ugly streaks, and after a while the mosquitoes began.

Hayer had left word at the hotel where the regiment had been quartered the night before; someone met me at the station with a note from him. It was almost midnight. I couldn't go to that hotel, though; I had a room reserved at the new one. So I went to my own room and wrote him a letter to thank him – what with the mosquitoes and the dictionary, it took an hour – and then I fell into bed with silly superfluous blankets on it. The soldiers, I said to myself, would be across the river tonight in the French Congo. Would I find my trunks? Was the hotel going to be terribly expensive?

At the thought of the money, I shuddered and opened my eyes. There were little slits of light shining through the shutters of the door. Oh, I can always get money somewhere, somehow. ... I fell asleep.

Monday, January 26

Kinshasa. I've been here four days waiting for the boat, which leaves in another three. Kinshasa is a big town, growing bigger by the minute. There are about twenty-five hundred Europeans here: Belgians, Portuguese, Italians, some English, and a handful of Americans. There are a lot more natives and the native town is big, but doesn't show up well.

The big trading companies have concessions with houses on them, some of them depressingly like the suburban parts of London. I've seen three national monuments, and I am afraid there are more. Plenty of industry – textile mills that weave the local cotton into cloth used by the natives, and mineral water is manufactured here too.

I'm up on all this because this morning a reporter and another Belgian took me on a sightseeing tour; they were shocked that I hadn't seen more of the sights, and I'm glad they did it or I should never have known enough to go to see the rapids. You stand on a hill and look down at the Congo, which splits up around little islands and flows behind them in slow streams full, they tell me, of crocodiles. Suddenly the river hits the rapids and you see how fast it's going: the water comes down with terrific speed and makes a loud roaring noise. Across on the French side there are blue mountains, far off – the green of the trees and the white water and the blue are brilliant, especially at sunset.

Friday, January 30

Last night, Madame, the little secretary of one of the oil men, a nice girl who speaks English, asked me to dine with her husband and two friends – employees of the boat line, a chief engineer and a wireless operator. We got slightly squiffy[3] and we danced, though it was fiendishly hot, and I felt a little better. They were nice people with a position to keep up and we called one another by our first names, and I kissed Madame good-bye when we parted at the boat.

I have a cabin to myself, thanks to a little graft on her part, and it's the only cabin like that on the ship, which is jammed with priests and nuns and new mosquito-fodder from Belgium. It is a tiny stern-wheeler, the ship is, and we are just entering the narrow part of the river, with mountains closing in. So far the country has been the same as at Kinshasa.

All aboard! Loading one of the steamboats that plied the waters of the Congo River. Many of these vessels had begun their working lives in Europe and the United States before being disassembled and shipped to Africa.

---

3 British slang term for being drunk

The cabin is tiny even for one. We tie up at night, after ten o'clock, and we'll be plodding along like this for ten days. I'm warned that I will be thrilled to death. I hope so. Last night I wasn't; it was so hot that I thought I would rather die than lie there any longer, but even my desire for death was languid and unpassionate. It's the first time in my life that I grew slippery with perspiration just lying in bed. I wiped and wiped my face and arms till my handkerchief was sopping, and still I sweated. And people were embarking all night, shrieking at one another.

In the cabin next to mine, they were talking English with a thick accent, discussing some girl in Freetown and warning one another not to let the wife hear about it. I was ill, too: something like dysentery, but it would be too early for that to develop.

Yes, now the river is getting better. We're passing an island thick with trees and bushes and up ahead the water curves around between hills. It looks something like the Mississippi, but perhaps that's because of the boat.[4] From the native village there is a constant throbbing of drums.

Thursday, February 5

Now the shore is always a wall of jungle: tall trees, some of them as twisted as the oaks in Kensington Garden or in Rackham's pictures,[5] and some of them great palm trees, stiff and unyielding. All through them are the vines, twisting around and filling in the spaces with thick green.

The little wood-posts where we stop are only tiny clearings with grass-thatched huts. When we don't stop, the children run along for

4 Many of the steamboats plying the waters of the Congo River in the 1930s had begun life on the Mississippi River and were sold and transported to Africa after they were retired from service in the United States.
5 Arthur Rackham (1867–1939) was a celebrated English artist and illustrator of the day.

a few feet, shouting at us and dancing up and down, and skinny little women stand there and stare, making Y-shapes with their babies strapped to their backs, leaning one way while the babies lean the other. Most of the people are almost naked; the children always are. I wish I could be. But the tsetse flies are a nuisance, and they would be more so if I weren't wearing clothes. The worst kind of bite is given by a tiny black fly; it carries no germs, but its bite has a painful sort of itchiness that starts all the other bites throbbing, the old ones that I should have forgotten.

We ran head-on into a beautiful tornado yesterday afternoon. Everything was dark and muggy. It had been depressingly hot, and then a breeze started and lightning flashed marvellously, forked gold in the dark green sky, and the rain came down in a fury. The boat didn't stop, although the engineer ran to suggest it to the captain because the engine was under water. We weren't really in much danger because the storm was head-on, but up in front they were swimming in the rain.

Night fell an hour early, and it rained so much that we had to stop and wait for the moonlight. We were late for the post where we stayed the night. The rain stopped at last and when the motor died the lights went off, and the river was silver and the long disappearing shores were black, and in the coolness every one slept heavily.

WHEN WE COME TO A SHALLOW SPOT in the river, the markers start calling out. You can see them by leaning over the top deck: one wears a helmet backward and his white shirt has a long rent in it; the other wears a bright red skirt. They sit on either side of the bow, holding sticks marked with white, and one dips his in and calls the number, then the other dips his; they make a chant. Sometimes the black passengers bring out a drum, a long one made of a length of tree-trunk. They prop this up between two of them, and while one strikes the skin, the other slaps the wood, making a staccato accompaniment. They play loudest when we sail up to a wood-post, and the Negroes on shore wave to them and shout.

At Bumba, where we stopped last night, they have a special appearance. The District Commissioner told me that they've been a very brave and warlike people. Some of the young women wore queer-looking curls at the sides of their heads, so that in the back they looked quite flat-headed. Two old women were completely bald, and their heads looked like almonds; they shone in the sun. They wore nothing but skimpy skirts, and their breasts hung down to their navels; they folded their arms over them.

All along the river, there are dugouts with little houses built up in the middle, made of two or three mats slung over a support. The people in them live that way all the time; they build fires on iron plates. They fish and go up and down the river selling palm oil and fish and anything they can get hold of – "The Jews of the river," the captain called them. There was a cluster of them this morning around the mouth of a little stream, with nets and slats built up to catch the fish.

Last night at the wood post, the natives were playing with a tiny animal that looked like an armadillo, except that the tail was longer. It's called a pangolin,[6] as nearly as I could make out. It has a long tongue and eats bugs, just like an anteater, but it belongs to the rat family, I think. They wanted to sell it for fifteen francs, and both the captain and I were tempted, but I don't think we'd be able to feed it enough bugs on the boat. It was a queer looking animal, but the Negroes are queerer. Especially by firelight as I saw them last night.

They're bigger now and more grotesquely marked on their faces, or perhaps it's because they're so naked that they look strange. At night, with their eyes shining and the ridges of tattooing on their foreheads standing out strongly, and their brown bodies almost glittering in the lamplight from the boat, they make me wonder uneasily why

6 A scaly anteater that is indigenous to areas of Africa and to southern Asia.

we're all intruding in this country anyway. What do they think about? It shouldn't be so hard to tell. They are animals, but articulate animals. And their eyes – I never noticed their eyes till yesterday. Some of them are narrow and bloodshot, startlingly intelligent and fierce, especially when they are quarreling. The captain had to settle a quarrel the other day between our quartermaster and the head of the wood-post. The quartermaster was turning an honest penny with his stereopticon, giving the inhabitants of the village a show for a franc apiece, and the head man objected because he said it interfered with the business of loading wood: the boys weren't working fast enough. Baillon settled it by telling the quartermaster to do his exhibiting up at the other end of the boat so as to leave the laborers without distraction. They departed more quietly, muttering insults at each other.

Thursday, February 12

I have been here in Stanleyville two nights, all readjusted, and now some plans are made. A Mr. Thompson met me at the boat with a letter from Patrick. He's been transferred to Penge,[7] as he hoped to be. This means he is the only European in town – "Better for me and worse for you," as he said, but I don't think it's worse for me. Penge is too far inland for a car to get there, though, and now I shan't buy one either for him or for myself. That relieves me; I couldn't have afforded it, not possibly. But he is waiting in Avakubi, hoping that I can get there in time to go with him on the three days' journey in the bush. However, I can't.

I could have gone today, early this morning with an Englishman who's going back to Kenya, but he couldn't take all my luggage, and I couldn't go ahead without it. This means I do the three days alone when I've been set down by Thompson after ten days – I'm going with

---

7 To further obscure Putnam's identity Hahn called Penge "Sanga" when she revised the *Congo Solo* manuscript.

him on his next trip of inspection on a roundabout way through Buta, by way of the elephant-hunting farm. Very lucky for me. He's been awfully kind and asked me to stay here at the Consulate instead of at the hotel.

Finding notes from Patrick like this along the way is very funny and makes me feel something like a pilgrim, led from spot to spot with occasional kind messages dropped by God from the sky.

The captain of the boat took me yesterday to see the falls at Tchopo, and I took photographs, and then we drove all over looking for the elephants that are clearing the ground for an aviation field. We found them coming back from their bath in the river. They're the small kind with huge ears, and they had a most uncanny way of melting into the landscape. I was right on top of them before I saw them.

Monday, February 16

We drove up here to Buta[8] yesterday, taking turns at the wheel and going pretty fast. We crossed several rivers by means of pontoons. They are rafts built over a lot of parallel dugouts; the blacks paddle them all together, singing while they work and shrieking for cigarettes after we have landed. At the Aruwimi [River] we had enough time to eat our cold chicken on the pontoon, and I noticed with a gasp the way Thompson ordered the natives to stand off because of their smell. He held his nose, which I consider rude. They didn't seem to mind, though. It is a peculiar smell, musky.

Buta is pretty, but awfully hot. At the hotel where we eat, we were talking as fast as we could to some other Englishmen when suddenly I noticed that the waiter was a Mangbetu, the first I have seen. There were two of them: I stare at them all the time and they look rather embarrassed by my interest. The taller one is beautiful. His head and

8 Located about 240 km (150 miles) northwest of what then was called Stanleyville

the long, chinless, oval face make a shape that is more lovely than Nefertiti.[9] His face isn't marked by welts, though he has tiny tattooed patterns on his forehead.

THE CATHOLIC MISSION IS BUILT OF BRICK, long cloistered buildings surrounded by gardens. Most of them are schools for black children; they learn reading and writing and all those things, and the last forty years of African history – no more than that to avoid confusion.

The Brother who showed us around – white-frocked and bearded, kindly and portly – says he sees no difference from European children in their aptitude, unless it is that they're more docile and concentrate better. We saw the shops where they learn carpentry and ironwork, and there I'm sure they beat us all hollow. Tiny boys were doing their work very deftly, and I was jealous; I've always wanted to be a carpenter.

The outstanding thing about the mission is the zoo. They have a real okapi,[10] a lovely gentle beast. There are two baby elephants, very insistent that you notice them, and there is a pitiful wild beast called Lycaon, a wild dog. It has a dreadful cry, a combination scream and bark. I can't forget it.

There were all sorts of fruit trees and flowers. We drove away with a great cluster of bananas and a lot of guavas.

9 Queen Nefertiti was the wife of the pharaoh Akhenaton, who ruled Egypt 1353–1336 BC.
10 A member of the giraffe family that lives in the Congo rain forests. The species only grows to about one-and-a-half metres (five feet) tall at its shoulder height.

CHAPTER 3

PENGE

Monday, February 23, 1931

AVAKUBI.[1] ASIDE FROM THE SIGN, it's a very small settlement with a large number of natives lounging about looking much at home and idle. There are lots of them in white clothes vaguely like those of the Arabs in Tunis; they must be related, far back. I've read about them. The forest is all around us. Three houses on the main road; my own (the resthouse) is one of them. Patrick's colleague lives down the river a little way. The native quarter is farther up the road, and lots of new houses are going up there, native ones, near the hospital. No mosquitoes, but many hungry flies. The air is not too warm, but it is so wet it almost drips. It rains a lot and makes me sleepy.

Thompson left this morning, nervous and fussy about my being left alone without baggage, which hasn't come yet. Patrick went three days ago, leaving a note to explain that he couldn't be sure enough of our arrival to risk a longer stay. He left, also, two boys: one a large-faced man from the West Coast, named Stephen, who speaks English, and the other, Ngimu, the chauffeur, a recent acquisition from Buta. He sent supplies, too, and a bed and a mosquito net, fortunately. I am comfortable enough and eat well.

1 Located on the Ituri river, about 250 km. (160 miles) northeast of Stanleyville and 150 km (90 miles) upriver from Penge.

This is really the bush, they tell me. I share the resthouse, a dismal place where the wood of the ceiling drifts down constantly in a thick rotten dust, with inquisitive chickens and frantic bats, and I'm enjoying myself, though I miss the typewriter. It looks as if I will have an escort on the trip anyway. A friend of Patrick, named Hubert Smet,[2] an elephant hunter, often goes to Penge and will take me there if I like.

WHEW! He's just been in with the cheerful news that maybe all of my luggage is smashed and lying in the water sixty kilometers from Stanleyville. Because the next truck that left after Thompson got back has broken down. That would be mine.

I received the tidings with a surprising apathy. Let's see: what was in the luggage? Most important, my year's notes for the next book. This is very bad. I daren't think about it – and yet; even then, maybe it's not irretrievably lost. Next, the typewriter. All my clothes except three dresses, and, luckily, my bush things and boots. But this will be serious. Next the revolver, all my medical supplies, my engagement ring,[3] several books, underwear, stationery, compass. Hell, I'll never get home at this rate. Yet I don't seem to care. What's the matter with me? Am I crazy?

Smet stayed to dinner and sent his boy up for his own bottle of Pernod, which we killed by one o'clock in the morning. He says he's going to send Robert, his mulatto baby, to Brussels when it is six years old, because his sisters want it.

Just at dawn there was a big storm. I woke up wanting my blanket and saw the storm coming, because I had furtively opened a window in the bedroom before piling in – leopards may be leopards, but I had

---

2 A white man who lived at Mambasa, 280 km (175 miles) east of Penge. He made his living hunting elephants. The meat was sold to the colonial authorities as food for the native conscript labour, while the ivory went to markets in Europe. Putnam's biographer, Joan Mark, identified Smet in her book *The King of the World in the Land of the Pygmies* (University of Nebraska Press, 1995). Hahn called him "Wauters" in the expurgated version of *Congo Solo*.

3 Hahn had been engaged to an unidentified young man in New York, and the fact the relationship fell apart was one of the reasons she "ran away" to Africa.

to have air. Now I repented; the shutters began to slap against each other with a terrific noise, and I had to get up and try to make them stay shut, so I saw the rain come with a queer ghost-pale lightning and thunderbolts straight out of the Old Testament.

Tuesday, March 3

I am in Penge. We started at eight-thirty in the *pirogue*,[4] after the second boy suddenly decided he would rather walk than come in a motor-driven canoe when he couldn't swim. He shook hands with Stephen and started out alone. Stephen didn't look too happy either as he settled down in front of the main load with the other boys and two women. I was carefully deposited under a shelter made of canvas spread over a wicker frame and bound to the *pirogue* with raffia.[5] There was a chair there for Smet too, but most of the time he was at the back fiddling with the motor.

We came to the first rapids and aimed straight for the highest, most impassable part, a real waterfall. Stephen looked scared to death. We couldn't do anything there, of course, except to hold our own against the rush of water, so we aimed for a shallower spot and by means of poling got across without much delay. Smet said that the canoe didn't make good time; it was the wrong shape for a motor. "Did you see Stephen at the rapids?" he asked in a satisfied tone. "I did it just for him."

I saw some plants at the edge of the water, like puffballs of dead giant dandelions but yellow like hay. Smet said they were papyrus. After the first of the trip I didn't see any more, but that doesn't mean much because we didn't often hug the bank close enough to see what was growing. After a few hours and a few shallow rapids, we reached

---

4 From the Spanish word *piragua*: a kind of flat-bottomed dugout canoe that traditionally was made from a hollowed-out tree trunk.
5 A kind of soft and very durable hemp twine that is made from the leaves of the raffia palm tree.

a place where we unloaded and the boys carried everything, including the motor, about a kilometer overland to a village above some rapids that were too high to cross. Then we started to load up again.

The people of the village were all gone away except a few women who did most of the carrying; one old thing was especially unlovely, a skeleton with a snaky headdress, and she looked overripe for death, but she carried the heaviest loads.

We stopped at five in the evening at a lovely village on a high bank, with a house overlooking the river for us to live in. We had baths, and to celebrate my first night in the real jungle I dressed up in my best evening frock and was thoroughly bitten all evening as a lesson for being whimsical. My appearance fascinated the natives; they drew up at a distance and stared fixedly all the time, making *sotto voce* remarks that it is probably just as well I didn't hear. I don't blame them. When I looked in a mirror I was sure I had leprosy or smallpox because I was covered with small bright-red spots.

In the morning, Smet left me to make sure all the stuff was carried up the road, and he went with the *pirogue* to climb a really bad rapid. I waited around at the resthouse while the men packed, and for two hours I saw the crew struggling at the worst place, pulling with a liane[6] and pushing from behind, with Smet, a white-clad puppet, running up and down giving orders and the *pirogue* itself staying absolutely immovable in the middle of the foam and froth. When we left the river bank to follow the path, they were still there. At the other end, we piled up the luggage and sat down to wait on a steep bank covered with vines. One of the local girls waited with us. She was pretty, I saw after looking at her for half an hour – at first I hadn't thought so, but the impression grew. She was wearing nothing but a bead belt and a strip of cloth behind and a little one in front; there was a design of a snake around her shoulders and a small one to match around her forehead. She was very lively and kept chattering and jumping around

6 A type of woody topical vine.

in a little dance. Every now and then she yelled "Whooooooeeee!" for all the world like a high-yellow Harlemite.[7]

I watched her vaguely and swatted flies and ants and bugs and listened to the plaintive squawks of the two chickens, and after an hour I was glad to hear the motor again. The *pirogue* came along in a minute: Smet stepped out and said, "I'm tired to death," and he flopped down on the nearest case. He looked bad: a pale-green color. He said he had diarrhea and was very weak, and the rapids were terrible. He could hardly talk for a while. We looked through my medicine box, but I couldn't think of anything to give him, except sodium bicarbonate, and so he had a dose of that and rested in the shade for a while. It was terribly hot now, almost noon.

When he felt better, the boys loaded up again and rigged up the shelter farther forward this time, where it would be more comfortable. Smet rested pretty much all afternoon because there weren't any bad rapids now, and toward the middle of the hottest spell he said he was

all right again and feeling hungry. I was having a private torture with all the new bites on my arms; I suppose it's because I'm new to it, but they almost drove me crazy. If I scratched, they hurt. If I didn't scratch, they itched and felt terribly hot.

I was annoyed at myself because I couldn't really pay any attention to the river, and now it had become beautiful, oily-smooth for long stretches and rippled at the rapids. The marker up in front pointed out the course to the man at the engine, and we twisted and turned along the water wherever it was deepest, sometimes in the middle and sometimes hugging a bank.

In the evening, we came to an island with rapids around it. We skirted this and made for our stopping place, a village high up against the sky. The current was so strong that the men had to pole hard, and in the middle of it the sun burst out into color just before setting. The blue was banded, green near the horizon and shading into periwinkle

---

7 When Hahn lived in New York City in 1928–29, she frequented Harlem night spots and came to know many African-American musicians, artists, and writers. She created a stir by socializing with some of them.

up on the middle of the sky, and the clouds were pure orange and flame color. The trees along the south bank were dark green, while the ones to the north had turned absolutely black, so that they looked like black lace with the green sky showing through. All of this was reflected in the river in pools of color without shape, green and red and orange and blue melting into one another, and along the bank it was oily black. We looked very small and dark in the middle of it, because the banks were very high and so were the trees on top of them, and the river was wide and seemed wider in the dark.

Smet was ill again. When we reached the rest house he sat down again and closed his eyes, giving his orders and doing all the necessary talking with the head man in a very small voice. He thought he would feel better after his bath, but he didn't. He didn't eat any dinner, although he kept telling me to eat more. I wasn't hungry; I didn't feel terribly well either. We both drank coffee, and then I waited without saying anything for a couple of hours while he slept in the chair. I didn't want to wake him and I didn't want him to spend the night sitting up like that, so I waited. Finally he did go to bed, absolutely speechless with fatigue, and I turned in too, and I must have scratched my arms in my sleep because they were bleeding in several places when I woke up in the morning. But I was feeling better and so was he. There were two tadpoles in the water Stephen brought for us to wash in. A whole phalanx of natives lined up to see me clean my teeth, and they watched every stroke of my arm and everything I spit out with the same rapt interest. Smet said, "If you were alone you would never have a minute to yourself. They would be in the rest house all the time, looking."

One old man with a basket on his head trimmed with chicken feathers made up songs and danced to them, laughing very hard at himself. He was the town jester, a privileged person because he went everywhere he wanted and peered at everything, singing about it and giggling, while the others stayed huddled up together at the side. The ones who helped carry the boxes crowded down after us to the boat to be paid. Smet carefully counted out the money from his little burlap

The river view of the hospital at Penge

bag: the franc pieces are tied in bunches of five with red string and the fifty-centime pieces with blue. Everything was settled at last, and we pushed off.

It was an easy trip now, and a short one. Soon we were near Penge and I could see Patrick's house very clearly because the trees have been cut down around it and it's about a hundred meters high from the water. All the way along the banks there were bunches of people at intervals, staring at us or shouting. When we came near the landing place Stephen stood up and said, "Look, Missy. Massa come!"

Suddenly I was terribly excited, and then I saw a lot of little *pirogues* humping along toward us, and then we passed Patrick at full speed, paddling like everything and grinning his widest. I stood up and yelled, "Doctor Putnam, I presume?" and he yelled back, "You've no business being here until six o'clock tonight."

We all piled out at the bank, talking at high speed with Patrick leaping from French to English and back again, depending on whom he was talking to. Now and then, he shouted in Swahili, which he is just learning, at the boys who were carrying. We climbed a steep bank to the road and walked up to the house, talking all the time. It's a nice place that used to belong to the Administrator when Penge was more or less of a trading center: it's built of Congo-manufactured bricks that crumble easily, and there is a veranda all the way around. Other small houses nearby are being fixed up for the boys. One, the best, is on the edge of the river and has a wonderful view, but at present it is occupied by goats and chickens and would need a lot of fixing. Patrick said that later on, if I still insist that we will quarrel if we live in the same house, we might fix it up for me. At present, though, he sees no reason why we should quarrel or why I shouldn't make out perfectly well sleeping in the study and wandering around at my own sweet will.

"I never thought you'd get here; not once in a thousand years," he said. "But now that you're here I'm going to chain you down. Lots of people *said* they'd come, but you're the only one who did." So I began to feel very proud of myself.

And then I saw Chimp again. I had seen her last in Brussels. She cried and threw her arms around me. I don't know if she really remembers me (it's been more than a year) or if it's just that I'm white and she remembers white women. Anyway, it was very affecting, though I've heard bad things about her from everyone but Patrick. She bit everyone in Avakubi, I think, and Smet hates her. I suppose she'll bite me soon. Meantime, everything's all right.

The houses would shock Thompson to death. On the side of the verandah there's a huge pile of junk that might come in handy some day; it's a most indiscriminate mixture of boots that don't fit, pieces of cloth, and odd bits of broken machinery, etc. On the corner table are a few specimens of dried beetles and worms that Patrick is going to send back to Europe when he gets time. Books that Chimp has torn up are lying around waiting to be fixed. The floor is freshly strewn every day with matches, the tops of which Chimp has eaten off. [8]

---

8 At this point in the narrative Hahn inserted two sentences to bridge the gap created by the deletion of eighteen paragraphs to which the Putnam family had objected – down to a paragraph that begins "Someone blows a bugle ...' (see p. 44). Hahn reverted to the original description of her arrival at Penge in "Stewart," which was published in the October 22, 1966, edition of *The New Yorker* and reprinted in Hahn's 1970 book *Times and Places*.

As I was speaking with Patrick, commandingly he said over his shoulder, "Abanzima!"[9]

When she approached, giggling in a shy way, I took her out-stretched hand. My gesture was mechanical; I was overcome with surprise and dismay. I could see that my Undine, my maiden of classic tragedy, was no beauty. Why, she was an old woman! The teeth showing in her welcoming smile were filed to points; her bare breasts were shriveled, and her head – this was the worst shock of all – was shaved smooth as a billiard ball.

In a daze, I walked up the bluff with the others, in single file, quite forgetting to observe that my tin boxes had at last found the mode of carriage they had been made for; they were all neatly balanced on African heads.

We came to the house, which was large – that is, by Congo standards – and went into a room with many books and boxes in it, a wooden table and a desk, camp chairs, and a cot with sheets and a mosquito net.[10]

Members of the household filed in to put down the luggage, and when it was all there we started opening some of the things Patrick had ordered. Chimp kept getting in the way until Patrick took her out onto the verandah and chained her there.

---

9 Hahn first met Putnam at a party in New York City. He had told her the story of his romantic involvement with the young Mangbetu woman who had nursed him back to health when he was gored by an elephant's tusks while he was on a hunting trip in the Belgian Congo. It was unthinkable for Putnam, Harvard-educated and the scion of a socially prominent New England family, to bring his love back to the United States with him. However, determined to be with her, he had returned to the Belgian Congo to live and work. In Hahn's eyes, this made him was a hopeless romantic whose love for his undine – a sprite who, by marrying a mortal and bearing his child, might receive a soul – was something beautiful and pure. For narrative purposes, in the expurgated version of *Congo Solo* Hahn renamed Abanzima "Dubesema."

10 Earlier in the century, Penge had been an important trading post and administrative centre. The house in which Putnam lived was of brick construction and had been the home of the resident Belgian colonial official. Putnam had set-up his medical clinic in the settlement's abandoned two-room schoolhouse.

Abanzima, with her hair regrown. Courtesy of the Peabody Museum of Archaeology and Ethnology, Harvard University, 2001.24.7416

By this time I realized that we were being watched by a large, rapt audience out on the verandah. We were actors on a stage. The audience was quiet, but I could hear some sounds – heavy breathing, a soft whisper, an occasional inadvertent squeal of wonder. Patrick did not seem at all self-conscious about the watchers. Imperturbably, he went on opening crates and I, in loyal imitation, unpacked.

Presently, Abanzima came back with a tray. She was followed by two more women similarly laden. They cleared off part of the table and set down food for us to eat. Evidently, it was for Patrick and me alone. When I asked if Abanzima wasn't going to eat with us, Patrick shook his head and said she didn't, except on special occasions. The locals were very casual about their food, he explained. Abanzima stood watching me, her small brown eyes attentive as a lip reader's. When she caught my eye, she burst into a high cackle of laughter, covering her mouth and rocking her body. Patrick smiled – a thing he didn't do often or easily – saying, "She likes you."

Oh, well, perhaps she wasn't so very ugly after all, I decided. Nor was she as old as I had thought. It was cicatrisation that marked her face and her chest, not wrinkles, as I'd at first supposed, and I was getting used to it. She'd cut her hair, Patrick explained, to make it grow better.

As I was eating a meal of chicken and rice with palm oil, I took stock of the other two girls, each of whom had come forward to offer her hand as soon as she set down her tray. The taller, Nambedru, is a tall girl with a head somewhat elongated, though not much. Her hair was parted and plaited in strips, or stripes, that ran from front to back like the marks on a melon. In fact, her head would have look exactly like a melon if it hadn't been for her eyes. They were beautiful – enormous, set very wide apart and slightly tilted at the outer corners, above high cheekbones. Sissy, the other girl, was small and had a pleasant rather scared smile. Both she and Nambedru were cicatrized and both had filed teeth, like Abanzima's – another feature that I had learned by the end of the meal to take for granted.

Nambedru brought a teapot and filled our cups, serving Patrick first, as she had done all through the meal. "They always serve the men first," he explained. "It would only confuse them if I tried to change the custom."

Nambedru looked critically at the table and leaned over to take away a ketchup bottle, and Patrick tugged playfully at her ear and said something that made her giggle wildly. She retreated in a coltish stumble, and he watched kindly, saying, "She'll learn. She is still pretty young – just came from her village a month or two ago."

"Oh, they never know, but I should guess she's about fourteen. She and Abanzima are Mangbetu, you know – they're cousins of some sort. It's a very interesting tribe. Its region is farther north. You don't find many around here. They have a custom of wrapping their babies' heads with tight bandages as soon as they're born, and the skull is deformed while it's still soft. You've noticed how long her head is? I don't know why Abanzima's isn't the same, but her mother died in childbirth and probably nobody else took the trouble to wrap her head."

I said that was a good thing, naturally assuming that a man would not care for a melon-headed wife, but Patrick didn't understand. He merely shrugged and said that the practice didn't seem to affect Mangbetus faculties in any way.

"And is Sissy also a Mangbetu?" I asked.

"No," said Patrick. "Sissy comes from this village, in a way. Her father's from the local tribe and her mother's a pygmy. You could see it if you knew pygmies – those turned-out lips and the lighter color of her hair. I only got her last week."

At the moment, the implication of that speech was lost on me, for I supposed it was merely Patrick's way of referring to servant hiring.

SOMEONE BLOWS A BUGLE IN THE MORNING, and all the boys line up for inspection and a little drill. The roll is called four times a day. The most soldier-like is the tiny guardian of the hospital, who takes his work seriously and is really very smart and efficient. I think he's about nine or ten. Of the others, Stephen seems to be cock-of-the-walk; he won't drill properly and keeps making jokes. This is because he is the foreigner and rich. He is rich because Patrick can't very well lower the wages he used to get when they were in Douala, and they're on a much higher scale than the boys here. Patrick has offered to send him home again, but he doesn't want to go, naturally. He says that wives cost only three or four hundred francs here, which is a great improvement on the price in the West – two or three thousand.

Everything strikes me as funny. I keep stumbling over a new animal. I had met Chimp, a small monkey that lives in the kitchen, a strange, gentle, furry, sloth-like beast called a paresseux,[11] a baboon that is tied to a nearby tree and always clucks, the famous donkey, and

---

[11] Hahn misspelled the name of this species of tree sloth, which is indigenous to the rainforests of the Congo, spelling the word "parasseux."

a tortoise that is tied to a water-faucet in the back of the house. "Is that all?" I asked Patrick.

"Huh? All the animals? Oh, yes, I think so," he said.

Then later on I called, "If that's all, you've got rats. I just saw a white one. At least I think I saw it – it went awfully fast."

"Oh," he said, "that would be the guinea pig." And he went on with whatever odd job he was doing.

"Well, then, I guess I can have a dog," I said. "The captain of the *Micheline* promised me a puppy if his dog had puppies. The only thing is, how could we get it up here?"

"I hope he can find some way of doing it," said Patrick, heartily. "We need a dog."

However, there has been one casualty. I found it too difficult, scratching Chimp and the paresseux at the same time, and I handed the little beast to Patrick to hold. He was talking at the moment, and went on talking for some time. So did I. A few hours later he called in to me, "Say, what did you do with the paresseux?"

"You had it," I answered. "I gave it to you hours ago."

"Did you? I don't remember. ... I guess it's crept off somewhere. That's too bad; Abanzima likes that animal very much. Well, it will turn up. It's been lost before. It finds some place and goes to sleep, and it's terribly hard to find."

It hasn't come back yet, but I am hopeful for the best and stepping very carefully.

Smet went on to his house, which is about a kilometre farther on, and found that the natives have stolen everything he left there: a lot of cartridges and shoes and salt. He is especially angry about the cartridges because they are hard to get here without a lot of red tape. He's probably going back tomorrow.

Yesterday morning I went up to the hospital. It was Injection Day, when everyone with syphilis or yaws was to come to be treated. Patrick's only been here a week and it was his first day for injections. He first had to study up to make sure of the dose because he has a new kind of arsenic compound and doesn't want to make mistakes. The hospital is just a big two-room house that used to be a schoolhouse in the old days. Crowds of people were waiting. Patrick separated them into contagious cases (with the children who had yaws) and the tertiary cases, who waited in the other room. Then he got to work. He has a few helpers who wear blue jerseys with red crosses on them. The patient lies on the table and they tie a cable around the upper arm to make the vein stand out. Then they let go and Patrick sticks the needle in, very carefully, and shoots in the dose and tells him when to come back, then takes on the next one. He was so careful that it took him a long time. The yaws he showed me: warty growths on the bodies of the children, filled with very thick, sticky pus. One little girl – pretty, too, but then all the children are pretty – had leprosy; the first time I've seen it. It was a very small withered-looking spot. Poor kid. But Patrick says that they have a sort of benignant form out here: the withering is very slow and not painful, and people seldom die of it. He told me, too, that it isn't true that fingers and toes drop off. It's only that the bones melt away and the fingers shrink down: they look as if they had dropped off, but they haven't.

Smet and I waited for him at the house, but he was so busy he sent word for us to eat lunch without him. We went back afterward at about three and found him still working. He was soon finished, though, and came back and ate lunch, and afterward we went up in Smet's boat to see the Falls, a little farther, along. We took Chimp but she stayed with the *pirogue* when we got out. We walked a long way on the rocks, and at one place I slipped on a wet stone and sat down long enough to collect a lot of ants. For the next hour I was grabbing and slapping and pulling off my clothes, much to Smet's amusement. The Falls here are the real article; they've scoured out a channel along what looks like a weak sedimentary bed that is almost vertical, and they're terribly strong.

We went back to Smet's for dinner, and afterward I fell asleep while they were talking, so Patrick and I walked home and forgot Chimp. A few minutes after we got here some boys came and said she had bitten Smet, and would we please send for her. Patrick sent two boys and a bottle of iodine.

"I suppose he tried to take something away from her," said Patrick. "Maybe she had his bed and he wanted her to get off."

"Well, I don't exactly blame him in that case," I said thoughtfully.

"I suppose not. My judgment's warped when it comes to Chimp," he said.

I think I'll walk up now and see how Smet is, and if it was a bad bite. I hope I don't lose my way.

Thursday, March 5

This morning, I was working and saw a newcomer on the veranda, peering through the window. This didn't surprise or disturb me, as there is always a crowd gathered there to see me and I'm beginning to develop the same haughty indifference to it that a goldfish must feel. However, this gentleman came to the window, raised his red fez and said, "*Bonjour*, Madame." Then he made a long speech and I had to call Stephen to translate. It seems the King of Penge had come to pay a call, and the King himself came forward at that and I looked at him. I'd heard of him before from Smet, who thinks he is a congenital idiot. I must say he rather looked it – a tiny man with a weak face; but he was dressed in white, with silver buttons, a red fez, and a stick. I said with Stephen's help that I was glad he had called and that I, too, said "*Bonjour*." I didn't quite know what to do after that. He said that he was my friend. I thanked him again. What I should have done, Patrick explained later, was to invite him into the office to sit down and have a cigarette, but such a simple idea didn't occur to me.

I walked off and looked wildly through all my luggage for a suitable present. There was nothing but a nice necktie and I didn't want to give that away. Meantime, he chatted with Stephen. Then I thought of the one thing that never fails to please white people; I asked him if I could take a photo. He said yes and looked flattered. He announced that he was going now to see Patrick at the hospital, and so I accompanied him with the other chap, the tall attaché. All of this interview was carried on in the face of some difficulty, as Chimp, most disrespectfully munching fish she had stolen from the kitchen, was terrorizing the King by brandishing her chain at him, and a man with a big feather headdress and a harp was trying to sell me eggs at the same time; six of them in a big green leaf.

Patrick was very busy at the hospital, but he washed his hands and greeted the King, and told him that he'd be much obliged if His Majesty would tell everybody to stop peeking through the windows of the anteroom of the clinic. This His Majesty did, and then Patrick told him to go away because he was busy, or words to that effect. The Royal Party withdrew, but sent word back from the house that the King wanted his cigarette, of which I had ignorantly defrauded him. I was awfully sorry and all for making up the deficit, but Patrick was mad and told Stephen, "You tell King him pretty small king. He no bring present for Missy; why Missy give him cigarette? You tell him pretty small king for beg."

This seems to have settled the affairs of state, and I turned my attention to the hospital, reflecting that after all the King did get what he really came for, which was a look. Patrick had some most gory cases to show me. There was a woman who thought she had syphilis; Patrick rather doubted it because none of the symptoms were right, but he explained to me that they always say they have it in the hope that they'll get injections of neotreparsenan;[12] they think this injection is a sort of magic medicine and good for anything. If it was syphilis, it would be a bad thing to wait to the secondary stage, which is difficult to cure. Patrick needs a microscope, he says, to tell about these things, and they won't give him one because they need all they've got at Headquarters.

12 An arsenic-based, water-soluble yellow powder that at the time was used to treat syphilis.

The head men at Sanga assemble to meet Hahn.

Patrick taught me how to give an injection in the vein, and I did one. There was a man there that I had seen before, who has the secondary rash all over. He's had one shot, and yet today when Patrick gave him the second, he had a terrific reaction and began to shake badly. He thought he was going to die. Patrick thought it possible and gave him some adrenalin. The man lay down on the floor and waited very quietly for the death he was certain of meeting, now and then grunting a little. But Patrick wasn't really awfully worried because he had had his worry once before – he told me about it – when Abanzima reacted the same way to a shot he gave her for yaws, and she called in everyone and said good-by and he didn't even have any adrenalin at that time. But she recovered immediately, and he thought this man would too. Meantime he was busy with others.

An old, old skeleton of a woman was sitting with her foot over a bucket, because she had a horrible ulcerous sore on her ankle. He took her last; it was the first time she had been to the hospital. He washed the sore with disinfectant and looked at it – it was about seven inches long and four wide, and had eaten away a great deal of the flesh. He cut off the rotten part, including two tendons, and she didn't even scream. She whimpered a little and stretched out her hands in the air, but waited and let him do what he wanted as if he were God and knew best. Then he packed it and bandaged it, and work was over for the day – only about an hour's overtime this time, which is an improvement on the other days; the work is going better.

This afternoon the man who had had the fit came up to the house, as well as he'd ever been. "I feel as strong as an ox," he said cheerfully. "When can I eat?"

Abanzima is thinner than I expected from the pictures. Thinner and less like the negresses at home, although the main difference, Patrick says, is that her head is shaved just now in mourning for a relative who is dead. But she may be thinner than she was when the picture was taken two years ago, because she smokes too much of the native tobacco; they use a two-meter long pipe made of a length of banana plant, and put a little clay bowl in one end. It needs two people to start it; one to puff and the other to hold the match at the lower end.

Abanzima and Nambedru came from another town downriver. They're both members of the same clan in Mangbetu and use that language when they talk. Nambedru is about seventeen (Abanzima, twenty-seven) and not at all pretty to my European eyes, but I suppose I'll get used to it. She has the Mangbetu head, long and pointed, and her eyes are very big and wide apart, tilted up at the outer edges. Her mouth is big and so is her nose, and yet her face is small. She has a funny, tiny, high voice and a cheerful laugh. Abanzima met and annexed her at Headquarters when Patrick was working there.

CHAPTER 4

HOME AND HOSPITAL

Saturday, March 7, 1931

THE RAINS HAVE STARTED IN. It was raining this morning, but it's stopped now and I've been able to put my monkey skin out in the sun for more curing because it smells bad. I found a nest of ants started in my woolen dressing gown last night; there has been a flight of flying termites, which drop their wings all at once and look like a cross between ants and little worms without them. I went out last evening and looked at flowers. There is a kind of yellow snapdragon or sweet pea, and there's a small shrub with leaves like oak leaves and thorns, and a fruit that looks like guava or pomme rose.[1] There is a tree with brown dead-looking clusters of fruit; lots of this all over. In general, though, there aren't many flowers.

I stayed out for the sunset; not very colorful this time except for the sun itself, which was a brilliant, angry orange.

The women are beginning to get used to my evening bath. The first few evenings I felt more like a performer on a stage than I have ever felt before, even when I was one. The little bathroom opens to the back veranda and has no door; they heat water over the fire that is always burning on the bricks, and pour it directly into Patrick's tub.

---

1 The fruit of a shade tree native to India and Malaysia, which was exported to Africa and the Caribbean by British merchants in the late 18th century (also known as plum rose or rose apple).

Then they bring a lantern and set it at the door so that they can all see freely, and they sit in a rapt semicircle while I undress and get in. Themselves, they hardly ever bathe that way; they take the water out into the brush and slosh it over themselves with their hands. But my clothes interest them. I gave a green beret to Patrick one day, and Abanzima has always been most scornful of it. She changes her clothes about three or four times a day. The whole costume of the native dress was probably the original of the ensemble, Patrick said last night – a long skirt, which can, if necessary, be worn as a simple dress, wound around under the armpits, but is usually only a skirt gathered up and tied at the waist; a blouse with short sleeves set on a wide band, coming down to the top of the skirt, and a headdress of the same material twisted around with the ends tucked in at the sides. They don't sew much themselves, but have a tailor in each town with a sewing machine.

Patrick has a bad cold, which he insists will last for at least eight days. The entire household is more or less in the dumps, except me. The tiny girl has a chest affliction and stays in bed quietly, which is a bad sign because they don't go to bed until they simply have to. Abanzima hasn't been well for a long time: her head bothers her. She's getting better, however, and laughs more than she did at first. Nambedru is suffering from a highly complex set of sulks which, Abanzima tells Patrick, can only be cured by his making her a sort of second official cook instead of merely a "boy" – i.e., a servant, waiting on table and sweeping and making beds. I can quite see her point.

Patrick and Ngimu between them have fixed the phonograph, which was warped out of shape. We have evening concerts now, and the boys and their wives come up and listen, motionless, until the machine is closed and put away for the night. Stephen is ideal for working it: he likes to do it, and we simply arrange the records and give them to him to play. Their favorite is the Paul Robeson record "No Room to Hide Down There" and "Didn't It Rain" and a few other spirituals on the same disk. It's the only Negro record Patrick has. It's fun to watch them. They love it.

The most alert of the *infirmiers* [male hospital attendants] is a Mobudu boy called Mautea, about fifteen-years-old. He has the same features that Nambedru has – a lengthy head, very thick lips and extremely wide-set, slightly tilted eyes. I think, myself, and so does Patrick, that the eyes are so wide-set because they are pulled apart by the head-lengthening process. I am going to watch all the long heads after this to see what the eyes are like. Mautea can typewrite the hospital forms and speaks a little French. He asked Patrick yesterday for permission to learn to ride the bicycle, which was given him, and he practised boisterously all afternoon. "Have you broken the bicycle?" Patrick asked him later. "Not yet," he answered cheerfully. He was sergeant yesterday, in charge of the drilling, and they had an extra careful one because they've been getting slack. Owing to too much giggling and lack of discipline, Patrick made them stand at attention for ten minutes, rewarding them afterward with a cigarette apiece. But when they got the order to relax, after the ten minutes, and were told they could all do just as they wanted, the whole ten of them immediately set to scratching.

I played with Chimp for a long time yesterday. She pretends to bite my hand and at the same time hold her own hand to my mouth for me to bite, or sometimes offers me her foot instead. This is rather awkward: I simply make the motion of biting, however, and she is satisfied. I never get tired of her imitations. What does a chimpanzee think about? Does she know she's a chimp, or does she think she's a human, a sort of extra-unfortunate human whom everyone beats? The baboon never imitates. I must watch the tiny monkey: I don't know it very well.

When I say a word in Swahili, the servants are delighted. Abanzima's learning a little English, too. They've made a new joke about Chimp, calling her "*Bula Matadi,*" which is their phrase for the Government, because she never listens to anyone or takes any advice.[2]

---

2 "Bula matadi" is probably an expression from the Kikongo dialect that relates to the bulldozers the Belgian colonial government used to break rocks and stones for roadways. It is a wry reference to the administration's use of brute power to impose its will.

Sunday, March 8

It is Sunday, and market day in the village. Patrick wants to improve the market, which so far has been held in a horrible sunny place; a few old women selling bananas. He plans to persuade the King to move it into the shade and to stimulate trade; next week he's sending Abanzima down with a lot of fishhooks, and I intend to go along with anything I can find; extra shoes, etc. We went this morning with a few things; the whole household. Abanzinga rode the donkey, and constantly all the way, more for the histrionic effect than because he was afraid, he kept yelling, "Oh, my master! My master!" Patrick rode circles around the cavalcade with his bicycle, and Chimp followed him begging piteously for a ride, and the rest of the ménage stretched out behind, with me in the lead – giggling, as usual. We made a formal call on the Sultan and he came with us to the market; Patrick purchased some manioc flour and I took photographs of everything. Then the donkey was called into use: two great bunches of bananas were slung across his back, though he kicked vigorously, and Patrick got on to see what would happen. He bucked all over the marketplace, and everyone scattered widely. The old man with chicken feathers in his hat went one way. The lady with Arab blood and a veil went the other. In between, several hundred people were going in a zigzag direction while Chimp climbed a very tall tree in record speed. When Patrick was at last unseated, there was a roar of applause. Going home, Nambedru was put up on the donkey, though she protested even more than he did. She rode for a short time, hunched miserably and whining in her funny falsetto voice, while I almost burst laughing. When she got off she joined me in the laugh, and we came home without any more accidents.

Vandevelde, the Administrator from Avakubi, is here. An *infirmier* is sick, and I offered the other day to help Patrick at the hospital. He gave me the clerk's job of writing out slips for the patients and keeping the records up to date. Mautea, erstwhile clerk, helped with injections. There are two Injection Days a week, and they're by far the busiest. The man who'd been so knocked out came up for another, and they

54

Patrick Putnam (squatting) engages in some market-day bargaining

The market-day crowd dressed in their finery

gave him a very small one, which didn't seem to hurt him at all. I noticed the old lady with the sore on her leg, waiting for another dressing. Patrick said she'd been up every day, but the sore wasn't healing. He thought it was probably a sign of tertiary syphilis; she grew weaker and weaker, and, if possible, thinner. She could hardly move now. He was worried because the care of her leg took up much more time than it was worth, speaking from the point of view of the community. And yet he couldn't neglect her.

To make matters worse, the five soldiers of the Administrator, not having anything to do here at Penge, looked up all their old ailments and came to hospital with the demand that they be attended to immediately, as they were superior beings. The Administrator himself looked in for a minute and seemed properly impressed. We had made plans to go in the late afternoon to the swimming beach Smet had pointed out, for a dip as soon as the sun wasn't too hot. But as it turned out, we couldn't make it.

At noon, ordinarily closing time, Patrick gave me a lesson in intramuscular injection in the buttocks, for people who haven't good enough veins in their arms. I did two: a little boy and a woman, and my hand shook disgracefully, but they didn't seem to mind. Then he sent me back to take care of Vandevelde while he finished up, dressing the old lady's leg and giving her a shot of sulphotrep [*sic*],[3] very weak, to combat the possible syphilis. He came late to lunch, very preoccupied. The old lady, he said, had gone into a coma and he had arranged for her to stay at the hospital, sleeping as she was on the table and having the sore dressed twice a day instead of once. He talked again of the impossibility of neglecting cases like that, although ethically he should. After lunch he went back to her and stayed until evening, coming back to announce that he had been cutting the sore all afternoon. He has a bad cold, but didn't complain.

3 (or sulphotep): A pale yellow liquid that smelled like garlic and in the 1930s was used as an anti-clotting drug. Today, it has been identified as being carcinogenic and is no longer in medical use. Hahn misspelled the name of the drug in her manuscript.

At dinner, which the three of us always have together, a boy came and said that the old lady was dying but that her husband was with her. Patrick said that he couldn't do any more, to let her die. He turned instead to his customary chess game with Vandevelde, while I watched and read, alternately.

Vandevelde went home at eleven. I went to bed. Patrick went to hospital to have a last look around. I was suddenly waked by his holding a lantern over my face, and as I opened my eyes he said: "Can you stay awake?"

I mumbled, "Sure. Why?"

"Put on something warm, then, and prepare to do it. The old woman isn't dead yet. If she were, I wouldn't mind, but as it is, I think I'd better stick around and see what can be done. I need some one to talk to me, or I'll drop off."

I put on a bathrobe and slippers and we walked down the road with the gasoline lamp. "Her husband's there, sleeping on the floor with a mat," he said. "He's a young man. He says she's been a good old wife to him, a hard worker, and he hates to see her die. He's never slept with her, but she's a good worker."

It was really cold. We found two fires in the hospital, one next the table where she was lying and the other in front of the watchman's chair. She was fast asleep, breathing steadily but with a peculiar gasping, and her lower lip moved each time. It was the first time I'd seen her when she wasn't grimacing with pain, and she was so frail and skinny that she looked like the skeleton of an embryo. Her husband, on the floor, sat up with his arms around his legs and looked at us interestedly. She was more or less coiled around a kettle of hot water that Patrick had put there, which kept her warm locally, but otherwise her flesh was cool. Mautea was the watchman for the night.

Patrick tried to feel her pulse, but was afraid he was counting his own. I felt his and counted aloud, to compare it. Hers was weak, but faster. He'd given her some stimulant that was keeping her alive, and now he gave her adrenalin. She seemed to improve. After a while, during which we kept awake by talking to each other – the red brick floor seemed to make me drowsier, just looking at it – Patrick decided to try an injection of salt solution. We mixed up a proper stew under his direction, and then, keeping it hot by putting the container in a dish of hot water, he spent a long time trying to find a vein large enough to stick. But it was useless, so he said he would do it subcutaneously. He had to sit on the edge of her table while Mautea and I stood by with the lamp and container respectively. He'd made her husband get up on the table next her, to keep her warm, though the husband protested vigorously that now was not the time to sleep with his wife, especially as he never had. The injection went incredibly slowly. Mautea held the container high or low, according to instructions – to make it easier, he'd set it on his head sometimes. My arms grew terribly tired holding the lamp. Patrick must have felt much worse holding the needle steady. Then the gas lamp went out, empty, and we had to use the oil one, which isn't so good – we haven't any more gasoline here. To complicate things I had an attack of stomach cramps and disgraced myself by taking time out to sit down. But that passed too.

Mautea retired for some sleep. The husband was quiet, but didn't sleep – I saw his eyes peering at us every time I looked at him. She went on gasping and sleeping. We talked disjointedly about everything in the world; finally turning to the subject of Pavloff, Patrick's superior, and an autopsy he once conducted, or didn't conduct, in a poisoning case. This involved a long and juicy discussion of poison symptoms, during which the injection was finished.

"Are you going to go on sitting here?" I asked Patrick, who had sunk back in the chair with obvious intent to spend what was left of the night.

"No, I'd better go on home."

We left the lamp with Mautea and walked home by moonlight. It was about three o'clock and he stumbled on the road. I fell asleep the minute I got into bed.

At six we all got up and went to hospital again just for a look. She was exactly the same. He left orders for her to be given an enema, because he wanted to feed her that way with beaten egg and milk; and after breakfast he went back to take care of the regular work. I went to sleep again for a while. When I woke up, he was home again and said that she had died during the enema. He didn't have time to sleep in the morning, nor yet in the afternoon (though I did) before we went on a swimming trip.

I went down to the landing in Vandevelde's *tipoye*,[4] a sort of sedan-chair, and I enjoyed it. Patrick had rigged up a strange craft, laying four broad planks across two parallel *pirogues* that were paddled by two men, and we had cushions on the raft-thing where we could sprawl at ease. An assortment of men came along in a big canoe, with the *tipoye*.

At the rapids just before we came to the beginning of the road to the Falls, we had a hard time and Vandevelde poled while Patrick got out and pushed in the water. Then we crossed the river and got out. There was some confusion about the proper road. I took what turned out to be the right one, while Patrick and Vandevelde took another way. Patrick shouted at me to follow, which I did, forsaking my path and going back to find that they had disappeared. I shouted, but the Falls roar so loudly that no one can hear anything. So I went a third way directly by the riverbank, slipping on mossy rocks and occasionally calling out mournfully without reply.

I found Patrick at last, but Vandevelde had strayed. We came to a small sandy place that we thought must be Smet's bathing beach, but though I stopped and put on my bathing suit, Patrick went on to reconnoiter. He left his clothes here. So did Vandevelde, who came along in a minute. Then Patrick came back and said he'd found the real beach, which was much better, and he told us to hurry up and get our swim, because it was getting dark. We followed him: I in my shoes and carrying my clothes. The others left theirs and walked barefoot. It *was* a nice beach, and after a little while I stopped being afraid of crocodiles, though I jumped every time I bumped into a log.

4 A sheltered seat hung between two poles and carried by native porters, was a favoured means of overland transport for white colonial officials who traveled to remote areas.

It was marvelous swimming. The water was warm and the sky was getting dark and a storm was coming up, so the wind blew and the lightning flashed, and yet there was no rain.

We decided to stay until dark. Patrick was sure the boys would send someone with a lamp, if it grew late enough. It was better to stay in the water than to get out – warmer.

However, though it grew late no one came. The boys were too stupid or tired to come, and they couldn't hear us shouting.

At last, we started back to find the clothes. I was in luck because I had my shoes; the others didn't, and besides, Patrick was getting cold. We had a hard time after we reached the first clearing; it's always dark in the bush even at noon, and now it was pitch-black except for the lightning. I began to think of leopards. So, I think, did the others. We did find the clothes, though – it was Vandevelde who did – and now we all had our shoes, but couldn't find the road back because it was too dark to see. I wanted to go back by the river, the way I had come. Patrick was unwilling; he hadn't come that way and wouldn't believe it was any good. He was all for waiting for lightning and groping back through the forest. We did try it for a while, but if we ever had the road we lost it immediately, and it was so dark that we couldn't even see one another, and kept wandering off.

It was impossible walking; you bumped into waist-high fallen trees with every other step, and kept stubbing your toes. Vandevelde agreed with me that the river way was better. When Patrick gave in at last, we went to the river and found that it was quite easy and fast going if we were careful of moss. However, although he admitted it was all right, Patrick was now fired with the idea of finding that road before we got back. He left us without our noticing – he was last – and disappeared.

Vandevelde and I, stopping to hail once again, heard the boys answer close by. We turned around and looked for Patrick, but couldn't find him. So we hurried on to the clearing with the *pirogues* and he told some of the men to go back and look for Monsieur – we found my little flashlight in the canoe, which would help. They didn't want to go. They were afraid of leopards and snakes, but they had to. After we had waited a long time they brought him back – he had heard them coming and hid behind a tree to scare them. We all scolded one another and started for home. It was a fast trip and perfectly lovely.

CHAPTER 5

MATOPE

Saturday, March 14, 1931

VANDEVELDE LEFT THE DAY BEFORE YESTERDAY, after vowing that he would come back in eight days, when his work was finished, for a really pleasant rest. We feel proud of ourselves for making him like us. Ordinarily in Africa everyone hates everyone, and so this is a welcome change. I've been very busy with a new charge. It's not really my charge, but I feel responsible. The little boy on whom I practised for my first shot came back last Thursday for his second treatment. He hobbled very painfully and his toes were all tied up with raffia and old leaves. Otherwise, of course, he wore nothing but a little rag of a belt. Patrick said that his feet were full of jiggers,[1] probably; so after his shot we unwrapped the toes and looked. They were very bad. He had three places where the jiggers were gathered in masses, and his big and little toes were ulcerated. "That's from neglect," said Patrick. "He's probably an orphan. Otherwise his parents would have dug the jiggers out as he got them." One of the *infirmiers* got to work with an ivory pin, and I watched fascinated because I hadn't seen the opera-

---

1 Tiny, six-legged larvae of sand flies. These parasites breed in poor hygienic conditions and affix themselves to the skin of the host, usually the feet. Their bites produce a wheal that is accompanied by severe itching, If left untreated, jiggers cause flesh to deteriorate, resulting in deformities and even death. Jiggers continue to be a major health issue in many areas of sub-Saharan Africa.

tion before. The boy, who was named Matope, started to cry. As the jigger was extracted whole, Patrick told him to kill it himself, which he did ferociously. But the process was a long one, and at the end of a painful hour we had only about twenty of the beasts out and a lot more to come.

Matope had to be held down, especially when his ulcers were washed. He shrieked over and over, *"Basi kwenda, bwana!"* ["Let me go, sir!" (Kinguana)] I felt very sorry for him, especially when I remembered that he had come to the hospital of his own volition – a hell of a way to treat a good boy like that! Besides, he was young – only four or five. I was amazed to hear myself saying to Patrick, "Let me take him home. He oughtn't to walk on those feet."

Patrick agreed, after a little thought. We'd have to take care that Nambedru didn't catch yaws, and that he didn't infect the ground with his jiggers. So we had him carried back to the house and put the matter up to Abanzima, who said it would be all right. Meantime, Matope, whose original self-control had been completely shattered by pain, went on sobbing quietly because he was laboring under the delusion that he was going to jail for having so many jiggers.

To quiet him, Patrick handed him a banana. He shook his head vigorously; "I've just had my injection," he said.

"Bright boy!" cried Patrick. "I'd forgotten."

He wrapped up the kid's feet in bandages and gave him a bowl of antiseptic to keep the worst foot in, all afternoon. Now and then I took a look at him, sitting on a cot on the back porch with his foot in the bowl, and his eyes very large, looking at the cooking preparations. I gave him some beads to string, and he made himself a necklace. In the evening he had something to eat and grew more cheerful.

When I sat next him a while, I saw that he was shivering. It was dark and getting pretty cold. So I turned all my trunks out, trying to find something to give him, and I found a woolen under-vest. It was more like a nightgown on him, but he seemed to like it. That night, Patrick got one of the Red Cross blankets, and we put him to sleep on a mat next my bed, on the floor.

Hahn and her young friend Matope

Next morning, I thought I'd better go with him to the hospital. He followed me obediently, though he looked dubious at sight of the building again: once inside he began to strut, proud of his new clothes and reassured by the presence of relatives who had come up to find out

64

what was happening to him. They told Patrick that his father was dead and his mother had gone away with another man. Patrick scolded his great-uncle, an old one-eyed man with a beard, for neglecting Matope's feet so badly, and said that he would keep the boy four or five days for treatment, after which he could decide for himself whether to go home or to stay here. The old fellow excused himself on the grounds that he had only one eye and couldn't be expected to see jiggers: both he and Matope's brother, a full-grown man, seemed cheerful enough at the prospect of leaving him with us. Matope got some cigarettes from me and gave them to his relatives, then waved goodbye loftily. He stuck by me all morning at the hospital, though as his turn drew near he grew a little thoughtful and suggested that he go back to the house. He shrieked with redoubled vigor at the treatment. As a matter of fact, he's coming along nicely – the jiggers are dead and have thrown their eggs out, and the ulcers seem to be healing. However, he didn't run away in the afternoon, but stayed in the bureau most of the time and learned not to be afraid of Chimp.

Matope is fascinated by the drill of the servants and comes hobbling out whenever he hears the bugle. This morning he burst into tears when I told him to go to the hospital; he announced firmly that he would not go, and when Patrick told him that he must, he wailed bitterly. Chimp put her arms around him and clucked. At last he left, fortified by the promise of a piece of honey-bread; he and Chimp walked up the path together, hand in hand, and once in a while Matope stumbled on the hem of his gown.

Tuesday, March 17

Sunday six of us almost went up to meet out respective gods. Patrick had rigged up the motor on the most likely looking *pirogue* he could find; building a framework on the back to screw it on. The craft itself was small and very unsteady; a slender U-shape in cross section. He shouted to me to cut to large pieces of honey bread for us to eat in lieu of lunch, and to bring them along. We were all eager to see how the boat worked. A gang was gathered at the starting place: Bwama Asumani (the best and the largest of the village head men), Abanzima, Nambedru, a lady from town, a distant aunt of Abanzima who visited us on the way back to Wamba, Ngimu, and, of course, Matope, who sticks to me like a barnacle. Everyone was cheerful except Nambedru, who was having one of her grouches. Patrick and I have given them all new names that they don't know about, so that we can talk about them without suspicion. Abanzima has had hers for some time – ever since I arrived, in fact: she's Prudence. But we have given the others their own, too.

Nambedru – Ophelia.

Sissy – Diana.

Matope – Angus

Patrick went out for a little spin around by himself and discovered that the motor worked all right, but that the canoe was very, very tippy indeed. Asumani was inclined to try it out, but he hesitated a little, at last confining his contribution to a boatman, ordered summarily out of a passing fishing canoe, to be our marker and general pilot.

"Want to try it, Mickey?" Patrick called. "I warn you, we might get wet."

This was no terror for me so I climbed in and sat down. It *was* tippy.

My faithful shadow Matope tried to follow, but since Sissy had been promised a ride, we thought that one child was enough. I gave my bathing suit to Matope and told him to take it home, as I didn't want to lose it in case we should have to swim. With Sissy and the boatman, we started out. We hadn't gone far upstream when the motor died, at the same time that we discovered that our boatman was one of the dumbest individuals in Africa and, moreover, had a bad ear that took his attention off the business in hand. Patrick had told him carefully not to try to point out the road, but only to warn him about rocks. This he was to do by pointing his paddle, as the motor made it impossible to hear anything. He couldn't remember, though: he kept on brandishing the paddle and pointed out the road. This made Patrick so angry that he shifted position suddenly to throw another paddle at the man, and the canoe almost capsized just as I caught sight of … a log? A log with two bumps on it, sticking out of the water, and another bump up in front?

I looked closer, hardly daring to turn my head suddenly. Just as I saw what it really was and my stomach almost turned over, Patrick saw it too and cried out, "Gosh, did you see that crocodile?"

"Yeah," I answered simply, and turned my agonized attention to the canoe. I didn't do anything. I just sat there and felt sick. It was at this moment that the motor stopped. … I've seen crocodiles before, of course, right in front of the *Micheline*. But never so close, and never so intimately. I could smell this beast: a horrible sticky, fishy smell. And it wasn't even looking at us: it just lay there and waited. I looked at the canoe and saw as if it were for the first time that we were only about six inches out of the water, and my elbow occasionally dipped in when there was a ripple.

Patrick went back to the landing to see what was the matter with the motor. He looked and said that there was nothing. Then he asked Abanzima if she didn't want to come along; she accepted with alacrity, and so did the lady from town. We wanted another boatman, but Asumani had gone away and there weren't any other men around. Thus, augmented by two more passengers, we started out again on what Patrick called a voyage of exploration. The motor ran well: we all held our paddles ready for the first rapids: the boat lurched as if every inch would be its last – at least in an upright position – and I sat there wordless, shaking, in the last stages of fright. I have never been so frightened for such a long time at a stretch. It was the same feeling that I have had when a motor car skidded into a ditch, or lightning struck somewhere near me, but I have always thought that it was like the lightning flash itself, so poignant that it couldn't last more than a second. Now, however, I was afraid for a stretch of time, and I stayed on the crest of the emotion. It was a queer feeling. I didn't stop thinking. I thought, all the time: for a while I imagined what it would be like when the crocodile grabbed my leg, and I wondered if everyone would scream as he was dragged under. This made me begin to shake so hard that I stopped thinking about it. Then, without slackening in my fear, I began to shape the words to tell about the crocodile if I should get home and start to write about it in this diary. After a moment I thought this rather funny. And yet I was still sincerely terrified.

I noticed that my stomach was out of order and wondered if that was the fear or the physical effect of the smell. I began to reassure myself idiotically by thinking that after we had crossed the first rapids we would probably be safe – "If I were a crocodile," I said to myself, "I would be too lazy to climb rapids." Then I remembered that I had been swimming just a couple of kilometers away from that place: I had been swimming there twice and we were planning to go again this afternoon if we could get the boat that far. I resolved never to go swimming again.

Meantime, the canoe went on and my legs were stiff from trying to obey Patrick and sit like a sack, instead of attempting to balance. We reached the rapids and stopped the motor. He had to get out to push. Abanzima got out too, taking off all her clothes but a little white petticoat. The boatman too. ... I knew what I ought to do, but for a few minutes I couldn't do it. Every time I opened my mouth, I remembered that smell. At last my mind forced my tongue: I said, "Hadn't I better get out, too?"

"No," said Patrick. "We need some weight to steady it. Stay there, you three."

I watched them and waited almost placidly for the first shriek, the first one to be dragged under. Nothing happened, though Patrick shouted directions so suddenly sometimes that I thought he was caught. I crouched there and went on shaking. My mind worked busily, and to my eternal shame be it that I was making plans all the time what to do when Patrick should be eaten. Could I walk back to camp along the banks – that is, if I wasn't eaten while swimming ashore? If so, I thought I could wait there until Vandevelde came back; he could take me to Avakubi. Yes, it would be all right. ... I drew a deep breath and then suddenly thought, "As soon as you get back safely, you're going to be ashamed of all this." Then I thought, "I know it, but I haven't any time to be ashamed now. I'm scared." And a further conciliatory afterthought, "I don't *want* Patrick to be eaten, even if I am saved. I like him." But oh, dear, oh, dear, it was an afterthought. Immediately afterward came the memory of Vandevelde's remark one evening: "I am not afraid of being killed, but if I should lose a leg or an arm, I would shoot myself in the head." Yes, I thought, he was right – and yet wouldn't he change his mind if, for instance, his arm was bitten off by a crocodile? And by the way; was I going to be able to hold on forever without being ill or was my stomach feeling a little better now?

Suddenly my stomach was all right, and I saw that it was a beautiful day. How I love trees! What a wonderful world! I had snapped out of it.

All this time, and it wasn't so much time after all, Patrick and the boatman had hoisted the canoe up pretty well. But we were now faced with a lot of small rocks just below the surface of the water. Patrick went ahead and tried to pull up a few, to dig a channel. Abanzima began to lament vigorously. "I'm doing something terrible, but I don't know what," Patrick called to me. He listened carefully to her wailing and then understood. "Oh, if I pull up rocks I'll make it, rain," he explained. "All right; I have enough out of the way now, anyway." We all glanced at the sky: there were some clouds, as a matter of fact.

But the *pirogue* had passed the worst part. All would have been well now if the boatman hadn't suddenly, for no reason that we could see, pulled it the wrong way so that it was caught broadside and whirled around in exactly the wrong direction. Patrick lost his temper completely and threw something at the man, then told him to come on back and help right the canoe. The man was so frightened that he began to cry and refused to come. He grimaced exactly like Chimp, and I was angry with Patrick. I forgot my manners and said, "Don't be so hard on him."

"Well, damn it," said Patrick, "did you see what the idiot did? Did you ever see anything so stupid?"

"It doesn't do any good to throw things. He's just an animal. Don't be so hard on him."

"He's got to learn to come when I tell him. Even Chimp does that."

It seemed funny, again, to be arguing about ethics in midstream with half the crew standing in the water. We both laughed and then the man came and helped pull it right. We started upstream again, all sitting in the boat, but we had shipped so much water that we began to sink. Luckily we were very near shore, and we stopped and bailed the water out; that is, Abanzima did, very deftly, with a big green leaf. I was just ballast on the entire voyage. The boatman kept crying and feeling his ear. I was sorry for him but afraid to show it.

Upstream again. We stopped at the usual place and Patrick said that the women should all go along to the bathing beach, which is above another rapid, and swim while he and the boatman went out on another tour to see how high they *could* get. Abanzima didn't want to go, but when I started ahead they followed. Patrick had assured me that they wouldn't be shocked at my lack of a bathing suit so long as we were alone. I'm not so sure, because they more or less expect me to hold to my traditions; still, they followed my example when I pulled my things off (I was soaked anyway) and we all ran into the water. I had completely forgotten the crocodile. The beach was sunny and pleasant. We splashed around at a great rate: the lady from town was so pleased with everything that she did a little dance; standing ankle-deep in the water and wiggling all the muscles below the waist and none above. We laughed a lot. Sissy kept diving for my toes and then running when I chased her. We sat on the shallow bottom and the others cleaned their teeth with sand, rubbing it in with their fingers and offering me some in their hands. I did it too, with almost no hesitation, and it wasn't so bad as I had expected.

Every now and then Abanzima looked anxiously downstream for the little puff of smoke that meant that the boat was still upright. She always found it. After some time, the canoe itself appeared safely above the last rapid, and soon Patrick joined us, swimming at

Putnam's motorized pirogue out on the river

The view of the river from the *barza* of Patrick Putnam's house at Penge

a modest distance to preserve the amenities. He shouted to me, "I think that we'll manage to get home all right if the weaker sex will control themselves in the canoe and stop shifting around. It was much steadier without all of you."

I let this insult pass almost unchallenged because I felt very guilty. Perhaps I *had* been wincing a little too obviously.

Going back was amazingly easy, partly because we knew the channel now. No one had to get out, even. Sometimes we had to paddle a little and once a back stream almost sent us ashore. I thought I saw a crocodile again but didn't say anything. After we landed, Abanzima said that she had seen it too – all the natives had – and that it was a different one from the first, and even bigger.

I STARTED TO TEACH MATOPE THE ALPHABET, but he's not very bright about it. For practical things he's amazingly apt and quick to obey orders, but so far he's not too eager to learn to read. He resents my reading, too – at least I think he does, though he shows it only by a sort of dumb loitering in my neighborhood when I sit with a book. However, both he and Chimp are up at hospital this morning, so I'm free. I played the phonograph for Matope, the first time he'd heard it, and he's mad about it. Patrick asked him today if he wanted to go home or to sleep here, and he said he wanted to stay. I have given him soap and told him to wash his own clothes, and he does it very satisfactorily.

His wardrobe is growing and we keep it on the lower shelf of my bookcase when it's not in use. There is the nightgown thing (my woolen vest), a pair of pink pantaloons (erstwhile my bloomers) and the raffia used for keeping them up, a large dirty handkerchief that I must tell him to wash, his string of beads, and a magnificent red buckler-effect that was sold to me in London as a spine-pad to wear with my bush shirts. He is now educated to the extent of taking off his clothes when he goes to bed. I think he likes the nightgown best, though he wore the red buckler to market on Sunday morning and made a great hit. He pads along behind me and greets his old friends with a lordly gesture or an airy shake of the hand. He knocks Chimp around very roughly, but she seems to enjoy it, and last night when Nambedru and I were putting him into his blanket, she came lolloping in and bit Nambedru, thinking that we were hurting Matope.

After work yesterday at the hospital, Mayanimingi, a ten-year-old *infirmier*, came up and handed me a note and then ran away. In very sprawly letters, I read: "*Musieur Mandam Do ne mwa tabaki basi mini.* … Mayanimingi." We made it out at last: "*Monsieur, Madame, donnez-moi tobacco.* ["Mister Madame, give me my tobacco."] That's all. Mayanimingi."

"*Basi mini*" means "That's all." His own name means "very hairy," but he isn't. I don't know where he got the name. I gave him a cigarette and put the note away carefully.

The man who makes dresses came up yesterday with his machine and put in a busy time making aprons for the *infirmiers*, and sheets for us. The bolt of white cloth that came up from Stan[leyville] has had a disturbing effect on the girls, who can imagine no good use for cloth except to make dresses. Every bit of cloth that isn't used like that, they consider criminally wasted. The other night Nambedru, after seeing the cloth, dreamed that an uncle of hers who was dead had appeared to her and asked her why she and Abanzima weren't mourning for him – i.e., wearing white clothes. She reported it to Patrick, who unsympathetically demanded of Abanzima why she wasn't wearing the white clothes she already had. Abanzima explained that mourning clothes had to be new.

"The queer thing about it is," he said later, when he was telling me about it, "I think she really did dream it. But it shows how cloth runs in their minds. They're mad for it."

I found out yesterday that the tailor makes the women pay twenty francs for each dress that he makes. That's a lot of money, judged by their standards. I asked Patrick why the women didn't learn to do their own sewing.

"Oh, they wouldn't think of it," he said. "Such a notion would never enter their heads. They've been brought up to believe that it's a magic art vouchsafed to a few men. Every woman in the Congo has her dresses made like this." If so, they're certainly not like the Navajos.

Navajo men and women make their own shirts and trousers and skirts. They may rent or borrow a sewing machine, but they do the work themselves.

Lots of times I find myself remembering the Navajo country [around Sante Fe, New Mexico]. I feel just as I did when I was living there; so many things remind me of them, especially the unconscious, unwary expressions of these people's faces. I suppose most aboriginals, if that's the word I mean, have something in common: if you take anyone and rub off his civilization he is still a man underneath, and unadorned he looks more like other men. Though a "savage" isn't really unadorned. Schweinfurth[2] says civilization leads to simplicity; the savage usually deforms himself with tattooing or colored mud or teeth-filing and the civilized man leaves himself as he is. He doesn't, though. As I remember the Indians, they didn't go to much trouble about themselves except for their hair ... but they did take baths sometimes. If I go on like this, trying to grade "cultures," I'll be measuring skulls with the most futile of the anthropologists.

Sunday, March 22

Matope's costume is completed, and a prouder little Negro never strutted over the earth. I was really afraid he would burst when I put the fez on his head. He managed to refrain from smiling until he got out of the room, but a moment later I saw him peering anxiously into my tiny hand mirror, adjusting the fez to a more becoming angle and

---

2 Georg August Schweinfurth (1836–1925) was a German botanist and traveler who explored the region of the upper Nile River basin known as the Bahr al Ghazal and discovered the Uele River, a tributary of the Congo.

grinning proudly. It's had one effect: he took another bath this morning, which makes the second in two days. Immediately after he had had a good look at himself he picked up the hippo whip and asked me if he could take a walk down to the hospital – to show off, of course. I told him to go ahead; he was gone such a long time that I'm sure he went all the way to town. Patrick's pleased, too, and says we must have another kaftan made to use while this one is being washed.

Matope kept the fez on until the very minute he went to bed, and that minute he put off as long as possible, though he fell asleep over and over again, sitting upright. While I am bereft of Patrick for company at meals, Matope has taken to coming in and eating with me: his head does not come up to the top of the table, but he sits there staunchly and tries to eat whatever I give him. Most of the European food he finds difficult, but he can down any amount of rice. I had to order him to bed at last most peremptorily, and I gave him a special hanger to put the kaftan on at night. He went to sleep smiling, though his foot has been giving him trouble again.

We had a *mokanda* [a message (Lingala dialect)] from Vandevelde, who is having a good time, though he's bitten to death, checking up on the work of the previous Administrator and unearthing any number of mistakes. This pleases him immensely. He says he'll be back here in five or six days. I hope Patrick will be up and about again – he's worse today with a bad stomach ache, though the cold is better.

I led the cavalcade to market again this morning. I put on all the jewelry I have except the bracelets I'm saving to give away on special occasions. I wore a khaki skirt, red jersey, Deauville sandals, no stockings, huge brass earrings, a coral chain, and three rings. The helmet over all gave the finishing touch. Abanzima wore a chenille blouse, a Javanese batik cloth for a skirt, and ditto for a headcloth. Nambedru and Sissy looked about the same as usual; Matope, of course, had his new clothes on.

We arrived rather early due to having hurried to stay ahead of the donkey, which was attired in his new saddle and bridle: the market hadn't opened so we went up to Sultan Saidi's house. He bade us welcome and brought out chairs: a grand armchair for me and a mat at my feet for Matope, who squatted down exactly like a dwarf in an Aubrey Beardsley drawing.[3] Opposite us were ranged the headmen, looking lustfully at Abanzima's basket of cigarettes for market. Patrick had told me to be sure she sold the packages for three francs fifty: she got sore last Sunday because the prices of other things were too high; and she jacked up the price of the cigarettes to four francs, with no sales as a result. I kept an ear cocked in her direction. I sat in a lordly manner, wishing violently that I knew more Swahili (though my vocabulary's coming along) while Asumani chattered and kept the crowd giggling. I think it was moving day in the village, because people kept walking by carrying furniture.

Saidi's wives lurked behind him and stared at me; I, in turn, stared at a woman walking on the highway in white high-heeled slippers which were put on the wrong feet, and a pink European dress trimmed in coarse lace with headcloth to match. The most elaborate ladies had umbrellas; so did some of the men. The more I see of the snaky head-dresses they have here, looking very much like the cootie cages we used to have at home, the gladder I am that Abanzima's head is shaved and that Nambedru and Sissy wear their hair neatly plaited in plowed field furrows over their heads.

Even Matope combed his hair this morning with my little green comb and looking-glass. He imitated me exactly, even to twisting his head to stare critically at the effect from the side. Combed out, it looks longer than I expected, but it curls up again almost immediately and regains its unborn lamb appearance. Hair and its bewitching proper-ties are very important commodities here.

---

3 Aubrey Vincent Beardsley (1872–1898) was an English artist whose sensitive, highly imaginative style and hedonistic – and sometimes macabre – subject matter place him within the European *fin-de-siècle* artistic movement. Although he died at the age of twenty-six and his artistic career lasted just six years, he earned a well-deserved reputation as one of England's most innovative illustrators.

When Patrick cut my hair he was particular to have only Abanzima sweep it up, and no one was allowed to know where she carried it to dispose of it. If someone who doesn't like me should get hold of it, anything dreadful might happen. Matope cut some of his hair off the other day and gave it to me; two little tufts of wool; but I don't know what he meant by it, though he smiled affectionately.

We sold all the cigarettes at the quoted price, and bought eggs, sugarcane, melons, and bananas. A rather poor haul: there was no oil for sale today. We haven't really any right to sell anything because we haven't a license, and besides these prices on cigarettes are less than the store prices. But Patrick wants to give local trade an impetus, and it's true that the market has picked up wonderfully since we came.

The whole question of trading with the natives is a difficult one. All government officials, or anyway all the important ones, have a right to levy tribute up to a certain limit, so when Vandevelde, for instance, travels, he gets his chickens and fruit practically free. But as a result, the people naturally hide everything edible that they've got, and Vandevelde wonders why the country is so poor. Smet does the same, though he can't go to quite that limit, as he has no authority – he insists on buying food at his own price, a price he considers fair. But the natives naturally take the simpler road ; they only say they have no chickens or bananas, and it's a constant struggle for him to get enough food. Patrick says that it's not worth the few francs that Smet saves. He would rather pay three cents more per chicken and not argue five hours a day. As for Vandevelde, it certainly showed that Patrick was right: while he was here we didn't have a thing offered for sale, and our diet was most limited; but the day after he went away, we were swamped with things. Naturally, Smet resents Patrick's paying high prices; he thinks it spoils the natives for him. But they aren't really high prices. They're fair prices.

Patrick thinks that halfway measures are too much trouble. If you are going to extort, he says, extort honestly and don't try to cover up your tracks with a few *centimes* that are to all purposes just as good as nothing at all. Take the food outright or pay decent prices. I think I agree with Patrick. I'm not sure, of course, how right he is in his estimate of what is fair. But so long as it's as cheap as it is, even at his scale of living, I think I'll side with him rather than with the others. If I couldn't afford those noble sentiments, perhaps it would be a different matter. I'm afraid my convictions have a way of fluctuating with my income.

Saturday, March 28

This has been a very busy week. We've had an important guest, and a family row.

Important Guest: That, of course, is Vandevelde. He looked fine: brown and strong, and said that he'd walked most of the way because the *tipoye* was uncomfortable. He'd spent one day waiting for buffalo: had seen one but not managed to shoot it. Otherwise, he had done everything he intended to do in less time than he'd expected, and was in a good humor. In one way I was sorry he'd arrived early, because Patrick's cold had come back in full force and he refused flatly to go to bed while Vandevelde was here. "He might mention to someone that I was sick," he said. "Someone would tell Melius, and Melius would say to himself, 'Putnam is a sickly fellow,' and it would go on and on from there. No, I won't go to bed." So he stayed up until about one-thirty that night while we all talked at high speed. We had a long argument about the compass that Lindbergh used on his trans-Atlantic flight; Vandevelde and I trying to explain why it was a new idea and failing miserably. Then Patrick described the game of foot-ball. This took hours and I fell asleep twice, but Vandevelde seemed to be interested. He was glad to have some one to talk French to again.

We talked late over dinner, about crocodiles and government and elephants. Vandevelde delighted Patrick by giving him permission to shoot one elephant a month for the Government: it's a sort of job he can give three men in his district, and they don't have to buy permits. For the first time since we've come, we heard the wild chimpanzees that night. I noticed it first and thought it was our Chimp; it was exactly like her cry when she's angry – a shrill, "Yow, yow, yow!" I said, "When did Chimp get loose? Or is it a wild one?"

Patrick stopped talking to Vandevelde long enough to say, "Why, so she is loose. It's the first I've heard of it. Oh, that's our Chimp all right."

I was interested enough to go and look for her. No, she was tied up and fast asleep in her tree. It was the wild ones, and at the thought that there actually was a tribe of them nearby I was thrilled. A tribe of forest people that I could never know, no matter how many Red Cross hospitals I should install, or trading posts.

Abanzima nodded when we asked her.

"Why is there a child crying?" asked Patrick. "Is it being spanked?"

"Yes. They're having a dance: a big dance in a circle, and when one of them cries like that it's because he's been dancing wrong and the others are beating him to teach him."

Vandevelde took me with him one morning to hear a squabble that the headmen were having, or at least that's what it turned out to be. In the first place, he went just to get information. Saidi had fixed up a new house for the audience with a raised platform of bricks on which was the table for Vandevelde to write on, chairs for us behind it, and a ring of chairs for them all around. The platform was separated from the rest of the room by a railing, and altogether it was very much like a throne room. Sometimes goats tried to walk in, but the sentries at the door kept them out.

Abdulla sat all alone on the other side of the platform, because he was quarreling. He claims to be the rightful sultan. Of course, I didn't know what they were saying, except now and then, but that wasn't all the business they transacted, though it was the most important. One of the headmen is very old, with a cracked voice and a wall eye. He is Asumani's uncle. When it was his turn to talk (they stood up to give their speeches in front of the table, while Vandevelde wrote down what they said) he made a very dignified speech. He was wearing an Arab *kanzua*[4] of brown cloth, with a mantle over it trimmed in silver braid, and a white cap. Lots of the talk was about relationships and of who poisoned whom. For instance, a well-known political fact is that a near-relation of Saidi's killed the reigning king not long ago.

I can't imagine anyone of that blood having the nerve to kill a goat, but they say it's true. While Asumani was talking, Abdulla said something that made him mad, and they began to shout at each other, leaning over the table and the papers and waving their hands. Vandevelde, who never got either angry or excited, looked at them gravely and told them to quiet down, but they didn't pay any attention. At last, Saidi was moved to exert his kingly influence: he told Asumani to desist, and then when he was ignored, he took Asumani's shirttails and pulled. He looked more like a futile little monkey than ever. Vandevelde called it a morning at twelve, and we went home.

This morning Patrick finished a job he's been having the men to do for some weeks: he's built me a little room on the veranda. It has walls of bamboo and leaves; a window cut into the leaves and tied back with raffia; a mat hung up for the door; a hanging shelf suspended by raffia; a soap dish made of a tin can; a candlestick ditto, reflector and all; and a bureau that he bought the other day from a carpenter. He had put a lamp next the bed and lighted it to show me how I could read there, and he'd fixed the candle and even sat the teddy bear down on the dressing table (made of the box the motor came in) and when I looked at it for the first time, the prettiest room I've ever had, he said, "And if you aren't surprised and delighted I'll knock your head off."

"I think you're the nicest person I've ever met," I answered hastily.

"All right, then: I'm repaid for my half-hour's work. Come on out and look at the garden."

---

4 A Swahilii word for the long white cotton or linen robes, probably of Arabic origins, that men wear in areas of East Africa.

The girls have been clearing the burned space in the bush near my house, and now it's a good-sized bare plot. A new shipment of seeds came in the mail the other day and stimulated their interest; they've gone to work in good style, taking off their dresses and working as if they were born to it – which, as a matter of fact, they were.

Patrick's given them most of the garden for their peanuts and things; he set me to work on the European side. That is, he spent most of the day working, to show me how. It's great fun; I haven't done it since I was a kid. We've had a long strip of earth, hoed and raked, and chopped with machetes – I have Ambedu, the big fat man, to help – and planted it in two rows, one of radishes and one turnips. On the side, there are four little hills with cucumbers planted in them. Someone has to stand guard all the time against chickens.

Family Row: I almost forgot, and that's the most exciting thing of all. Patrick gave two lengths of Melikani cloth[5] to the servants, who kept insisting that they needed it for mourning. "You understand," he said to Nambedru, "if you're really mourning, you must shave your hair and do it properly."

"Oh, yes," she said, probably thinking that he would forget. And he did forget until one day he noticed her unplaiting her wool. She had it all brushed out and was just going to do it up again when Patrick came by and saw that it was filthy, two inches deep, he told me, in clay. Then he remembered and brutally cut it off. I didn't know about it until I saw him carrying the hair out to bury it. He told me, and I said he was a brute, but I really didn't think so until I saw Nambedru, who was sitting on the back veranda with a fierce scowl on her face. She looked perfectly miserable. Then I *was* mad at Patrick. And so, evidently, was Abanzima, who suddenly did a right about-face in her sentiments, and in a fury of feminism and sympathy cut off her own hair and even poor little Sissy's. Altogether, Patrick was an unpop-

5 A type of unbleached calico.

ular man. "Well, if she wasn't in mourning, why did she lie to me?" he protested.

"Oh, you're right enough, legally. But it was cruel."

"Not so cruel as you think. You're taking a European woman's viewpoint. You don't understand the Native," he added, grinning and imitating Thompson.

"I guess I saw Nambedru's face! You can't pretend that she's pleased," I said.

"She's not pleased. She's mad. She wants to be elegant. But she'll get over it more quickly, for instance, than you would in her place."

"If you cut off my hair, I'd poison you!"

"So? I must try it some time and see. ... No, there's one good thing about it. They're not quarreling any more: they're too mad at me. Funny thing, Abanzima's taking her side. I suppose I'll never understand human psychology."

"Good old Abanzima," I said sincerely: "I've never liked her so much."

He pushed away his book and stood up to go to work. "I'm a henpecked man," he murmured sadly as he walked off.

CHAPTER 6

DEATH AND THE CENSUS

Monday, March 30, 1931

THERE WAS HIGH JUNKETING IN TOWN in the afternoon: we saw a procession walking down with a Belgian flag and an orchestra, and so we followed and found a splendid wrestling match going on. The challenger stood in the clearing before Saidi's house, and there were two orchestras sitting on neighboring verandas. Saidi's wives were all lined up on his porch, but he came out and sat with us, giving us chairs. There was a sort of contestants' box where the other men waited. Their wrestling rules are new to me. They mustn't touch the opponent's legs with the hands; the overthrowing must be done by twining the legs and jerking, or by sheer force of the arms on the opponent's shoulders. Or, more likely, a combination of the two. Whenever a boy was thrown there was a glad shout, and then a host of men and little boys came dancing out with a comic sort of step, running a short distance, brushing the ground once with a bunch of grass, and then running back again. Some of the tiny boys who did this were all painted up and decked with beads. They were clowns, I'm sure, because a sort of ringmaster would now and then seize one and ask him questions or make a silly speech about him, while the clown stood frozen in a dramatic attitude. Once, they frisked over to us and the ringmaster said, "This man is strong: he can beat the whole town," while the man stood rigid with one arm out at an angle, staring into space. Then the ringmaster swatted him on the back and said "Good journey!" and they both laughed and ran away.

There was a dance last night, too, in one of the other little villages. We heard the drums all through dinner, and afterward, when Patrick had gone to bed, I went to the back veranda to have my coffee, and they were having a little private dance there – Abanzima, Nambedru, Matope, Bani, and Betuganai. One of them kept playing the little harp, and it looked very much like a Virginia reel. They stood in a circle, and one would dance up to another and then dance back again, the other following, and then the one who had been called would in turn dance up to someone, while the others just did any little leaping step, staying in place, that they felt like. Sometimes they all danced together to the center.

Somebody suggested that we all go to the big dance in town, so we started out; the boys carrying lanterns. It was very much like the big more stupid dances at home at the pueblos [when I lived in New Mexico]: a circle dance, with the women shuffling around in a circle about the orchestra, and lots of people singing. Sometimes they wriggled their buttockses, but most of the time, they just swayed back and forth. They each had one hand on the shoulder of the woman ahead. None of my own party would dance, but we watched a long time.

Monday, April 13

We've had a death in the hospital. It was last Thursday, on Injection Day, and I was there helping with the register. Things were going smoothly, though Patrick had reported to me the Monday before that he had had three rather bad reactions to the needle. Thursday the work was almost finished, and he'd left the hospital to do some errand back at the house, when I suddenly heard a noise in the corner and looked up to see a young woman who was sitting in the "finished" section, the ones who had already been injected, having a bad fit. She was trembling and moaning. As I looked, she began to cough and vomit, and she was having convulsions of trembling in a few seconds. Her husband, Hamari, was holding her by the shoulders.

I told Matope to run quickly for Patrick, but the boys said that Mautea had gone already at the first sign of the fit. Patrick seemed terribly long in coming, though I suppose he wasn't, really. He gave the woman adrenalin, but by the time the needle for it was ready she had already become quiet, stretched out on the ground and breathing in the same way the other woman did, the old one who died. Suddenly Hamari, who had been kneeling at her head, began to cry: "Oh, Zabibo, my wife, my wife, my sister! Oh, Zabibo! I told you not to come today. I told you not to come today. I told you not to come because you were sick last time."

He kept wailing and saying that until Patrick's heard him and said sharply, "What's that? She was sick from the needle last time? Why didn't you tell me?"

"I did," wailed Hamad. "I did. I told you. Oh, Zabibo, white men don't hear us when we speak. Oh, Zabibo!"

He beat on the ground rhythmically and wailed. I began to think I would cry in a minute. Zabibo was still breathing, but Patrick said her heart was weaker and weaker. There was a big crowd in the hospital, and yet I noticed much to my surprise that they weren't paying much attention to the affair. The *infirmiers* had stopped injecting, of course, but the patients went on chatting with one another, and now and they laughed at something that was said. Zabibo breathed more quietly. Hamari stopped wailing because he was out of breath. Matope came up and put his tickets in my pocket to save carrying them home for himself, and he smiled at me as he did it with the same childish unconcern that he always showed. He hardly glanced at Zabibo.

Hamari began crying again. "My wife, my wife, my wife. Don't die! Don't die!" He felt her hand, and at the same time Patrick said to me, "I think she's dead now."

Hamari stopped crying and looked inquiring. Patrick nodded, and then Hamari underwent a change: I couldn't help seeing it. While she had been dying, he was really in anguish. Now she was dead and he had a ceremony to perform. In a mechanical way he began to wail, in long drawn cries that were more like chanting, higher and higher and longer and longer until it really had become a chant, a chant like the imitation ones on the stage, most especially the wailing of the slaves in *The Emperor Jones*.[1] The other people in the hospital paused at last and looked at him as if to make sure that he was doing it correctly. Then they went on with the injections! From all I could see, Patrick and I were the only worried people in the place. Patrick, just to be safe, took all the tickets of the people who hadn't been shot yet, and reduced the doses that were written there, on the off-chance that something was wrong with the medicine, but now that he had more time to inquire, he came to the conclusion that it was his own fault. Zabibo had been one of the dilatory patients and he had sent for her, to find out why she hadn't come: she told him that she had been sick. And he had thought she meant she was menstruating, and so he had written the customary increased dose of injection on her card. It was just a little misunderstanding, but it had been fatal.

He didn't have much to say. I tried to convince him that she couldn't have spoken very plainly, but he wouldn't take that consolation and only remarked that if it had happened at home, they would have given him five years for it.

At the end of the morning, the family came to get the body. All her sisters and aunts and everyone sat around on the floor and on the ground outside, wailing in that same chanting way: some of them with their hands to their heads and their faces turned up, calling and calling, and under the whole network of voices was Hamari's bass, regular and pitiless – "Mama! Mama! Mama! Mama!"

They carried the body back to the village at last, walking slowly and plainting more softly. The last thing I heard as they disappeared over

1 *The Emperor Jones*, written in 1920 by Eugene O'Neill, was one of the first American plays with a lead role for a black actor. The plot deals with the leader of a West Indies island whose subjects rebel, drive him into the jungle, and finally kill him.

86

the hill was Hamari calling, "*Mama yango!*" ["Mother is dead. (Kish-
wili dialect)]

And none of the others, the ones who weren't related, paid as much
attention to that funeral procession of their friend as I would have to
a passing black hearse in New York.

☙

OF COURSE, WHEN IT COMES TO speaking of malpractice," Patrick
said to me, "the whole thing is malpractice. Lining people up like that
and shooting them as fast as we do. The entire system wouldn't bear
much inspection."

"Can you think of any better way to meet the problem?" I asked.

"No," he said promptly.

Tuesday, April 16

I've had a great deal of excitement this week. Smet organized a hunting trip, which was to last at least for four days. He was going alone
with Boniface, his chauffeur, and two pygmies, taking Patrick's discarded rickety *pirogue* and paddling by hand up the river. He had to
wait two or three days, of course, for the pygmies to be rounded up
and brought, but when he announced that they were actually at his
house I chirped with excitement and seized my camera and rushed
down there. There were three pygmies, really, in the charge of a wiz-
ened little bushman. Two were disappointing: they looked only like
rather small men, and Smet apologized for them and said that they
were really only half-pygmy. But the third was a little beauty. He was
actually tiny, and well-proportioned, with broad shoulders and a very
muscular body. He had a little beard and his eyes were very poppy, as
they are in the description that Schweinfurth gives. He stared at me as
hard as I did at him. Smet says that they never talk when they're hunting; they just say "yes" and "no," and he has never seen them asleep

more than an hour at night; they're always cooking and eating. They're nice people and never steal anything but salt. And it's no use paying them money for their services because they don't know what to do with it: he gives them salt and native iron. He had a lot of the iron piled up at the side of the house, balls of it mixed with slag.

"Hunting is nice," he said, "because at night when you're sitting at the fire, the boys talk more than they do other times. They ask questions about Europe, too. Do you know what they think? They think that we are cannibals in Europe, and that most of the tinned meat is human. It does no good to tell them no." He promised to take me on the next trip – he didn't take me on this one because it was a reconnaissance, and I'd have been in the way – and then he left.

And he appeared at the house next day, with bad news. No elephant tracks at all, and the jungle was too hard to cut for him to go any farther. He had an attack of fever, but he'd managed to get one buffalo and had, marvelously enough, transported it in that poor old *pirogue*, although they had almost capsized. I think Patrick doubted that he'd tried very hard; he just grinned as Smet retailed his dreadful experiences, and then he went to hospital. Smet told me that he thought he would start for Avakubi the next day, as he was tired and disgusted. I said all right, and then he blew up in a perfect fury. He was mad all morning, until I teased him into laughing. He is really worried about his house, I guess, and the real trouble was that he wanted me to come down and visit him in Avakubi. I don't want to do it, so the next two days were spent in an itinerant warfare. He resents my planning to go on Patrick's census trips, and assured me that I wouldn't enjoy it at all. Still, I said, I wanted to judge for myself.

It ended with my starting out yesterday with Patrick for Salumbungo's, where we are now, and Smet was still in Penge, but I don't think he'll be there when I come back on Sunday.

The expedition itself took so long to get started that I was minded of all of Cameron's troubles on his trip, when his men would manage

to fool around for days at a time.[2] Patrick had ordered ten porters.
Only eight turned up, but this is natural, because most people order
more than they need so that they'll get almost enough; Patrick wants
the headman to get used to believing him when he says something. He
sent for Halafu and asked where were the other two? Halafu promised
to send them immediately. There was a long wait, so Patrick sent for
him again. He'd gone to his plantation. Still determined, Patrick had
him come in and he said he'd told the men to go, but they'd run away.
Very well, said Patrick, dig them up again. Meantime, I waited and
waited and waited for the servants, who with me were supposed to go
ahead in the morning. Patrick was to follow when the injections were
finished. It took two hours for us to get organized, somehow, and we
started off – the three girls carrying light loads of their own food, and
Matope my camera and Patrick's revolver. When I saw my typewriter
still on the ground, I asked about it and Abanzima said that Ngimu
was to bring it later.

We were almost out of hearing of the house when Patrick called
the girls back and gave them hell. Ngimu wasn't coming at all, and
Nambedru was to carry the machine. They looked perfectly furious,
and Patrick said rather apologetically, "I guess they're out of practice."
I protested and said that I'd rather carry something myself, especially
as my machine was causing the trouble. I suggested leaving it, but
he was really mad at them, so at last we started again, all the ladies
heavily frowning. I called back sarcastically, "You haven't the *fimbu*[3]
handy, have you, for me to drive the slaves?" and he answered un-
daunted, "I wish I had, but it's lost."

---

2 In 1875 British explorer Verney Lovett Cameron (1844–1894) became the first
European to travel across tropical Africa from east to west.
3 A long wooden-handled whip of hippopotamus leather, common in the Congo
and in former Portuguese colonies in East Africa; from the Spanish word for
"rope's end." Also known as a chicotte.

My sympathy for them waned, however, as Patrick relented and sent a man after us to relieve Nambedru of most of her load, and still they lagged very much. I tried walking behind them, but it was too slow. This surprised me, as Patrick had been taunting me with my slowness whenever I go down the hill to the *pirogue*, and had even suggested that I do not try to walk, but take the *tipoye* instead.

After the first stop, I left them behind and went on ahead with Sabani, my boy, behind me. We overtook and passed the porters after another short rest in the shade. It was nice walking: my first view of the big trees. We crossed one big river and many, many little ones. There were pygmy tracks. It was so shady that I really didn't need a helmet.

I didn't know how far it was; it was supposedly a two or three-hour walk. I began to get hot just toward the end, when the forest grew sparse and the sun was in the middle of the sky. We reached Salumbungo's about noon, I think. It's a tiny place with six low long houses and a covered place in the square. The headman greeted me and said that we were to live in the covered place, as Vandevelde had done the same thing on his trip. I wondered slightly at this, and told the boys not to unpack till Patrick came.

I waited a long time, listening to the porters' gossip and wondering what in hell had happened to the girls. A heavy rain fell after a while, relieving the heat. The girls arrived in the middle of it, more than an hour behind me. Matope came soon after I did. I hadn't realized he was so close behind, and he was almost dead from weariness and had been crying. He pretended not to hear me when I spoke to him, so later in the afternoon I scolded him and said he'd have to go home if he didn't obey me. I added, against all my own principles, that he acted like a woman instead of the man he was, and he assented humbly.

The rain increased in strength. The porters put leaves on our roof, which leaked badly, and the little flies started to bite. At last Patrick arrived, streaming with water. He had Antea with him, and Sada and Chimp. Both simians were too tired out to do any mischief for a while. Patrick's pedometer said that the walk was about seventeen

One of Hahn's favorite infirmiers, possibly Sabani.

kilometers – not enough to make so much fuss as the others were doing. Patrick was in good spirits; he scorned my coffee and ordered chocolate. I said, "This is our house," and he said, "The hell it is. Where's the head man?"

The headman was awfully surprised that we wanted a house. White people never do, usually, because they are such funny little boxes, without windows and with very small doors, which are hermetically sealed when they crawl in at night. However, Sabani put up my bed in

one of the little kennels, and then we had supper under the roof –
most cheerfully crowded now, what with the girls opening boxes and
building little cooking fires all over the ground, and Chimp romping
around stealing everything, and the bush people sitting outside in the
dark, peering at us.

Then Patrick discovered that the last porter had never arrived with
his bed. This was really serious. Ordinarily he would be able to sleep
on the ground, on banana leaves; but the leaves were all too wet now.
He said that he would manage with one camp chair, I could use my
own blanket as a mattress, and the girls could use the mattress as a
buffer between them and the banana leaves. I suggested that Matope
bring his own mat and blanket out of the rest house and sleep with the
servants, sharing his bed with Nambedru. He ran and got his bed obediently when he was told, but he wept woefully at the prospect of
joining the common herd like that, and the ladies said it didn't matter;
that Nambedru didn't want him anyway. So he went back to glory and
to me.

It took hours to get settled down and sleepy, of course. And then
just as we did reach some semblance of peace, the porter arrived with
the bed! We didn't use it though: Patrick just took the blankets out.
The porter said that he had heard elephants. Instead of being a nice
man and sending for Smet, Patrick went out this morning for himself,
starting in the early dawn, and he hasn't come back yet.

Saturday, April 18

The village spent a pleasant afternoon gossiping with Patrick in the
arcade. Patrick didn't get an elephant, by the way: He followed them
all morning and came upon them twice but they strolled off without
giving him a chance to shoot. The girls walked to the next town, seeing
a pygmy dance on the way, and brought back a load of horrible-
smelling elephant meat. Camp was very odoriferous when they fixed

their supper. Patrick and I walked down to the river and had a bath after the sun was almost down: I think today will be equally hot. Everybody who needs it is being given a shot today. They are a pretty healthy lot: no syphilis and a few cases of old pain. Patrick was listing the headman's wives (all but one either dead or run away) and after he had written twelve or so the old man said, "You're going to get tired of doing that. I had sixty wives."

He used to be rich; it was the slave trade, carried on by Matope's ancestors, and the Rubber Régime that brought him down from his high estate. There is still a strained atmosphere between the Banguana and the bushmen. One of our porters was highly insulted when Patrick asked him if he could understand the bushman's language, and I heard the headman being very rude indeed to one of our city slickers yesterday while Patrick was gone.

The headman's last and favorite wife was brought out for inspection yesterday; dug up, protesting, from a grave that seemed to me hardly premature. Her skin hung in folds. She must have been quite fifty, or maybe even more! She certainly seemed much older than her husband. And she was annoyed, too: she was still muttering when her inspection was finished and she was given a clean bill of health.

Sunday, April 19

We fretted around all morning yesterday, and at last decided to be really zealous and come on the next village to do more census taking, and incidentally to see the pygmies. We started out at noon and Patrick and I went ahead, having a good walk through the forest and coming into the village so suddenly that we hoped the pygmies wouldn't have gone. The village is much better than Salumbungo's; it's richer, probably; the people are better-looking and more numerous; the houses are bigger and cleaner, and all of them have verandas. The town itself is built on a high bare hill, so that there is a view and a feeling of being free from the surrounding woods. One man is a very nice chap with a pleasant, flat-nosed face, and although he said at first that the pygmies were gone just that morning, he offered in the end to go and see if they really had gone very far. He might have been actuated in this by the fact that Patrick gave the one pygmy we found, a woman, a generous present of salt. She was terribly shy, but she liked the salt. Patrick made a little speech to her and said that I had never seen pygmies so that he wanted her to stand close to me; he pointed out that she had never seen a Madame either, so it was a good chance for both of us. For the space of a few minutes we inspected each other solemnly. Then our friend returned with five or six of them: two men, one a bearded old white-haired chap of quite four feet two inches, two women, and a *jeune fille*. Since we have neither beaten nor eaten them, they have grown bolder, and this morning I see quite a few new ones sitting under a nearby roof, watching us.

Yes, this is a better village. Even the goats are friskier; we had to take all our things into the house last night to save them from being eaten. Patrick intends to start back tonight with Antea, sleeping at Salumbungo's so that he won't have quite so far to walk quickly next morning: he has to be at hospital by nine or so. He is leaving me to see that the rest of the party navigates the long walk more or less successfully on Monday. It is very complimentary of him, but I feel nervous about it.

Monday, April 20

It is over. Patrick didn't start on his own trek until about five: he had much work with the people who had just come back from carrying food to the road workers, down toward Avakubi. At the last minute he entrusted to me two small children who were to come back with me and get a week's injections; they had eaten, so [they] hadn't even had one. They would have gone with him: it was his first idea, but they cried so much that their father intervened and promised faithfully, faithfully, faithfully to turn up with them in the morning, to go with me. "I like you," Patrick said to him. "You are a good man. When you say a thing, I believe you. But woe to you if you deceive me and do not come tomorrow with Madame. I, thy God, am a zealous God. ..."

No, I exaggerate slightly. Still, that was the general idea of his remarks, and the father nodded so hard that a chicken-feather almost fell out of his headdress.

Left alone, and more or less in charge, my spirits rose rapidly. I did a little dance just for myself and Nambedru while I was putting on long stockings for dinner; Chimp acted well all through the meal and obeyed me when I told her to stop reaching for things; and after dinner when it grew dark, I began to sing to her as she was going to sleep in my lap. Alifani, the *infirmier* who'd been left with me, came into the enclosure to write a couple of hospital tickets by the light of my lamp. Sabani followed. One by one the Banguana came in and sat down near the fire, and then the bush people came too. They began to talk to me. I've never seen them so friendly. It is true, then: they are nicer on a trip. Sabani was more or less spokesman, but they all talked and I learned a great deal of Kingwana. They asked me the English words for things, and they wanted to know if Patrick and I came from the same homestead, and in what direction my home was. Sabani asked me if I was going to take Matope with me when I went. I said I didn't know yet. Then he said that he would like to come too, if he could, and I said that I would think it over. It would be a splendid idea if I could afford it: maybe I can. Because he can bring Matope back again, and he's a nice boy and very helpful and good-natured.

Abanzima wasn't there. She was rather mopey and went to bed early. I followed much later, and after foiling a determined effort on Chimp's part to crawl in with me, I composed myself for what turned out to be a restless night. Perhaps I was excited at being alone with the Negroes; I don't know. I heard Abanzima's slight snore across the room, and Matope's occasional sniffle, and then I thought it was

Matope's new vest

morning because I heard birds singing, but it was only two o'clock, and they were crickets.

We all got up very early and I found out almost immediately that I had nothing to worry about. In the first place, Chimp had continued her good behavior – i.e., she had slept in Patrick's trunk instead of in mine. I am a nasty person, and this pleased me immensely. In the second place, none of the porters commandeered from the neighboring village had run away. As a matter of fact, two of them were pygmies, so this was really astonishing. But I suppose they're afraid of their bushmasters. Thirdly, everybody packed up and set off in record time; we were on the road an hour after I got up. Fourthly, Chimp mounted her porter, the smaller pygmy, with no objection whatever. One fly in the ointment was that the kids hadn't shown up and couldn't be found, but I'd expected that and wasn't much surprised. Alifani waited

96

behind in the forlorn hope of catching them later. Abanzima and I stayed a while to let the others, more especially the kids, get a good start. It was raining slightly which made the path awfully slippery, but the air was cool.

We reached Salumbungo's in a very short time and didn't stop; I just shook hands with him in passing. I kept behind Matope and Sabani kept behind me, and Matope went slowly but even at that Abanzima seemed to have dropped behind. Then Sabani told me that she was sick from the elephant meat and had decided to go slowly. I said I'd wait for her, but he said it wasn't necessary; she wasn't very sick and Wollaga was staying with her, with his wife. So I plodded on.

I almost dropped with surprise when Sabani suddenly announced gladly that we were almost at Abedi's plantations, at the edge of the Penge district. We'd been walking for only an hour, it seemed to me, though it must actually have been three. We stopped at the plantation village and waited for Abanzima, who arrived soon after and announced that her stomach was very, very sick indeed. I gave her a cup of coffee, very hot. All the people living in the village were glad to see the porters, and everybody seemed to like Chimp, and gave her bananas.

The last trek was hot because now the big trees were pretty well cleared out. The porters, glad at being home, sang and joked and shouted at one another, and we walked the last hour very tunefully. I reached the house shortly after noon, absolutely incredulous that we had managed thirteen miles or so in a morning. I am still in a warm glow of affection for everyone, especially the expedition behaving so nicely: Ngimu and Abanzinga greeted me as if I'd been away a long time, and I love the Negroes. Besides, the wine man brought two bottles of good wine today, the stipulated day, which is unheard of. Patrick gave the pygmies their choice of money, tobacco, or salt. They took salt. He gave them extra large portions and promised more to them anytime they should want to come back. We kept one for medicine; he's very poorly and covered with rash and I hope he doesn't run away. Meantime, we plan to go via the boat to Ketshui's next Saturday, with three men to pole and only Patrick, me, and Chimp as passengers. The others will walk. I've little doubt of our getting there safe, if not dry, but I don't have much hope that we'll be able to battle the rapids coming up again.

CHAPTER 7

MALARIA

Saturday, April 25, 1931

I HAVE JUST FINISHED (no, not *finished*, though I wish I had) with an exciting affair. Patrick left at noon with Mautea, Abanzima, and the river captain who brought some mail. They went in the motor *pirogue*, and we all, except Patrick himself and the captain, walked a couple of miles to the landing place below Abdulla's, the crocodile place, while the *pirogue* traversed the worst rapids. They picked up the other passengers there and departed for census at Ketshui's village, the place where I slept the last night on my way up here. I stayed here to make things easier and to keep the household more or less all right; it would be too much of a drag, we thought, to take so many as we did before. I didn't really mind; I'm still afraid of the *pirogue* and I saw another crocodile today. Yellow, yellow, yellow. Anyway it didn't worry me; I came home, ate lunch and read Stanley[1] until an hour ago. It began then.

Somebody came up and told me Antea was very sick (he has been sort of off his feed for several days). I went to the old jail, where he lives with a few dozen other people, and they were all there. A woman was holding his head in her lap, but it was a hard job because he was

---

1 *Through the Dark Continent* (1878) by Sir Henry Morton Stanley is an account of the early travels in Afria of this celebrated late-nineteenth African explorer and mercenary.

tossing and raving. He kept calling "Sun, sun," and then groaning and vomiting. I was scared but tried to imitate Patrick's offhand manner. It looked like malaria, a bad case. I ordered him to be given quinine and sent everybody hither and yon for hot water, the Kingwana dictionary, my own notes from the Hygiene Lectures in London (Sabani had to bring all my library for me to pick it out), and then I gave him quinine and hot lemonade. He came to and said now he was cold. He had no blankets: I made them put three on him and sent for Ngimu, who speaks a spot of French, because I don't know enough Kingwana. More people kept coming and Antea said he was going to die. I sat in the middle of the crowd in the horrible dark little room trying to read my notes calmly. Blackwater fever, perhaps? In either case, he evidently needed sodium bicarbonate. I have a little: we tried to give him some, but he vomited again. At last he grew quiet and rolled up his eyes, but he wasn't dead. Somehow I didn't even start to be afraid then. I don't want him to die because he's my favorite *infirmier*.

I wrote a note to Patrick telling him the symptoms and what I was doing, and then I tried to think of a good man to send. Angbedu walked awfully fast on our last trip: he's a good strong man though a leper. I sent Ngimu to tell him to carry the note (six hours' walk, I think Patrick said it was) and when Angbedu arrived he said he didn't want to go. "I'm a Monguana," he said, meaning that one Mobudu more or less meant nothing in his young life. Also, he was busy. Ngimu translated though Angbedu talked to me, too, pleading but stubborn.

"Very well," I said. "Go away. When the Doctor comes back I will tell him. I will also tell the Administrator." Ngimu added – I understood it – "Are you crazy? When a man is dying and a white person tells you to go, you must go." Angbedu looked more stubborn: I was puzzled as to what to do next, and so I lighted a cigarette I didn't want, and looked haughty. Ngimu, very indignant, said he'd go and fetch another workman. Angbedu, however, stood there and looked as if he wanted to justify himself. I couldn't understand him anyway, and it struck me that whatever it was wasn't important in the face of illness.

I think he was sore because he had to work hard on our last trip, too. He is a good workman, and I was sorry we were coming to the point where he'd have to be fired. I said, "Don't talk. Say yes or no. Are you going? Say yes or no." He talked some more. "Say yes or no," I yelled – well, almost yelled. He said nothing. "Very well," I said. "Go away."

I began to type my letter to Patrick. Angbedu stood there a while and went away at last. I stopped typing and wondered what next.

Ngimu came back and said two more men had good reasons for not going – sore feet or something. I sent for them. One I believed: the other I didn't but told them in my most ominous accents to wait for Patrick. They went away. Sabani and Matope came to ask what was the matter. I looked as if it were nothing – I had sent Ngimu meanwhile for Saidi – and told them that Banguana were lazy men and that the Administrator would soon be here. I said that if Saidi didn't get me a man I'd have the Administrator have all the men whipped who refused to go. I meant it, too. … What I think happened then in the village was that Ngimu remonstrated once more with the men. Meantime, I looked frantically through the dictionary for enough words to talk clearly to Saidi when he should arrive.

In the middle of my wait, I did one foolish thing: I brought out my gun – still looking haughty and indifferent for the benefit of two men peeking through the door – and loaded it in a leisurely manner. Of course, I wouldn't have dared break the law, but there's no law against bluffing.

Saidi never came. I don't know if Ngimu even reached him, perhaps so. But Angbedu came: he walked in suddenly and said, "Give me the letter. I'm going." At the same moment, Ngimu came back with another man, one of our porters on the trip, who was willing to go. But I remembered that Angbedu walked wonderfully fast: I thought it was best to accept his surrender. "Good," I said. I gave him some cigarettes, two packages, and added, "If you get back fast tomorrow I'll give you francs – three francs. Good-by."

I went on typing, all the servants glanced at me uncertainly and walked out, and then I mopped my brow. In the middle of the mopping they came again and said Antea was fighting them off and pulling off his blankets. By the time I got there he was calmer. He understood me, and he had told them to get me. He didn't say anything. I gave him soda again and he vomited, but then began to hold it. He swallowed when I told him. He even took his quinine dissolved in water. I've sent him a lantern, and I'll go back again after dinner. If he's still bad, I'll stay there tonight.

They got a specimen of his urine: it looks normal so it might not be blackwater, anyway. But I won't let them move him to hospital. I hope, I hope, I hope he'll be all right. Thank goodness Sabani and Nambedru and Ngimu are being nice and helpful. But the dependence is terrifying; the way they think I can do something.

Sunday, April 26

Antea quieted down last night the way the books say a person does after an attack. I ate dinner and had Matope eat with me. He tried to persuade me to go to the dance they were having in Abedi's village; the drums had started at five and were sounding loud. "You don't want to come?" he said incredulously. "But it's a *good* dance."

I said no, I would stay home, but that he could go if he wanted; everyone could go when my dinner was finished. We're short on light because I sent the only good oil lamp to Antea, so Nambedru had to carry a candle while I kept the gasoline lamp.

Everything was quiet after they went. Even the sentry hadn't turned up yet. I thought I was completely alone, so I was startled at stumbling over patient little Nambedru on the back *barza*,[2] sitting in the dark and boiling bananas. I retired to the front and went on read-

2 In East Africa a *barza* is a public meeting place. In the Ituri Forest region, the noun apparently had dual meanings. One was as the shaded porch area of a building, while the other was as a kind of quasi-judicial community hearing akin to a Small Claims Court at which the local official of the Belgian colonial administration sat in a public place to hear and adjudicate petty disputes.

ing Stanley. All his vicissitudes interest me much more now that I can identify the places: We are very near Starvation Camp here. It was very hot and close, with rain brewing, and I was tired to death for no reason at all. It was a comfort when Nambedru came out and asked permission to look at the Montgomery Ward catalogue. We discussed ladies' fashions in a sprightly manner until nine, when I went to have another look at Antea. He was sleeping well. A young woman who had appeared in the afternoon was keeping watch: a pretty girl with good clothes. She had tied a blue handkerchief tightly around his head for some reason: it was soaked with sweat, for which I was glad. I remembered that Patrick had told me Antea had brought his intended concubine to be looked over, and that Patrick had been unfavorably impressed because she looked "expensive." This, then, was probably the girl. Well, she was taking good care of him, and Alifani was there too, and Antea's little brother sleeping at the entrance. I told them to call me if he got bad, but that I thought he would sleep all night. Then I went home and to bed, but couldn't sleep.

The others came home and Matope, seeing I was awake, borrowed my torch to put his medicine on his feet. "Sleep well," he said, crawling into his blanket, and he added just before he slept, in a reproachful tone, "Madame, it was a very good dance, very."

WOKE UP THIS MORNING to hear Ngimu and Wollaga discussing Angbedu's wickedness. Nambedru joined in the chorus, "*Eko mobaya, eko mbaya, eko mbaya, kabisa.*" ["It is bad, for sure." (Swahili)][3] I saw through the leaves how Ngimu ran over to the prison with a bowl of hot water. I was panicky again and got up, though the first cock had just crowed. No, they said, Antea was still sleeping well. … I was

3 One of the difficulties in translating some of the African words Hahn used in her narrative is that Swahili and the various dialects of the Ituri region are primarily spoken, whileHahn recorded words phonetically, as she heard them. As a result her spellings are not always to be found in dictionaries.

beginning breakfast when Ngimu brought Faki to the *barza* with the load of tools Patrick had ordered brought down today to fix the motor to come upstream again on Tuesday.

Everything was there but the adrenalin, which he had ordered brought along instead of taking [it], as it was needed here yesterday. No one knew a thing about it; then I remembered that Antea was always in charge of such things. Poor Ngimu was dispatched again and found it in Antea's room. Faki, of course, had a lame foot and complained bitterly at having to go. I was merciless. I couldn't see anything wrong with his foot and he hasn't been coming to hospital for it, anyway. His wife went, too; he looked so aggrieved and limped so exaggeratedly that I forgot to send Patrick another note. Now I'm worried: perhaps his foot was really sore? Well, if so he can send his wife. Still, I'm worried. Especially as Ngimu very characteristically, after helping me bully him into starting, shook his head sadly and said, "*Mallally, Madamu. Mallally mingi.*" ["He's sick, Madame." (Swahli).]

Went to see Antea, who had just waked and was in his right mind. Most lugubrious, but looks better. He may have another attack this afternoon or tomorrow: meantime he told me where the quinine was in the hospital: locked in the cabinet, and Patrick, the poor nut, has taken the key with him. I gave Antea his morning dose with my own four capsules that Patrick left me when he took the bottle to hospital.

CHAPTER 8

ANGÉLIQUE

Wednesday, April 29, 1931

I AM GOING CRAZY WITH THESE KIDS. Anybody would think Sabani
was just Matope's age, or even a little younger. And him a grown man
with a beard … The trouble started the other day when Sabani over-
heard me wearily trying to persuade Matope to learn his letters. Fired
with ambition, he asked me to give him lessons, too. That pleased me
and I began with a will. He asked for Matope's alphabet book to take
home with him that night, to study. It's a crude sort of book: I made it
myself weeks ago, and it's been gathering dust on my desk because
Matope hasn't touched it. So I said sure, take it. At dinner that night
he suddenly burst out to me, sitting on the veranda peacefully chewing a chicken leg, and said, "Madame, Matope's taken the book and
hidden it!"

I called Matope and lectured him severely, making him give up
the book. Sabani took it home and studied. Next day, Matope
entered a formal, private complaint. He wanted his book back; he
wanted his book. "Well," I said, "I thought you didn't like it. If you
use it, you may have it back again. Do you want to use it? If not, let
Sabani have it."

He promised to study like a good boy if I'd only give him back his
book. I did, and of course I made Sabani another. This time I made
a small one and for trimming drew a border on the cover in red

crayon. The two of them spent the afternoon in perfect amity, chanting on the back porch, "A, B, C …"

Lovely, I said to myself, in spite of my aching head. I do like youth, eager for knowledge. Lovely!

Today, Sabani has gone so far ahead that I've promoted him to syllables. The trouble started then. I should really have two classes, I suppose. Matope looked darkly at Sabani, and just now Sabani has come in to appeal to me: Matope, he said, insists that they swap books. He likes the little book better, and he had said that it was my order. I called Matope. Severely I said, "Yesterday you wouldn't give up your book to Sabani. You said, 'I like my book. I want my book.' Very well, you keep your own book and shut up about it."

He is now sniffling persistently in the corner. I think he cries too much. I just told him to go outside if he wanted to finish it in peace; if he cries around me anymore I'll whip him. So he stopped crying.

The expedition got home last night just before dark. Patrick has bought a splendid big canoe from Ketshui and made the trip up with no trouble at all, though it took six hours. Well, there was one incident – he was going slowly up the side of the river, looking at the motor instead of ahead, and a branch knocked him off, right into the river. He says that he never swam for shore so fast in his life. He's lucky.

What punishment should be given the lazy men who wouldn't go to Ketshui's? We've been talking it over. I am in favor of Patrick's first idea: i.e., to make them all walk to Ketshui's, starting at five o'clock when they should have gone before, and come back the next day; if they're not back by the right time, to fine them. That is, of course, to give them their choice between doing that and quitting the job entirely. Patrick thinks perhaps a whipping would be better. He teases me for having been afraid and taking out my gun; when I admit that I was afraid of Angbedu, he laughs. But he says that he realizes now how sick Antea was; he thought I was exaggerating when he read my note and didn't give it more than a couple of thoughts. Antea would probably have died, he says, and they'd already closed the window to wait for the end. Now we know the reason for the attack: Antea had been slightly sick, as I said, and had allowed a friend here to persuade him to take the bushman's treatment – i.e., he was bled plentifully at the temples and then went down and took a cold bath in the river; Right after that the attack started, naturally. Well, he'll be on his feet soon.

An indignant and very large lady came up to the house the other day and announced that she had been mortally insulted by Agalanga, one of our men. He had seen her, it seems, on her way to the Walessi River, where there is lots of *banki* growing. *Banki* is Indian hemp [introduced into the region by Arab slave traders in the eighteenth century], and it's forbidden by the Government, as they think that smoking it is equivalent to smoking opium. But of course everyone smokes it anyway and says nothing about it to the white men. Well, she was coming back when Agalanga saw her and said, "Hello, old girl," or words to that effect. "How about letting me have a little dope?"

What followed then is not very clear. She maintains that she drew herself up and said with dignity, "*Banki*? What is *banki*? I am a respectable woman, and I know naught of such things."

Agalanga said, "Oh, come off it! Be a nice girl and give us some."

The lady's nephew leaped to her defense and called Agalanga unpleasant names, and as a result she came tearing up to the house, demanding justice. Now, this was while I was alone, and I didn't know what the hell it was all about. I found *banki* in the dictionary all right, but I didn't know why it was prohibited, or even that it *was* prohibited. Ngimu, for reasons I will explain in a minute, was no help at all. He couldn't even tell me anything about *banki*. So I told her to wait until the Doctor came back.

She did, coming upon Wednesday and telling the whole story again. Patrick called in Agalanga, but first he told me that he could guess just what had happened – Ngimu is an inveterate smoker and had without doubt put Agalanga up to it. No use dragging Ngimu in, too, though. The following conversation took place:

Agalanga: "I didn't say a word about *banki*."

Lady: "You did, you did, and I have a witness to prove it. And I'm a respectable woman, the *ménagère* of a white man in Irumu."

Patrick: "What's that?"

Lady: "Yes, *Bwana*. We have two children in Europe."

Patrick: "Well, well!" (Translates the story for my benefit and looks more kindly upon the woman.)

Jeering voice from outside: "That's a lie. She's just been with the white man a couple of times. She's not his *ménagère* by a long shot."

Lady (very belligerent again): "What scandal is that?"

Patrick: "Let it rest a minute. ... Agalanga, what happened?"

Agalanga: "Well, I saw this woman walking along, and I greeted her. I didn't say a word about *banki*. I simply said in a polite way, 'Welcome homes from the Walessi!' And then for no reason at all, the child started abusing me."

(Crowd on verandah cries, "Ohhhhhhh!" almost wordless from the indignation at the lie.)

Lady: "That's a lie. You said to me, 'Where's the *banki*?' I'm a respectable woman. ..."

Patrick: "Wait a minute, Mama. ... Well, Agalanga, you know perfectly well that you shouldn't insist on taking *banki* from ladies. After you had asked her once, and she said she didn't have any, you shouldn't have insisted. You shouldn't have asked her three times."

Agalanga (very excited): "Three times? I didn't ask her three times. I asked her only once."

Patrick: "You didn't ask her three times?"

Agalanga: "Only once, Bwana. Only once, I swear."

Patrick: "Then you *did* ask for *banki*?"

Agalanga was suddenly silent. Patrick said, "Well, it's none of my business. I'm not a judge; I'm a doctor. If Agalanga had insulted you, Mama, and you hadn't spoken badly to him, I would punish him. But you've each insulted the other: I think it's about even, so I'll call it a draw, and anything you do about it is your own affair. Next time one

Matope (on left) and a friend

of my men insults you, tell your nephew to shut up and come up here right away and tell me. Do you hear? Enough. It's finished." He added, "There's too much *banki* smoking going on here: it's a bad business altogether."

When they were safely out, we were free to laugh as hard as we wanted.

A STRAY DOG HAS TURNED UP FROM SOMEWHERE, and Matope is playing with it. Instead of calling, "Here, here," he calls, "Oss, oss, oss," and the dog seems to understand. To chase animals away – goats or chickens or dogs or chimpanzees – you call "Ish, ish." They understand that too.

Saturday, May 9

A day that started dully shows promise now of some development. It rained like everything this morning and cleared up only for Vandevelde's departure, near noon. Hardly had the chanting of the porters died away when Sabani came rushing to me as I sat frittering away the morning with a detective story. "Madame! Madame! There is a Madame!" he cried.

Incredulous, I sat up and looked at the path from the village. There most certainly was a strange white man talking to Patrick and a helmeted woman standing by. It's been two months since I've seen any whites but our own little circle, so to speak. I ran to find my hat and rushed out to meet them. A skinny dark man with a big nose was talking to Patrick in slow drawling French. He was introduced as Monsieur Dupin, and then he brought forward "Madame" and presented her. Madame is a silent fat mulattress with a Mongoloid sort of face, a pretty face. She had little to say. We walked back to the veranda and Patrick went backstage to order another lunch brought up: she hesitated when I offered her a chair. He called her "*la petite.*"

"Your daughter?" I asked naturally, and then was embarrassed when he said, "Ah, no. A sad young woman, that. She was to be married and her young man has deserted her." He said to her in Kingwana, "It is strange for you to sit near the Madame, eh, Rosa?" She mumbled something, looking at the ground. ... Nambedru waylaid me as I started into the house, and said, "Is the Madame your sister?"

"Who are they?" I asked Patrick on the back *barza.*

"I told you they were coming, didn't I? No? I thought I did. He's working on the new road and they've come from Mombasa on the way to Avakubi."

He seemed a pleasant chap. He piled into lunch and talked volubly. A pure Walloon, he called himself; a miner. He was one of two children, he told me, and started work at eight years old. Now he's a widower with a sixteen-year-old daughter in Belgium. It seemed strange to be talking to a white man whom I didn't know. He seems to be an honest sort, if his downright condemnation of Patrick's boss is any sign. For some reason he hates the poor doctor. Very sweeping in his statements. When Matope came and leaned on my lap, as he always does, Dupin looked curiously at us and said, "You like the blacks, Mademoiselle? Ah, that is good. I like them too. One must be firm with them sometimes, but they are good people."

We went on to talk about native food, which is a thing that few Belgians ever eat. He goes Patrick and me one better by declaring a passion for *manioc*;[1] I could see a spark of jealousy in Patrick's eye.

The Madame looked wonderingly at me and the household peered enviously at her from the window. And in truth they had reason. She was dressed as a European, though she speaks no French – a cotton frock, a sweater, a helmet and, most surprising of all, stout walking boots. She was wearing a goodly amount of cheap jewelry; a pink barrette in her hair, rhinestone rings and two brass brooches. I wonder if she is his woman or if she's really on her way to find a refractory fiancé. No doubt she is wondering something of the same sort about me. They dine with us tonight.

Sunday, May 10

Patrick left early this morning for Kayumba's, expecting to be back tonight, but in case he can't do it he's taken cooking pots and blankets. He'll try to get back, though, since he hasn't anyone with him to do the cooking. It's a nasty, cold, raw day.

Our friends turned up last night for dinner and waited a long time on the veranda while I tried to make polite conversation. Patrick was winding up his work for the boss. Dupin was inclined to be philosophical about Africa, and I let him ramble on. He discussed the race question for a long time, saying exactly what Smet says in almost the same words. Since they hardly know each other, I guess it's one of the

---

1 A kind of tapioca pudding made from the roots of a tropical plant called cassava.

things that Belgians say to white ladies. "One cannot talk to them. What would you say? It is Nature – one has not one's wife – one has need of companionship, but one cannot talk to them. Now that I have stumbled upon my little one here, it is not so bad. She is superior to the negresses." He paused and beamed at the little one, who sat silent and uninterested in the flow of French. She was garbed for evening in a badly cut white silk dress and she looked rather bored. "You are evidently a woman of the world," he continued. "You understand such things."

"Some men," he went on, not noticing that I was laughing, "take Africa as an excuse to go to excess in all things. I do not like the cities in Africa, or the posts. Give me the great forest, the quiet river, where I may take two drinks of whisky if I please" – I hastily put the bottle within reach of his hand – "and there is no one to censure. I wish to be my own master. These others I do not understand. *Ach*, the cities! There the married couples quarrel always, the Madames and the Messieurs are always unfaithful. It is because after his first term a man goes back to Belgium determined to marry, and he marries in haste the wrong girl. When they come here there is nothing to do, so they quarrel. Give me the forest, even though I must content myself with the blacks." The little one held out her glass. "Only a little one," he said to her severely. "Her father," he went on, "built this house. He was once Administrator of Penge. She is the image of him."

"Is it true ?" I asked her.

She grinned and said, "I don't know."

I remembered Patrick's scornful comment when I had reported Dupin's first confidence about her – her disappointed matrimonial hopes. "That's a lot of hooey. Nambedru knows all about her: her mother was of the same tribe as Abanzima, and nobody can tell who her father was because the lady was promiscuous."

Food came, and so did Patrick after I had called him four times. Dupin helped the little one to her food, after helping himself, and kept a wary eye on her manners. He glowered at the plump elbow that she had put on the table. She didn't see it. A moment later, he touched it gently with his fork; she pulled it off hastily and scraped at her soup plate in confusion. Sure enough, we had manioc to eat. It was good. Dinner was rather painfully silent: somehow Patrick's bearded face has a terrifying effect on visitors. I felt rather depressed, and played our whole stock of records through before they bade us a polite goodnight.

Monday, May 11

Patrick came back before dark, seething with fury. His patients down-river didn't really believe he was coming; all but a few had eaten and couldn't be injected. He made them walk up here and stay over until today; then he injected those that he could and sent them directly back. Dupin said he'd seen several crocodiles from his vantage point on the porch of the rest house, and that one had followed Patrick's canoe all the way around until he landed at the beach. He was so positive about it, and called on Rosa so confidently to back him up that Patrick believed him and was shaken for a moment.

I was more than shaken. Patrick, of course, has since decided it wasn't the truth, but he's still considering the advisability of staying inside the boat after this when he wants to get back to the motor.

After dinner we drifted, or perhaps we were pushed bodily by Patrick, to the eternal subject of the *ménagère*. Dupin said that, believe it or not, for his first year and four months he didn't touch a woman. The idea of the black ones filled him with disgust. Yes, Patrick agreed, most white men seemed to be that way. ... And then, he said, then what happened? Did he have a change of heart all of a sudden, or little by little? Well, Dupin said, he remembered perfectly how it happened. The authorities at the mines kept insisting that he take a woman – it's their very sensible policy for keeping all their men satisfied with Africa – but he was stubborn. "I had a little boy to talk to, just like that one of Mademoiselle's," he said. "Evening after evening I talked to him, learning the language and trying to keep from

having the *cafard* [melancholy]. I sat like this, evening after evening"
– his head dropped back in the chair, his gaunt workman's face looked
sad and pensive with the eyes closed – "evening after evening."

"You didn't like Africa, then?" Patrick asked.

"I hated it. I thought … of my dead wife, my little girl, the cities,
the women. I thought, ah, if I were back in Europe! Then, what
wouldn't I do! And all this time, mind you, there was a woman in the
house. For three months she was there, put there by my boss, and I
wouldn't look at her. I couldn't. One night I drank too much whisky,
and when I went to bed, there was a woman there. …"

"Then in truth," said Patrick, "it was you who were seduced."

"Exactly."

"And how did you feel afterward? Completely reconciled?"

"No, I was disgusted. But after that it was not so bad."

"And now you like Africa?" said Patrick.

"Ah, I would not think of going back. I have prolonged my term the
second time, now; Europe means nothing. If I could not go back for
another ten years, I wouldn't care."

He talked of his latest troubles with the work; getting food for the
men. For some time they had to exist on only five kilograms a week, and
they were starving. He talked at length of how he treated them – "They
are afraid of me," he said proudly. "In the morning when I open my
mouth to speak to them, they tremble. No need to strike. I am not one
to strike when I need not. I myself tried the *fimbu* (chicotte) one time;
I had myself given twelve strokes, and I kept the memory for a month
afterward. But I think it is not the best thing to do. Ah, before I took the
woman, you may be sure I was terrible to the blacks."

Wednesday, May 13

Saidi's mother is sitting on the edge of the *barza* patiently waiting for
someone to pay too much for one of her very pretty colored mats.
That reminds me of Saidi's sad story.

The day before Vandevelde arrived, the little king did a very peculiar thing: he picked up his belongings and favorite wives, gave orders that the rest house should be well fixed, and left for a long stay in Mombasa. Asumani, too, has disappeared; it has been quite a month since his white teeth gleamed on the veranda. I found out why when Vandevelde came.

It's all that robbery of Smet's things at the Interfina. Two of his chairs have been found in Saidi's house, and Abdulla is an eager witness on behalf of the State. Asumani's overpowering passion for cartridges has been his downfall, perhaps. Abdulla, the wicked Abdulla, followed Asumani one fine day and saw him in the act of shooting at monkeys. The discarded cartridge Abdulla picked up and kept in hiding until the big tribunal in Avakubi, when he suddenly produced the thing and swore to what he had seen. Smet's cartridges without a doubt, said Vandevelde. "No, no," said Asumani – the Doctor had given them to him. They were a light blue and Smet's were a darker blue. (This unfortunately is quite true, and Patrick may be hauled up in court in Stanleyville for giving cartridges to natives. He signed a confession while Vandevelde was here.) Well, anyway, Asumani evidently has a guilty conscience because he too has disappeared, probably to Mombasa, and such a thing as deserting the post directly the Government agent is in sight is a tactless action. Vandevelde told us that he was intending to recommend Saidi's deposition, and to put either Abedi or Halafu in his place as Sultan. Poor little Saidi! Of course, he shouldn't go around picking locks and stealing chairs. The hopelessness of it is what impresses me. Whatever made him think that someone wouldn't find the chairs?

If he's deposed he will probably ask to go to some other village to live out the years of his disgrace in obscurity. I'll miss his timid little chinless face.

Saturday, May 16

I had just finished work yesterday when two peddlers suddenly interrupted my solitude. The one selling eggs I immediately dispatched indignantly to Abanzima, but the other one had a monkey closed up in a basket, and that I seized eagerly. I couldn't see anything about it except its face; I experienced that strange shock that I always get when a monkey looks at me. It was a small one, but I couldn't see much about it, so I took it to the hospital, first saying that of course I wanted it. Patrick was jealous that I'd bought it instead of leaving it to him. He squinted curiously into the basket and then cried, "Oh, it's a baby Sada!"

We took it out and put in on the floor. There was a blue bandage on its arm that showed something wrong; when it was unwrapped the arm disclosed a nasty mangled wound. The mother had been killed, the man said, and the baby caught the end of the spear. Patrick looked dubious about it. It's so young – about two weeks. Still, it can bite pretty hard.

He washed the wound and bandaged it and rummaged in his store of rubber goods, while the whole hospital looked on interestedly, to find a rubber nipple that would fit a whisky bottle. Meantime we sent for the first milk that's been extracted from our cow, and when I say "extracted" I mean it. It took five men to rope her hind leg and tie her up to get it. Well, the monkey seized the bottle and drank about half of it and stopped biting people for the time being.

I named it "Angélique" and took it home. It's a girl, so Sada will have to wait only four years for a bride – that is, if it lives. Another bandaging in the evening tired it out so much that I despaired. It, or rather she, could only hobble to the fire and fall asleep with her head against a warm brick. She was cold all the time, because it was raining and windy. I finally put on my woolen bathrobe and made her get under it, though I was severely bitten whenever her arm gave a twinge, and in spite of the fact that she has fleas I took her to bed with me.

Angélique with her bandaged arm.

There was no other way of keeping her warm through the night; the sentry always falls asleep and lets the fire die.

Patrick left this morning for Kayumba's, and he was reluctant to go away at this critical stage. I am more hopeful, because she gave me a hell of a night, and any baboon with that much pep is a strong animal. When she wasn't crawling around under the blanket, she was pulling my hair or going on a tour of investigation and ending by making a hammock of the mosquito net.

She spent all morning shrieking for food – the cow grew fractious, and it took three hours to get any milk – and then she managed to chew up and swallow a healthy piece of banana. She scorns condensed milk. Now she's so lively, in spite of a painful half-hour of dressing the arm this morning, that she yells insulting things at the chickens, and chases them when she can unfasten her rope. She is about eight inches long, excluding the tail, but large, powerful chickens flee when they see here coming at top speed, holding her wounded arm off the ground and limping awkwardly. Her head is still shaped like an embryo's and her fur isn't fur, it's fuzz. That vigorous night has had one effect: she knows me now and makes a dreadful noise whenever I go away. When no one talks to her, she keeps up a perpetual noise, a regular loud grunt. I'll have to do the dressing twice a day until Patrick gets back, and he's staying away a long time – till Thursday night. So if she dies, it will be my fault. Even such an atom of monkey needs three people to hold her when the wound is being washed. Patrick almost sewed it up but decided to wait a while. He had to cut off some dead flesh, and perhaps more will die, but it looked cleaner this morning. The whole forearm is stripped to the bone.

I tried to sleep today, and I feel a little better – almost ready for another siege. Things might have been worse. We have two gonor-rhea patients now, and it's such a difficult thing to manage when it's gone this far that Patrick has decided on strong measures. The less sick patient is Ngleza, poor old thing: he spends all his time now rolled in a blanket in the corner of the dispensary, making cheerful wise-cracks about the other patients and begging me to smuggle him some meat, as he claims that he's dying of hunger on his present diet of rice and bananas.

The other patient is Baruti, a young bushman; his case is so advanced that Patrick said I'd probably have to tap his bladder to save his life, before this census trip is over. He said I'd have to because Baruti undoubtedly would refuse to let a Negro do it, and he'd be more at ease if a white person wielded the needle. I protested that I would make a botch of it, but he firmly read all the directions to me out of a book, and I would have had to agree if he hadn't discovered that our needles aren't long enough. Moreover, a little judicious inves-tigation with a rubber catheter – there are no metal ones here – showed that Baruti's far worse off than he thought, so he told him to come with him as far as Ketshui's, or rather as far as the road-working station, where he's going on Monday, and from there go with carri-ers to Wamba, for a real operation by people who know how to do it.

Baruti, of course, wouldn't go. He'd rather die and not have any mystery about it. It made me think how very hard our own civilization must work to teach us to go to the doctor and to consent to operations. Surely my whole instinct, in regard to dentists, for example, is to let things take their own way. Only my education makes me go.

Sunday, May 17

Program yesterday: Four p.m. – Begin to think with horror of dressing Angélique's arm. Mind taken off this conversation by Nambedru, Sabini, and Matope re geography in general and Mambasa in particular. Great excitement manifest at appearance in Kigoma of a new man with a shop – hats, kaftans, shirts, etc. Abanzinga appears in a new red fez.

Four-thirty p.m. – Go to hospital to get solution ready. No water. Balabo says serenely that the water carriers forgot. Ngleza, in corner, philosophically starving for want of water to boil his rice. Very wrathful; send for Mautea, who blames it on Nasibo, who blames it on Yali and Sabani. Send for Yali, who gets water with Nasibo while I press Sabini into hospital service.

Five p.m. – Angélique carried, protesting, to hospital. Casualties: one chewed thumb and a torn bush shirt. Operation begins.

Five forty-five p.m. – Operation finished. Angélique in state of collapse that almost approximates mine. We both stagger home and lie down in respective beds.

Six p.m. – Entire force begins to catch calf, with intent to tie it up. I demand supper.

Six p.m. – Supper arrives. One plate of beans, one of pineapple leaves, one of chopped banana and pineapple. Matope joins me with much gusto. Chase of calf continues. Everyone very hoarse from screaming, especially the cow and Angélique.

Eight p.m. – Entire force desists from chase, owing to lack of light. I try to read *A Sheaf of Bluebells* by Baroness Orczy[2] and have reached "'M. de Maurel!' cried Ferdinande, 'This is an outrage!' He voice was choked with tears – tears of shame and of remorse for the past" ... when Nambedru and Matope come and ask me if they may have bread. I say certainly, certainly, and they go away. Back in a minute to ask if they may have butter. Certainly. Salt? Certainly. Pepper? Cert ... "'M. de Maurel!' cried Ferdinande, 'This is an outrage!'" ... Matope and Nambedru start squabbling about the butter. Salt is spilled. "Her voice was choked with tears" ... Matope and Nambedru begin to read letters to each other and call on me to arbitrate.

Nine p.m. – Give Ferdinande up and go take a bath. Make interesting discovery that Nambedru is accustomed to boil eggs in my bath water nightly. Upon reflection, cannot see why I should object. Discovery also of many small white worms in water, which Nambedru assures me are vicious beasts. She and Matope spend happy half-hour diving for them, spilling most of the water in the process.

Nine forty-five p.m. – Take bath while Nambedru modestly takes off her dress and holds it up to shield me from Ngbago's profane gaze.

Ten p.m. – Feed Angélique milk, which she takes while sleeping. Wrap her up securely in mackintosh, the one the goat ate most of, and take her to bed. Angélique goes on sleeping.

Midnight – Angélique rolls over, out of mackintosh. I put her back.

Three a.m. – Angélique tries to go walking, discovers that it is cold, and flees to my stomach to warm herself.

Five a.m. – Angélique sits up, rubs her eyes, and bites my chin affectionately. Feels call of nature and with unusual thoughtfulness tries to dive through mosquito net. Extricated without too much trouble: flees to *barza* and attacks milk bottle voraciously.

---

2 A 1917 novel by British writer Baroness Orczy who is best known the creator of the phenomenally popular 1903 play *The Scarlett Pimpernal*, which in 1905 she turned into the novel that became a series.

Six a.m. – News from Yafali that Mautea is down with malaria. Appoint Yafali officer of day, not without qualm, and go to see Mautea, who is being sensible about it and taking the right medicine.

Seven a.m. – Milking begins. I hastily go out for walk.

Seven-thirty a.m. – Return to find that calf has drunk all of milk. Calf is tied up and Angélique drinks water, not without urging. Ngimu complains of stomach ache. Prescribe anti-bilious pills. Try to read, after giving orders for Angélique's lotion to be prepared. "'M. de Maure!'" cried Fernande, "'This is an outrage!' Her voice …"

Matope complains of headache. Throttle impulse to throttle him, and prescribe aspirin. Angélique raising hell for no particular reason. She can't possibly be hungry yet. Almost time to dress her arm again, damn it.

CHAPTER 9

MONKEYS AND MEN

A NOTE CAME YESTERDAY FROM SMET, who can't come this month because his motor is broken. He asks me to come to Makuta Mbili, halfway down and a place he can reach by a couple of hours' walk from the road-head, and go on a long hunting trip from there. I can't spend a month doing it, as he suggests, but I shall go down for a week; down to Ketshui's in Patrick's *pirogue* when he goes on Sunday, and from there on foot with a porter to carry my box and things. I can come back the Tuesday after the same way. I hate to leave Angélique, but she can't go without milk and Matope promises to take her to bed with him; her arm looks so well that soon it won't need fresh dressing. I'm taking Sabani, as he wants to go.

The night before Patrick came back I was bored. Noticing that all the women had painted their faces freshly, I took my fountain pen and drew a lot of pictures on myself – triangles on my arms, a spidery-looking thing on the back of one hand, a skull and crossbones on my forehead and a heart on my chest. This fired my ambition, and I borrowed a dress-cloth from Abanzima and wound a big handkerchief on my head. Except for the color, I was a pretty good imitation, though my legs were bitten after I stripped them.

I'm reading a book Patrick borrowed from Morot, his friend at the road-head: *Le Coup de Bambou*.[1] It's about this region and the pref-

---

1 Hahn got the title of this book wrong or else it has been forgotten. It is not to be found among the holdings of major libraries in the North America or Europe. A Google search also proved fruitless.

ace started me thinking, in argument, about the whole proposition of colonization. Patrick and I had a long talk about it. He has very inflexible theories, but he doesn't seem to put them in practice. It's not the merciless exploitation of natives he objects to, he says: it's a law of nature and all that – dog-eat-dog: why shouldn't the Australians have killed off the Tasmanians? What he does object to is the hypocrisy of the people who are doing it. The people who use missionary motives, for instance.

Of course, this country isn't like Australia, I said. Here they don't want to kill-off the Negro, they want to help him increase, because they need his labor. It's nice to talk as Colonel Stammers does about making the tropics safe for white settlers, but until that's done you must have roads and sewers and trains, and the Negro's got to build those, and he's got to be beaten into it – that is, if you're honestly relentless for your own gain – and exploited and driven and occasionally, because of some inefficient person like Vandevelde, starved for lack of proper provision. Patrick pointed out there that the conservation of the Negroes is the Government plan purely; a good far-seeing one; but for the small private concerns it has no value or significance: they're working to get as much as possible as soon as possible and devil take the hindmost Negro unto the third and fourth generation.

First of all, I must decide how generous I am. My "noble impulse" – i.e., sympathy for humans and other animals – is after all a luxury, the product of a more or less comfortable background, the fruit of leisure moments when I'm not looking for a job or doing one and thus doing some one else out of that same job. Compared with the bulk of the human population, I've had many of those moments; therefore, I am shocked at greedy Belgians and other colonizers who are cruel to the Negroes. I should rather steer a halfway course and have contempt for them for murdering golden geese. That settles nothing, though. It answers only for the Congo; it doesn't answer for the Tasmanians.

Well, I must wait a few days before settling the world. I can't decide on everything this Thursday.

Saturday, June 6

Patrick called a tribunal the other day of all the important men in the district to see what suggestions they had for the hospital work. They asked for a woman *infirmier* to examine the women patients, and Patrick said all right, to give him a girl to train. Then they asked for a private room to have their own injections; they don't want to be treated just like the others. He said all right. Then they told him that there's been a lot of criticism about the injections; they want him to promise that the *infirmier* who gives the needle must have slept alone the night before, as when he's been with a woman the needle has a bad reaction on the patient. "How can I regulate the *infirmiers* like that? They'll lie to me," Patrick said.

"Why it's simple. If the needle makes the patient sick, then the *infirmier's* been with a woman: all you have to do is to send him to Avakubi, to jail."

Patrick looked slightly doubtful. "Perhaps. On the other hand, maybe it's the patient's fault for eating before the injection, or smoking."

"Ask the patients."

"I do, every day. You know as well as I do that they lie when they've eaten. How can I tell when they are lying?"

"Nothing's easier," said Halafu. "Suppose it's Masuri, here. If I say, 'Masuri, do you want the needle today?' and he says 'No, Bwana,' I say 'Why? Have you smoked today?' Masuri will say, 'Oh, no. I haven't smoked.' 'Well, then,' I say, 'why don't you want the needle?' He'll say, 'Oh, I don't know. The needle hurts.' Then Masuri's lying. Aren't you, Masuri?"

"Well, I'll tell you what I'll do," said Patrick. "I'll make the man who gives the injection sleep sentry at the hospital the night before. They never bring their women to the hospital; I've gone there many times and never seen a woman with them. So it will be all right, won't it?"

"Yes, that's quite all right," they all agreed.

Wednesday, June 10

I didn't go on the hunt after all, because Smet decided there were no elephants and he himself arrived here on Saturday, having paddled from Ketshui's. He tried to persuade me to give up the Mambasa trip and come with him instead for a month at Bomili, which is way west of Avakubi and would be a month's job. He persisted, assuring me as usual there was no reason to go to Mambasa – he knew it well; a dull hole, just like Penge, etc., etc., Whereas Bomili was a lovely land, full of elephants. He would talk about very little else, and my patience had become so short that for a while there was really bad blood between us. Especially as he said the minute he saw Angélique, "He will die soon." For the rest of his two days' visit – he couldn't stand any more time than that in idleness – he made uncomplimentary remarks about her: I reiterated by taking her everywhere under my arm, and talking to her lovingly. Things reached a crisis when he tossed her a lighted cigarette. Of course, she picked it up by the hot end and dropped it with a startled squeak, and he laughed.

I lost all control of myself sand fell upon him, tooth and nail. Naturally, I didn't do much damage, though he didn't defend himself – he's made of granite, and I couldn't even make a dent in him. He looked surprised, though, and stopped laughing. A few minutes later, he apologized and explained that he once had a monkey who put out lighted cigarettes by rolling them on the ground; he hadn't expected Angélique to hurt herself. He was sorry; really, he was. As for laughing, it had been thoughtless and he was very sorry. I grunted an acceptance of the apology: a moment later we were arguing again about my Mambasa trip, and at last I promised to go to Bomili afterward. His *ménagère*, it seems, wants to know why I don't live in Avakubi and save him the trouble of coming up here to see me. ... I think I shall probably poison him on the Bomili trip. I like him all right, but he is irritating. He argues every statement and disapproves of every plan that he himself doesn't make. The real trouble is that he's an active person and I'm passive; he would rather do work, any

Chief Abedi

work, if it's only carrying furniture up and down the river between beaches, than to sit and talk; while I'd rather do anything except physical exertion. He can't talk very well about his work, but our main trouble is that he doesn't like animals. Of course, he doesn't: it's silly for me to argue. How could a man be a professional hunter if he liked animals? On the other hand, how could anyone not be interested in a monkey? Angélique grows more interesting, every day. ... And yet I hate children, and other people love them. Smet does, for instance; he keeps talking about his son and I'm just as bored as he is by Angélique. Very odd.

There is a medicine down at Abedi's beach: four little wigwams made of leaves and filled with rice and fish. I don't know what it's about. I went down to look at it yesterday and then took a little walk on the path by the river and came across a trail of red ants crossing the road in a two-inch-wide band. I stopped at a distance of four feet to avoid any foragers or sentinels, and watched. Then I took a stick and tossed it across the trail. Immediately there was a cluster of ants on the stick, which took them off the trail for a minute and I saw that there were two sizes: the big warriors and the others, which, were only half as big. The warriors had pincers in front and their heads were swollen and black. They formed an awning over the trail of the small ants, by holding on to one another's legs and making a sort of network all the way across the road. It was this network that was demoralized when I threw the stick, so I could see the caravan underneath. The small ants were the ones who were making a good little foray to some neighbouring leaves, probably to get some food. About a foot on either side of the main caravan there were warrior sentinels every so often, sitting on leaves and thus getting a better view of the country. I prodded one with a match, and he grabbed it with a really strong grip. All of a sudden one of them found my leg, so I went home.

Patrick's a little worried about the first river we have to cross, as that is where Asumani's sister fell in from the bridge, or rather the long log that crosses it, and was drowned. The whole road is in bad shape. He told Sabini yesterday to take good care of us and not to cross the river if it was too strong. Sabini said that Madame wouldn't drown in the river unless Fate willed it; that her death was prearranged by heaven, so there was no use worrying.

"Very philosophical," Patrick said, "but not helpful. You take care, do you hear?"

CHAPTER 10

NO BANANAS

Friday, June 12, 1931

TABORA'S VILLAGE. I decided suddenly to come today because it's Friday: If I had waited until Patrick comes back from his weekend trip, as he wanted me to do, I should have been a week later. We are twelve porters, Matope, Sabani, Agalanga, Boni, and Nambedru.

I'm feeling fine again, and it's hard to believe I was so miserable at noon today. The reason was that we started late, naturally, and it's really a long pull. We walked six hours along a road that isn't shady very often. It's in bad shape, too, because there's little travel. At first, it was all plantations, banana palms mostly, and then we came to a little place where Agalanga, who goes ahead to prepare people for our coming, was waiting in a perfect fury. He has stepped on an iron spike planted in a piece of wood on the path, quite in the old-fashioned style of the bushmen. The guilty bushman was in great fear of me and kept explaining that his little baby had dropped the thing by mistake. I was angry at first, but after I had looked around I knew he'd told the truth. He is a blacksmith with a little forge and the spike was a curved affair; one of his tools. I wanted to buy it, but he was too afraid I was taking it to show the authorities. Sabani, haughty Monguana that he is, tried to take it by force, but I stopped him. A little medicine fixed Agalanga, and then I looked at the man's stock and asked him to keep a knife for me till I come back to buy it on my return.

I tried to walk slowly for the sake of the old Mahuma who's coming along for protection, but it really hurts me to walk slowly; I get twice as tired. I had to go ahead. The rivers kept me back just the same; I'm a coward on those log bridges and I crossed them slowly, especially a terrible one across the Itito, which Sabani says (I think wrongly) is bigger than the Ituri when it grows up. The bridge was a twisted tree, a long one but not thick, and first we had to climb over all the branches, far above the water. There was a liane swung alongside to hold on to. It was too slack to be any help, but I feel better with something in my hand like that.

There were short stretches of good forest with huge tress, but after leaving a deserted village where I ate a banana and drank some water the road grew really hard until this afternoon when we reached a small homestead of a genial bushman who gave Nambedru a dried antelope – *mboloko* – and seemed on the best of terms with my people. Then was the worst time, and Matope wept, and I almost gave up and sat down for a while just before we reached here, our camp. It's a Banguana place maintained as far as I can make out just for a station in this most uninhabited part of the Ituri Forest. Analanga or someone had scared the *capita*,[1] I think, for he bought me a chicken for nothing, and when I told him I'd rather buy it (I've no extra stuff to give for presents) my people were furious. Then they thought I paid too much for the food that immediately began to come in great quantities, comparatively speaking. I paid exactly what Patrick pays at Penge, but they know I could get away with less here. I could, but I don't want to. First, I'm soft. Second, I'm passing through this place again and I want to be able to buy stuff instead of snatching every leaf of *sombé*[2] from a reluctant Monguana. At the horrible sight of their depraved Madame paying nine francs and a

---

1 An apparent variation of the Portuguese word *capitão*, which means captain, leader, or commandante.

2 A dish of manioc leaves and goat meat in a hot sauce, popular in Central and East Africa.

packet of Alberts[3] for one large chicken, one small antelope, and an egg, when she could have had the same for eight francs – a difference of nine cents, all in all – Sabani and Agalanga came and told me that I was committing a great crime. I explained my more material reasons and they suddenly beamed and said, "Yes, Madame, I see. That's smart, really!" Sabini added, "They're awfully poor here. They'll be glad to see us again. Yes, that's smart."

What made the path bad was only that the short scrubby bush had encroached and there were lots of swampy places. I saw two things that were either worms or snakes: they looked like giant earthworms, but they were beautifully iridescent and when I wanted to pick one up, Nambedru screamed and said it was bad. She always says that, though.

Saturday, June 13

Yuma's. This was once a big village, but most of the people have been transferred to Avakubi and the rest will follow soon, following the Government's idiotic habit of shifting all the villages every year or two. The reason they do it is that they keep digging up new ethnological facts and theories; they want to divide the people up according to race now. It plays hob with the plantations, though, and all the *capita*s complain.

This is only a few hours' walk from our place of yesterday; it seems even less because the road is pleasant, leading through forest until it crosses the Ehulu, where you're practically arrived. The Ehulu is pretty big – we crossed in a leaky *pirogue* – and they said there are no crocodiles. I wanted to go for a swim, but a big storm was brewing, and Sabani advised against it. We came through two small villages,

3 A brand of cigarettes. R.J. Reynolds, the American tobacco company, introduced a brand of pipe tobacco called Prince Albert in 1907. It was one of the most popular tobaccos of the day, and the name was popular, too. Tobacconists in several European countries also introduced a line of products with the same name. Ironically, the original American tobacco sported the face of a Native American Indian on its packaging, *not* that of a European royal.

in the first of which there was a lot of trouble owing to Agalanga's zeal. I had bought four eggs: the old lady said she'd rather have salt than money. She objected to the amount of salt that Agalanga gave her, and I told her to take back the eggs. Of course, she didn't; she went on muttering and there it would have ended if a young relative hadn't passed uncomplimentary remarks about Mobudu bullies – i.e., Agalanga. They began to yell at each other and the Monguana, who was about half as large as Agalanga, pulled off his shirt and got ready to back up his statements. I would have liked to see a fight, but prudence forbade it. I had to shout at Agalanga three times to make him stop, and then the goat-whiskered old *capita* began to scold him while he looked very glum and repressed. So I had to shout at the *capita* too. He immediately became servile again – a Negro of the old school; it made me embarrassed – and I started out again hastily, after giving the old lady two cigarettes.

This chief is Abedi's brother, at least they have the same father, and he's so up-and-coming that I would never dare offer him salt in lieu of francs. I'll be running out of small money, though, if I don't watch out. Patrick and I forgot to count in Nambedru's *posho*[4] and I must give her ten francs this week like the others of his personal staff. The porters get a franc a day and no help from me, which is not like the usual business of the white man's buying bananas in bulk and reselling them to the men. Patrick's idea to save trouble. The men don't like it quite so well, but they pool their money and let their private *capita* do the wrangling, which serves in the same way. If my small money holds out three more days, I'll be in Mambasa where they can change the bigger bills and then we'll be all right. Pay for the porters' work isn't given until the trip is over; this is just *posho*. I guess the money will last: I have enough food now for the rest of the trip – two chickens, a leg of a goat, and a lot of rice and manioc, not to mention ten eggs. Yuma is standing here now, watching the typewriter. I guess he'll be begging for cigarettes in a minute.

4 Rations – usually rice – given to soldiers, sailors, labourers, and safari porters in lieu of pay in East Africa.

Saturday – posho day, when the road workers were issued their weekly food rations.

The Banguana villages end here, they tell me, and from now on they'll be all bushmen. Though there won't be any villages till we reach Omali's where we'll sleep tomorrow, and the *capita* says it's a long, long way with bad walking. We must get an early start, though of course we're getting used to it now. Matope still complains that his feet hurt. Well, so do mine. It's really cold now that the rain has finished and I regret having left my second blanket in Penge.

The country was good for walking today. It's getting hilly, which is a great relief after the miles of flat bush-covered country around Penge, and I like the big trees. Tomorrow we cross the river where Asumani's sister fell in and was drowned. Yuma says that what happened was the water was so strong it carried off the bridge just as she was crossing. He says it's all right now because the water has gone down. How would it carry off the bridge, though? The bridges here are just trees; they're not supported by anything. Well, I'll see tomorrow.

Tuesday, June 16

The first accident yesterday was when I slipped crossing a rotten bridge; my leg went through a hole and I landed in the middle of a procession of big red ants. It was uncomfortable, as I couldn't get out in a hurry. When most of them were pulled off–they hold as hard as they can – I noticed that my leg hurt a little. Later on, it hurt a lot.

Matope was so exhausted that Sabani fell behind and carried him. The path was well-traveled, which made it worse. At every creek the ground for yards around was trampled into a soup, and after an hour of it my morale almost gave way. Trying to grip on the slippery ground, and splashing through cold mud up to the middle of my shins and wondering what was the matter with my legs, made an ensemble of torture. I thought that surely I had been walking for hours, and yet when I looked at the clock it hadn't been so long. Now and then it rained. Nambedru, surprisingly enough, suddenly announced that her feet hurt and she was tired – this after only three hours. The others didn't mind the road at all.

We came to a place where they had cut all the trees to plant a garden, and then had left the trees lying there. However, the road led straight through, over the trunks and branches. I thought I'd scream if my legs hurt any more. Just at the end, a little stick whipped me in the face and I did cry, but no one saw it as I was ahead. Suddenly we came out on the white man's road. It was a new automobile road with tracks on it.

There was a man far off; we called him, and he told us that the white man was farther on at the end of the road. It was just noon now, the time I'd said that we would arrive, and I had thought it must be late afternoon. Now it was easy walking, of course, and by the time we came to the big house I was able to speak up as if a morning of mud-wading was a pleasure. The white man stood at his door, looking polite but annoyed. Belgians always look like that at first in the Congo.

However, he invited me in and gave me a chair, and the other members of the caravan sat down on the *barza*. Everything looked very new and scarred and rough-hewn: the road is red, cut through laterite,[5] and there were wheelbarrows and scales and mixing machines standing about. But the three-room twig house was comfortable. And there was no mud.

The Belgian said that the auto came twice a week; that I must wait two days unless I wanted to walk, and that, he said, wouldn't help much as the distance was three marches and I wouldn't get there any sooner. It's a truck, he said, and I could carry all my boxes and a couple of servants if I wanted. Nambedru has said that Patrick had told her I mustn't walk along a road if it was possible to ride; there are no trees to shelter it. All right, I said, nothing loathe – and now, where could I live? But there was no house except his. There followed a polite argument as to whether or not I should take his bedroom. I won out and had my things put in the storeroom: bed, Matope's blanket, and all. I paid the men's *posho* and told the porters that they could walk empty to Mambasa. They said good and could they go right away? So off they went, and Boni ran off in the other direction to see some relatives at the road head, and Monsieur found a house for Nambedru and the rest, and turned Sabini over to his own boy. Then I had a bath with a shower, and discovered that my big toes were in really bad shape. Monsieur, who by this time seemed to be an angel, gave me a pair of his slippers after cutting the blisters for me. He said that his feet always acted like that here.

His wife is in Belgium, because her liver is bad here. He has three children. He was in the war. We drank whisky and talked until lunch, which somehow didn't arrive until about three in the afternoon. I talked and talked and talked, the words poured out unbidden, I couldn't stop. It was the fifth white man I'd seen since coming to Penge. He's

5 A type of reddish-coloured soil rich in iron and aluminum, which is found in hot, wet, tropical areas. Hahn recognized it because she studied Geology as an undergraduate at the University of Wisconsin and in graduate school at Columbia University in New York.

alone a great deal of the time himself, and he had a lot to say, too. He was a plumber in Belgium; then after he came here they put him on this work.

We had cognac afterward, and at sunset we walked down the road again and looked at how the work was done. Dinner was at nine-thirty, and when it was finished I almost fell off my chair with sleepiness. I'd put Matope to bed already, following a sudden qualm of conscience when I remembered that after all Monsieur is a Belgian and probably has ideas about girls who travel alone. It's hard to remember all the time to be careful. Anyway, Matope was asleep on the floor, and I crawled into bed and dropped off in spite of my aching knees. I woke this morning when the bugle blew at five, and then I rolled over and fell asleep again – like Matope.

Monsieur has a pet goat and lots of pigeons, of which he is very fond.

Sunday, June 21

Trouble, trouble, trouble for Monsieur. Three days ago came a letter by messenger from the Administrator at Mambasa. The road between there and Irumu is washed out, with the Government bus fallen into a ditch, and Mambasa is marooned without a car. However, the Administrator added brightly, there is plenty of food in the countryside for the road workers: send men fifteen kilometers down the road and there is a village with many plantains. Good! I decided to wait two more days for Agalanga's wife to get well and for Nambedru, too, and meantime, I was to take two of my own men and go with Monsieur and his porters to that town where there were so many bananas. Sunday – i.e., today – I would start walking to Mambasa, as the road might not be fixed for another week. Good. ...

We started out, with a *tipoye* because my knee still felt suspicious and the toes were still ulcerated. We had only four men for the *tipoye*, which is hard for them unless the passenger walks a lot of the time.

That I did, but I couldn't walk all the way because the knee grew worse. At eleven, we reached that village and found sixteen little bunches of plantains.

Characteristically, the Administrator had been slightly mistaken. Now Monsieur was really worried. He sent the other men into the forest to hunt for manioc against *posho* day and we came back here, arriving at five or so. No plantains for my people, who began to be frightened.

The next day I called them all and said that if they wanted to go to Mambasa and wait for me there, all right. I would wait here unless I could find porters for the loads; which Monsieur said I couldn't possibly; I would wait for the truck. Agalanga said he'd go as soon as his wife was well; Betugonai said the same. So did Nambedru and Sabani and Matope. This was flattering but I was worried. I'm tired of battling with Monsieur for food; he gives what he can, but that's not much.

Yesterday they decided again that they'd better go to Mambasa, after all, and wait for me there. Agalanga's wife is still sick but the others – Nambedru, Sabani and Betugonai – started this morning on the three days' journey along the new road. Matope still elected to stay, though he cried when Sabani went away. And now I've nothing to do but wait. I'm awfully glad I sent the porters last week; if I hadn't, everyone would have starved. Monsieur wants me to come back for a while after Mambasa. But, not for me! Not again, unless I have a truckload of food.

Day before yesterday, the men struck and wouldn't work without more food. Monsieur insists that they get enough food on Saturday to last the week, if they'll only have a little sense and conserve it. But they eat it all in three days and ask for more. In a way, that's true. (I saw a man yesterday, half-finished with a plantain, chuck the rest into the bush because he wasn't hungry at the moment.) I suggested that Monsieur give the food twice a week, and he says that although it's a lot of work, he'll have to do it. As for the strike, he settled that by means of shrieking and stamping around and help from the *capitas*. I didn't go along to see because I'd had enough of that on the road to the plan-tain village, when he found the whole crew taking a siesta and had to drive them back to work. But yesterday morning, the morning before the giving of *posho*, he came back to the house and suddenly gave up for a minute. I was shocked. He's always so hard with the men, and so gay and silly when they're not there, that I couldn't believe my eyes when he suddenly slumped into a chair and put his arm up over his face. A moment later he looked up and said, "Mademoiselle, some-times I am discouraged." He'd been crying.

I said, "It's wrong to push the road so fast when you haven't enough food for the men." I say that all the time, and he won't admit it.

"It's got to go fast. Too costly."

"It wouldn't be so costly if you had half the number of men."

"Then we'd go only half as fast, and the road wouldn't be finished next year."

"What of it?"

"Then Belgium would lose money."

"She loses money now, this way."

"Ah, but if the road waits, America and England and France will all say to the League of Nations, 'You see? Belgium is too small and too poor to develop the Congo properly. Much better give it to us.'" He stood up and walked around the room. "No! It would not be so bad if these small officials had a little sense. Already it is better than it used to be. On the railroad from Matadi to Kinshasa there is a dead man ..."

"I know," I said wearily, "there is a dead man for every tie, I mean a dead black, and a dead white for every five. Though why you're all so proud of that I can't imagine. And here they're half-dead of hunger, and you know it."

"They're stupid animals. Why don't they save their food?"

"I know one thing. I'm certainly not going to leave Matope here to grow up and work on the road."

He shrugged. "It would be a great mistake to take him away. The work is not hard." I looked at him.

"Truly," he insisted, "it is not hard. These blacks don't know what real fatigue is." He stopped, because he himself couldn't sound as if he believed it. "You would be making a mistake. There are many white children in Europe who are much more unhappy than Matope. Take one of them."

"You idiot!" I cried, "I'm not going around the world saving children for the fun of it. Or the principle either. 'What if there are white children who are orphans? I *know* Matope; I don't know your white children. I don't want your white children." We let it drop.

Today we were eating breakfast when he saw a man walking by with all his food in a basket on his head, en route to a house where he had arranged to sleep with somebody's wife in return for his *posho*. The husband had consented and a *planton*[6] had told Monsieur. That meant, of course, one more man on the *barza* every day crying, "Bwana, I'm dying of hunger." Monsieur called a guard and the man was dragged to the door. I went into my room until it was finished. Matope a few minutes later came in looking delighted – "The white man has been beating him!"

When I came out there was Monsieur, with bleeding knuckles and a wounded foot, and the man with his basket of food had gone. We went on talking about Rostand.

Thursday, July 2

Relief suddenly arrived Sunday morning – the Government truck! Full of plantains, it was, though Monsieur said it wasn't enough for half his men. All was excitement and hurry to pack and go, family and all. We started back to Mambasa in half-an-hour, and forgot only the butter dish.

Gee, it felt queer to be riding in a car again. It's been four months since I've seen one. It seemed to me that we were simply whizzing,

6 A personal servant or attandant.

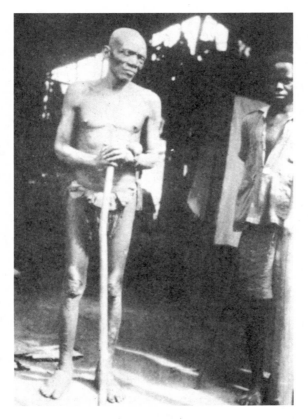

Njoka, a pygmy hunter

though really it was a poor old Ford truck and couldn't go very fast. Matope and Boni were grinning with delight, all the way.

The road is sixty kilometers long and exactly the same all the way – tall forest on each side, with here and there, at long distances, a bunch of houses and a plantation of banana trees. Lots of pygmies at the villages. We ambled pleasantly and stopped everywhere; at each place someone brought Boni a banana pipe, and the whole crew would take quick puffs of it before starting the trip again. That is to say, Boni provided the tobacco (my cigarettes) in return for the loan of the pipe.

Mambasa is in a clearing. That means that I had my first breath of really fresh air since I left Stanleyville. I didn't realize how stagnant and still the air is in the forest until a breeze blew down the road from Mambasa. It was more stimulating even than whisky. It gave me nostalgic thoughts of the ocean and the mountains. I was excited, ridiculously excited, and Mambasa is only a little post, a post like Avakubi. Still, I was excited.

We picked up my people on the way through the native village. Nambedru was thin and fretful, but glad I had come. Sabani almost cracked his face grinning. I found a couple of old friends from Penge. They told me that both the Agent Territorial and the Administrator were away for the day, fishing or something, but there was an old soldier waiting for me at the rest-house, and he had a lot of chained prisoners to sweep out the house and fix it up. I was all installed almost immediately.

A grand fanfare of trumpets woke me in the morning. In the clearing before the bureau all the soldiers and *plantons* were drawn up, and they saluted as the flag was raised. I saw two white men assisting at the ceremony by standing very stiff and dignified before the flagpole, and Matope said the Government had returned the night before. There followed an impressive drill, while I dressed hastily and ran out sans stockings to see the Administrator and present my papers. I was terribly afraid of him, after the report.

I needn't have been. He was a gentle man, very tall (or do all white men seem tall to me after these short-statured Negroes?), and he had a blond beard and a gently sarcastic way of talking. He promised me a chicken, strawberries (that I couldn't believe till I saw them, but they really arrived), and invited me to dinner that evening. After which I went down to the shops and talked to the Greek and listened to Nambedru's complaints. It seems that Sabani has not done well by her. I don't know just what is the trouble, and neither does Sabani. However, I told her to wait and let Patrick arbitrate; then I sent her to bed because she had fever again.

THE MISSION HERE IS A LITTLE TOWN IN ITSELF. My friends didn't build it; they're only keeping it up until the doctor who started it gets back from his leave. There is a hospital, brand-new, and several houses. There's one black *infirmier* who gives all injections; I talked to him for a long time and asked him to give me an injection of the doctor's medicine. He demurred. "It's medicine for black people, not for white," he said. However, I insisted and won out.

ONCE MORE, I BEGAN TO WORRY ABOUT PENGE. If the truck went the next day, I said, so would I – with my bed, Nambedru, Matope and Sabani. I would wait at Monsieur's for the porters and the rest of the things. Every one was pleased except Matope.

His mother had appeared on the scene. She's a little woman with a replica of his face; deaf and dumb, but very eloquent with her fingers. I understood almost everything she said. She wanted to keep Matope with her, and I advised him to stay there. (Not, I admit, without some qualms. The Greek says she's a prostitute – that isn't so important, but wouldn't he be hard up for food in that case?) Matope said no; he would go back to Penge. But she decided then to come along with us. Good, I said heartily, come on. After some reflection, she said that she would finish her work – pounding rice – in three weeks, and follow after. I don't know if she will, but we left it at that, and I gave her a cloth and ten francs and various odds and ends of salt and tobacco. She gave me a big dish of peanuts and two ears of corn.

I had begged passage on the *camion* [truck] for the aforementioned party, and besides that for Agalanga's wife, whose feet are in bad condition. They consented and gave permission besides to carry all my luggage along, so that the porters can walk "empty." That evening I got a note from Patrick, asking me what the hell, and would I please send a few men back even if I couldn't come, as he had run short of workers, sending me various messages. I sent Koto, Maliamungu, and Suedi, who brought the note, with a detailed account of all accidents. Also there was a note from Vandevelde saying that he and Pavloff and Doctor Melius were arriving at Penge either the third or fifth of July. I should hate to miss them; I can only hope that they'll be late in coming, or stay a long time.

Well, in the morning when I was all packed the Administrator announced that he and the Agent were coming, too, to help "Monsieur-On-The-Road" with his monthly payroll. I was pleased. Halfway there we encountered a fine big antelope, but when the chauffeur fired, the gun didn't speak, and the antelope escaped.

The porters should be here tomorrow. I told them to bring their food along. Also, I bought a whole bunch of plantains for Nambedru before we left Mambasa, and if she mentions hunger once more I shall slam her in the nose. I had to ask for food for Sabani and Matope, though, and Monsieur said, "I'm tired. ... Can't they wait till tomorrow?" But being practised now in persistence, I only said, "No, they can't. They haven't eaten since early morning." He looked surprised at my firmness, but the Administrator was there and he didn't like to refuse. Therefore, four kilos of dried bananas were carefully weighed out and given to them, and I know he hated to do it. I can't help it. ... I brought him two cabbages from Mambasa anyway, and an assortment of tinned stuff.

Saturday, July 4

Yuma's village again, and I'm overjoyed that the worst is over. I left Monsieur's house yesterday, unbeknownst to him. It was a dirty trick, but there were circumstances. He's gone up the road to work, and it's more than a mile. He promised to be back at eleven-thirty in case the porters had come and I wanted to be off. "Sleep at Omande's tonight," he said with an airy gesture. "It's only fifteen kilometers and he has a good house. You can be there in three hours at the most; as it's a dirty road it may take a little longer. You must eat before you go, so I'll order lunch."

Well, after he left I pondered and talked to Sabani and decided that wasn't practical. Omande is only halfway or a little more to Njoka's, and Monsieur doesn't realize how far the second march is as it is, without adding to it. He really doesn't know the forest at all. Therefore, I sent all the sick people ahead and when the porters arrived at ten-thirty they were rudely surprised to find that they must go on immediately – they'd looked forward to spending the night at Monsieur's.

I waited until twelve and Monsieur hadn't come. Walking in the forest after dark is no fun, especially when you've been hearing so many leopard stories. I wrote a hasty note apologizing and set off with Sabani and the lantern in case of accidents. I got to Njoka's just ahead of a bad thunderstorm, and he was waiting. "You stayed there a long time," he grumbled. However, after he had told me again what a big noise he used to be, he cheered up. So did I, at the thought that all the worst mud holes were over and done with and my toes weren't sore yet. Also that I didn't have sunstroke from walking in the afternoon. People seldom do walk after twelve, though it seems to me that in the forest it can hardly matter much what time of day you walk.

Sabani said on the road, "The white man's people told me that after you left he cried. He cried for you. I didn't quite understand it," he added frankly, "but I suppose he didn't want to be left alone."

"He didn't cry for me," I said. "He cried for his wife in Europe. Whenever he sees another white woman, he thinks about her, and he cries."

"Oh, I see ... Madame. How much does a white man pay for his wives in Europe?"

ɷ

IT RAINED ALL NIGHT, AND I OUGHT TO KNOW because I heard it. It's cold, sleeping in that open place, and my people were joyous for some mysterious reason and played a couple of zithers from midnight till morning. This morning they fell into a deep slumber just before it was time to start out, and Sabani was grieved when I woke him at six. "It's raining. Are you going to go when it's raining?"

"Certainly," I said firmly. He didn't dare to argue, but the captain of the porters said, "The Itito is big again – big as it was when Saidi's wife fell in and was drowned."

"Really? Well, I'll go to the Itito and see. If it's too dangerous, we'll sleep there."

He had no answer to that, and so off we went, though there was a lot of trouble about who carried what. It was really raining hard, and we were all soaked in a minute, but in away that's preferable to the heat. I didn't dare stop anywhere to rest – maybe my stiff knee is rheumatism; I don't know. To keep their spirits up, the men began to sing.

The rain is bad
Oh!
The rain is bad
Oh!
It makes the road muddy
Oh! Oh! Oh! Oh!

But Munganga is waiting
Oh!
Munganga is waiting
Oh!
The doctor is waiting for his sister
Oh! Oh! Oh! Oh!Agalanga says to Madame
Oh!

Agalanga says to Madame
Oh!
I'm dying of hunger
Oh! Oh! Oh! Oh!

Monday, July 6

Penge. There was a most flattering and satisfactory reception yesterday when we stumbled in, Sabini in the first stage of his long-postponed sickness. Just as we clambered out of the last ravine there was a great shout, then the whole family came galloping down: Abanzima first – we swung around each other in Mangbetu fashion – Nambedru next, hanging on to me, and then Chimp, coughing and dragging her chain behind her in great excitement. Patrick last in a crowd of grinning *infirmiers*, muttering, "You did good time. I was going to be shaved, but you came too early." He had put off his down-river trip until I arrived and ordered soup for lunch instead of porridge – oh, it was a welcome! We talked sixty to the minute. No white man had come. He's shot a great big elephant. Leopards have taken one of the baby goats and wounded the buck. There were four ducklings, but Chimp ate two of them. There's a new half-grown baboon, wicked, but not yet wicked enough to be chained up; and Angélique, alas, has completely forgotten me and clings firmly to Abanzinga. This is dreadful, but in a way it saves a lot of trouble, as she sleeps with him now, and it is his responsibility to feed her. The black-faced monkey it is, instead, who hangs onto me and squeaks if I put him down.

I must say, it goes to my heart when Angélique shrieks with fear of me, but I don't want to start taking her to bed with me again, and I must do that if I want to make peace. Patrick bolted his lunch, approved of all the new clothes we had picked up, took possession of the new red fez and went off in high good humor. It was not until he'd gone that I went out and found a brand-new cabinet awaiting me, a splendid white affair trimmed in black, with the windows and door screened against chickens and ducks, and a new floor put down. Bless his heart.

WE PLANTED THE NEW GARDEN YESTERDAY, me with two baboons hanging around my neck and arms except when they stopped to dig up the seeds I had just covered. (Angélique has returned to me; she divides her allegiances now.)

Unfortunately, Patrick suddenly got a photography enthusiasm and unlocked Chimp to take her picture. Afterward his worse nature got the better of him, and he left her unlocked, with the result that she ate all the sugar in the attic and stole our bread. He turned a deaf ear to the servants' complaints – that is, the more they complained, the less he locked her up, and by the time he capitulated at last everyone was furious with everyone. When he suddenly told me that he had a bad fever coming on, I wasn't at all surprised. He's in bed for the day, today.

CHAPTER 11

THE VILLAIN IN AVAKUBI

Monday, July 13, 1931

PATRICK IS VERY ILL. It grew worse yesterday, and when his temperature reached one-hundred-and-four [degrees Fahrenheit] he decided to clear the ground for action. For a couple of hours I was busy writing down directions of what to do if he became delirious – "Though it's not at all likely," he said. "Last year I reached one-hundred-and-six, and my head was perfectly clear. It's my stomach that hurts now, and my back."

We pulled down all the books and looked through them to see what he had. He was sure it wasn't malaria, because he had a swollen gland in the groin and because his fever never broke and he didn't sweat in spite of blankets and hot tea. Climatic bubo, he insisted – whatever that means. Then he suddenly saw a patch of red on his leg and thought it was probably erysipelas.[1]

On this premise, I took down all notes for a dose of digitalin and adrenalin in case his heart should go bad, a warm wrapping of wet sheets and fanning to bring down the heat, and injection of camphorated oil. We put everything in the room and had a lamp fixed up in case he should get worse at night. *Tout à coup* [suddenly] he changed

---

1 A contagious and infectious skin disease that also affects the subcutaneous tissue. It is characterized by inflammation of the diseased areas, with accompanying redness and swelling. It can be fatal.

his mind – it was malaria after all; peculiar because he's an old-timer. He resolved on a regime of quinine to begin next day, drank a dose of laudanum while discoursing learnedly on how bad such things were, and while still protesting that it hadn't the slightest effect on him, fell asleep.

☉

SABANI MADE A CONFESSION. He looked very mysterious as he said, "Well, I've got a wife now."

He has more than once hinted that I ought to buy him a wife, but I held out for Patrick's plan with Ngimu, which is to wait until the man has saved up half the sum by himself and then provide the other half. At present, Sabani is in debt to me for fifty-two francs. But it seems he gave the cruel parent a shirt and Papa counted forty off for that; there remains one hundred and sixty, and meantime Sabani's got the lady on credit. He looked very pleased about it. "She's living at my house today," he said. "Waiting for me."

Friday, July 24

Anyone would be excused for believing this time that the Doctor was really coming at last. We had three letters about it: Pavloff, Vandevelde, and Smet all wrote that he and Pavloff would come up with Smet and arrive here either Wednesday or Thursday. So Tuesday afternoon everything was swept and garnished to the last degree, and Patrick, who is much better, and I sat up late discussing what should and what shouldn't be presented unofficially to Pavloff. All the Negroes, especially the *infirmiers*, were excited: Matope was terrified because of stories he'd heard of the Doctor's fierceness. Everybody was sent out to buy eggs and because we haven't many chickens, we bought a couple of goats to kill later on. When no one came on Wednesday we told each other that they'd be here Thursday. All

Thursday morning I wandered about uneasily, not liking to write because the table was so beautifully cleaned up; not liking to play with the animals for fear of dirtying myself. Patrick was as bad. Noon came and nothing in sight or hearing. I insisted that we eat our porridge. At last at two o'clock some sharp-eared boy heard the "picky-picky" on the river, and there was a wild rush to fix another lunch – lobster out of tins and pineapple leaves and mayonnaise – while I arranged a whisky bottle with an artistic festoon of glasses on the side-table. The resthouse looked perfectly horrible but festive, draped with cretonne and things.

And then it was only Smet! The other two had failed to turn up at Makutambili where it was arranged that they all meet. Smet had waited two days and then got disgusted. He admitted that he suspected the Doctor was really afraid of Patrick's boat and sailsmanship. Patrick turned a bright red and decided to be really angry with the Doctor at last. With commendable control, he put it out of the conversation and said nothing more about it all day, and Smet took up his abode alone in the decorated *gîte* [a lodging, resting place]. It was only in the evening when a note arrived for Smet that I saw he was still excited; he thought it was probably from Pavloff at Makutambili saying that they had arrived at last, but it was only a note from Smet's chief hunter with the news that an elephant he had wounded was dead at last in a highly negotiable place in the forest. Smet left this morning to see about cutting it up; he'll be back in a couple of days.

Meantime, we say nothing about the Doctor. It's really very trying. They should at least have sent word to Smet. The hospital now is almost entirely out of all supplies.

Saturday, July 25

Another monkey! No one knows what kind this one is; it was dropped by its mother who was robbing a plantation and was suddenly surprised by one of Abedi's men into galloping off and leaving it. About ten days old, Patrick says. It's so small that it can sit in my hand in perfect comfort, but it has an enormously long tail. It's a silver color with a black face and curly hair; Asumani says it will be a "magistrat" monkey when it grows up; bigger than the baboons. It – or rather she – was in a state of complete collapse when she arrived; limp and dumb, with her head bent back and her mouth open. Patrick insisted her back was broken. I insisted that she was hungry; that was all. After Patrick had looked her over in his most professional manner he sent for splints and camphorated oil and needles, I carried her off and gave her warm milk and had the great satisfaction of proving my point because she straightened out and gobbled the milk and started to scream in a most healthy manner. She was afraid all day, though. Today she's most friendly. Patrick gave her to Chimp to nurse, and Chimp hurt her, so we took her away. That marks the end of Chimp's governess days, and Patrick feels badly about it because he's often said that he'd trust Chimp with anything but fowls, and now he can't. This morning Boy, the young baboon, kidnapped the child and ran all over the homestead before he was caught; the baby seemed to enjoy it. Angélique sniffs at her scornfully and raises hell whenever I give her the bottle instead of handing it to herself. The pig is growing really enormous and can defend himself against the dog now, but Angélique can't. A hundred times a day she comes screaming to me with the dog in hot pursuit, nibbling at her tail and her hind legs. By this time, the house is swarming with animals – the guinea pig has given birth, too – and it is difficult to keep track of the bizarre friendships and feuds that are current. I think I shall make a chart, thus:

	Likes	Hates	Fears	Holds in Contempt
Angélique	Abanzinga	Dog	Chimp	New monkey
	Me	Pig	Sada	
	Boy	Pat		
	Black monkey	Chimp		

	Likes	Hates	Fears	Holds in Contempt
	Matope	Nambedru		
Boy	Ngimu	Chimp	Patrick	Black monkey
	Abanzinga	Sada		Pig
	Me	Dog		
	New monkey			
Pig (Grover)	Everybody			
Dog	Black monkey	Boy	Chimp	Guinea pigs
	All humans			
	Pig			
Chimp	Patrick	All Negroes	Turtles	Everyone
	Antea		Monkey skins	
	All young mammals			
Black Monkey (Mangbetu Mobaya)	Patrick	No one	Nothing	Nothing
	Matope			
Mickey	Everything but black monkey	Black monkey	Crocodiles	Black monkey
Abanzima	New monkey	Pig	Snakes	All Banguana
	Boy			

Monday, August 3

Ketshui's. I decided to go with Smet to Avakubi, but first we went to finish a job that he had neglected – the cutting up of his latest elephant. It was all done except the weighing and paying off. With only two of his men and Matope we embarked in the big boat, not bothering to start the motor, and poled downstream, working hard and growing warm and going very slowly. On the other side of the river a path struck into the bigger way leading from Avakubi, and brought us to a small bush village where awaited an imposing array of pygmies, each with his basket of meat. It smelled hardly at all. It was weighed and paid for and sent off to Morot in almost no time, and we got back to Kayumba's for a late lunch.

Two days of comparative inaction made even me restless and drove poor Smet crazy. Yesterday, then, in spite of probable qualms on his part, we packed up with intent to go somewhere and thus miss Patrick when he should arrive in the evening. I was delighted, but he was sorry. Still, go he must. Just before embarking he got news that he was afraid to hand on to me. ... One of his men had shot an elephant in the environs of Penge! He giggled as he told me.

Even then, I couldn't keep from laughing. "Go ahead," I said stoutly. "I'll wait at Ketshui's, if you'll take me there. Go ahead and cut up your old elephant."

"No," he decided, "I'll trust the boys. It is only a small one, and they can't do much harm. We will go to Ketshui's together, and then I will be near my hunters, and tomorrow I shall look for a new one. When the boys are alone they shoot only the little ones; I must find a big one and then another, and then I shall be free to take you to Avakubi."

So here I have waited like Baby Bunting, looking at the river and hearing great bangs of the gun, close by. He has come back with his hand cut and bleeding from using the gun the elephant broke up; he has wounded a very big beast, which is gone into the forest, followed by the hunters, to die he hopes, as it fell down twice when crossing the river from the island where he shot it.

Ketshui is gone to Avakubi for one of those many *barzas*; this morning a sub-chief sent us two skimpy bunches of palm nuts carried by a man half-dead of hunger. The nearer we go to the road the more the famine prevails. I made Smet give him food, but that doesn't help the rest of them.

It is raining hard, and I am sorry for Smet if he's caught in it, because he says the elephant tracks will be washed away and he'll lose the animal. All last evening he kept coming back to the subject of the elephant, and when he wasn't talking, he sat with his chin in his hand, trying to imagine what he would do if he were in the elephant's place, I guess. It was very exciting when he shot him, I think, though he only mentioned the details in the course of a long conversation. He saw this elephant alone on the little island near here. He shot him in the ear, and dropped him, but then the beast got up and started across the river, followed by the *pirogue*. He turned around and made for the boat, and the boys wanted to give up the chase and let themselves go down the current where he would be afraid to follow, and he turned and made for the other shore. That was when he slipped and fell once more in the water. He was staggering with weakness.

Smet left him and then came back here to call a boy to follow him at a respectful distance. In the afternoon, he took a light gun and told me he was going after small game, but he couldn't resist following the track. He came to the other side where he had lost the elephant and found his track again; one foot had only two toes instead of three. From there on it was easy to follow for a short way, but suddenly he found himself in the middle of a perfect maze of tracks; the elephant had found friends. Only by tracing out the two-toed track could he follow it at all. He walked for miles, but could find nothing. Once he saw a huge Colobus monkey and was aiming at it mechanically when he remembered that I don't like people who shoot monkeys needlessly, and he desisted. (Good, I said at this point; it's against the law anyway. "Oh, the law … " he answered.) He grew angry; it was a great big elephant and if he couldn't find the corpse some undeserving bushman village would get all the meat and ivory. The sun had set when he turned back; he didn't get back here until about eight o'clock and I had decided he wouldn't be back that night.

I heard him this morning, terribly early; I fell back and slept another century or two, and yet it wasn't six when I did get up and found him already gone. He is strong.

The elephant that broke the gun did get away completely. It wasn't Smet who saw it; it was one of the boys. He shot the elephant and it turned around and charged, pulling the gun from his hands and smashing it. The boy ran away and came back later to get it. He says he was caught by his feet, which were under a log that he couldn't throw off as the elephant was standing on it when he took the gun, and it's true that his toes are crushed. Queer, though, that he wasn't killed.

Saturday, August 8

The peaceful and somewhat archaic holiday in the forest was rudely interrupted. First, news suddenly arrived that Patrick, going to Penge from Kayumba's had turned over in his canoe and lost everything – rifle, camera, table, chair, clothes, blankets, and medicines. It was Mokwanzanza who came to Kayumba's after catching the boat again down in front of Adinotta's, who said Patrick had told him to tell us if he saw us – he encountered Smet there, still following the elephant. It was true, because next day Sabani came back and he had heard the news before me, on the road to Avakubi. I wrote to Patrick right away and told him how sorry I was, and in a sudden rush of remorse sent him fifty francs that I begged from Smet against a check. Before he got my note, though, he sent one to Smet, with no word for me, but a disturbing one for him. He confirmed the news of the disaster (luckily, he said, no lives lost – it seems that Yafali was driving, and ran the sticks of the shelter into a tree, as has so often happened before – this time it finished the job) but what he really wanted to say was, "Your wife has decided to go back to Avakubi, and was going to start walking this morning with Robert. I persuaded her to wait until day after tomorrow, in order to get word from you. I don't know what is the matter; I think she finds it dull here in the country, and then perhaps she is angry about tobacco, chickens or Mickey ... Please send an answer immediately."

Smet was awfully worried. He had left his *ménagère* in Penge to visit relatives. She mustn't walk in the sun with the baby, and then, too, what was the matter with her? I told him he'd better go right away to Penge and find out. Since his elephant's hapless corpse lies nearby, he did not need any persuading, though he said wistfully that it would be simpler if I would come back with him. There are no porters at Ketshui's, he said, and the road through the forest to Goffin's house, where I could take a motor car, was filthy, and altogether ...

"Altogether," I said snappishly and unfairly, "it's not my fault if your domestic affairs drive me out into the cold world." I reflected a trifle tardily that it was my own domestic affairs more than his, but I was sore.

"She is always like that," he said at last despairingly. "Never satisfied in a place; always wanting to go away. It would have been better not to bring her, but Patrick said he wanted to see the baby, and I thought it would such a nice holiday with her. Well, never again!"

There was nothing for it but to call the *capita* and demand porters, though I felt like a dog. Surprisingly, he had enough to give me. I sent a note ahead to Goffin, asking him to hold a *camion* [a truck], and we had a gloomy supper interrupted by the necessity of making many arrangements – me borrowing money from Smet, and trying to figure out someplace where I could stay in Avakubi if the *gîte* were occupied – his wife had the keys to his house, but he gave me a key that he rather thought would fit. I was in a real rage, but tried not to show it. I don't see why I am such a shrew at times, but there it is ... Anyway, the poor devil was conquered at last and I managed to thank poor Nimrod with a good grace in the morning. We started out, my family and I, in a drizzling rain with the prospect of a nasty mess of mud to plow through in the forest.

The road wasn't so bad anyway. After about three hours – I slipped once and fell into a mid-wallow – we came out into the workers' village, muddy up to the waist and very wet. My legs were aching rheumatically. This end of the road is so much better than the one at Mambasa that it was a pleasure to look at it. Cheerful Negroes, clean clearings, motor cars dashing up and down to carry the rocks – who's responsible for this favoritism? There was a huge stack of plantains there, too. Someone has blundered with poor Monsieur at Mambasa.

I climbed down to the ground in the pitch dark, before Vande-velde's house. I hoped wildly that he had returned from Stanleyville, and my hopes were fulfilled. "Monsieur! Monsieur!" I shouted, and he came out on the porch, very surprised to see me. Of course, I was showered with comforts. The new *gîte*, a beautiful place with a bed even for Sabani; his own metal lamp; a big table and a desk: thousands of little things and, most important of all, a standing invitation to meals. Because I really hadn't brought anything like that.

My forlorn and neglected vanity began to sit up and take notice. I was in time for dinner with him and we talked at high speed until I fell asleep at the table. He's been busier than the afflicted paperhanger, and coming back from Stanleyville his car broke down in the bush and he slept two nights in a native village, with only bananas to eat. He had bad things to say of Pavloff, and so had I, gleaned from Goffin – how he has taken to beating his new girl with a *chicotte*, and how he is always drunk and sick. The new man is agreeable, he said.

And now I must go and see Pavloff, and be hypocritically pleasant while I sniff around the hospital.

Sunday, August 9

Sunday in Avakubi. ... An unwonted quiet in the morning; Vandevelde breakfasting uncomfortably in a collar and necktie; the three priests, white-frocked, walking solemnly down the middle of the street; the soko with a great flood of Negroes looking for food and – wonder of wonders – finding it. And me, deathly ill with a hangover. All bathed in a flood of golden sunlight, and a cool breeze blowing over the river.

I girded up my loins yesterday afternoon and sought the lion in his den; which is to say Pavloff installed in an old house, installed with thousands of empty bottles and a few full ones, sitting at table drinking Pernod with a cheery plump little curly-headed, curly-mustached chap, up for the weekend from Bafwasende. I walked right in and had a drink with them, establishing a sort of *entente cordiale* [A friendly or cordial agreement] with the new little man. Pavloff was well amidships, but dignified. I was shocked to see him – twice as thin as he was before, and pale with a green pallor. He was, as always, cold and puzzled; but I was determined to do something definite about him, because I am curious as to why he doesn't send the medicine to Penge. The Pernod turned the trick. I watched him get more vague and dignified, and tried to imagine him in the act of beating his *ménagère*; I found it difficult. Though he has the pale, expressionless, blue eyes that are capable of any cruelty. Meantime, however, relieved by the presence of a third person – he is ill-at-ease with white women – he loosened up: I could almost tell the time by the clock when he began to like me. He even referred light-heartedly to his bad luck with his *ménagère*, and how he had kicked her out. He always pretended to be Saint Peter before; he has changed.

It grew dark and I started to go. Pavloff asked me to supper, and I was suddenly brave enough to say, "Supper? With you? Never!"

The little chap jumped. Pavloff looked scandalized and frightened. I explained: "You will say bad things about me if I dine with you in your house, as you did before."

It was so crude that nobody cared, after a minute. I turned to the other man, smiling, and said, "He has a nasty little tongue, this man."

Pavloff said, "But I took it all back, Mademoiselle. I learned that it is the custom in your country, and I apologize. Now will you dine here? And I said "Yes." We all bowed and I went home to put on my best dress.

I want Pavloff to like me so I can discover the secret of the lost medicine. So I dined there in my most ladylike clothes; a rambling meal in a smoky, under-furnished, messy room with two men collarless, sweaty, and argumentative. I had to drink Pernod, Burgandy, and this poisonous Congo beer, and I enjoyed it. We all grew quite fond of one another – yes, I began to like Pavloff, or at least, to be terribly sorry for him – and since we were talking French, we stayed polite to the bitter end when we all walked back to my house at one in the morning, with a boy carrying a lantern and the rest of the post dead asleep.

I slept badly and woke up miserably ill. At ten, I went back to his house, as we had an appointment to show me the hospital in my capacity as unofficial assistant to Patrick. I found there the two young men, bleary-eyed and breakfastless, entertaining three priests who were decorously sipping Pernod. Another man dropped in; a State man for the road, pleasant-faced and clean and sober. It was a pleasure to look at him. He was a Fleming, I am sure. It was a queer assortment. We talked about prices of things, and the *capitas*, and monkeys, and Patrick's enormous quantity of mail every week – catalogues and things – and methods of transportation, and Antwerp, and the soko,[2] and Vandevelde because he wasn't there. Someone mentioned the time and everyone jumped up apologetically, and then Pavloff and the little chap and I went to the hospital.

It is a lovely hospital. There is even a laboratory for the microscopic work, and a centrifuge – I was almost rude, I felt so jealous.

---

2 A species of anthropoid apes indigenous to the area around Lake Tanganyika, discovered by the Scottish missionary and explorer Livingston.

There are six houses with six beds in each, and a regular village of *infirmiers*. He doesn't deserve it; he doesn't deserve it. The stockroom with the medicines!

I must have betrayed some of my feelings, for Pavloff, who is most unreceptive of impressions, said, "This week I am going to make up Putnam's cases. I've been so busy, Mademoiselle. ..." He promised to send a sack of potatoes for planting, too.

They invited me to lunch, and I unblushingly accepted. More beer before food, though, and we sang a few songs, and when I asked Pavloff to write Vandevelde that I was lunching there, he wrote, "Mademoiselle says please excuse her, as she is too tired from walking." I added, "It isn't true. Belgian beer is too strong," and a moment later we had a reply – "Mr. Pavloff, you are a little liar and everything that Monsieur Smet reports of you is false. Well – *Bon appetit*! I'm coming in for a cup of coffee after lunch."

We roared with laughter and Pavloff blushed deeply, and Vandevelde did come, and we practised shooting at bottles with a little rifle, from the back veranda. To look at us you would never think that we all said such nasty things about one another in private.

CHAPTER 12

ELEPHANTS

Saturday, August 15, 1931

SMET CAME BACK TUESDAY NIGHT, BAG, baggage, baby, and all.
Characteristically, he didn't come to see me, but managed to encounter me by chance on the street and gave me a letter from Patrick.
A friendly letter, thanking me for mine and giving news and asking
small favors, just as if I had never left him in a spirit of anger. I put it
into my bag and walked along thinking about things. Suddenly, I was
interrupted by Smet's voice – "*Je suis FURIEUX contre Putnam!*" ["I
am *furious* with Putnam!]"

I felt a vague anger at this, but asked why. It seems that Patrick had
neglected the baby, who hadn't had the right kind of food. I gather that
Robert eats at the table with his father, and that he couldn't very well eat
at the table with Patrick, as Patrick didn't eat at table but took all his
meals in bed while Smet was absent with me. Still, I couldn't see why it
should make much difference, when he has Katherine, his mother, with
him all the time. Smet is away from Avakubi most of the time, after all.

"It isn't only that," Smet explained when I said so, "but when she's
here she can get all the food she wants; she's at home, do you see? If
she needs an egg or a chicken for the baby, why, there are plenty of our
own and she needn't ask for it. If you ask Putnam for something he
intends to give it to you, but he forgets. Sometimes you must ask three
or four times. I don't like to do that."

I know just what he means, but I resented his saying so.

Smet came yesterday, smoked a couple of cigarettes, looked at the ceiling, and suddenly announced that he was sick to death of town and wanted to go somewhere. "I think I'll start up the Wamba road and look round for elephants," he said.

Eagerly I said, "May I go?"

To my horror, he appeared to hesitate. "I was thinking of taking very few things, and if you go along I'll need the cook and everything," he objected.

"Why? I can cook."

He laughed unbelievingly. "Well, I'll think about it."

"The hell you will," I replied. "Forget it. I'm sorry I asked. I'm going to Stanleyville instead."

"Indeed. How?"

"With the next white man who comes along. You watch me."

He took another cigarette and pondered. "Never mind; wait. I'll think about it."

"I don't want to go to Wamba," I lied. "I don't like you at all."

"I don't understand you," he countered.

We sauntered up the road and met Pavloff, returned from Goffin's and had an aperitif. Pavloff announced that he was sending the medicine to Patrick today, and I offered to help. So when I bade them good evening Smet said, "Then you won't go to Wamba tomorrow? No matter; I can wait a day. Sunday we shall go."

Mollified, I hurried in to dress for dinner, and gave the news to the family that we were going somewhere; I wasn't quite sure where. They were pleased as always, and so was I.

Thursday, August 20

There was a weekend influx of unshaven men in white clothes in Avakubi, and I woke on Sunday morning to find that the Administrator from Bafwasende had slept in the other room of the *gîte*. I had slept deeply after going to bed supperless; I had helped Pavloff pack cases of medicine for Penge, and I was tired. AND angry. Pavloff had evidently mislaid the requisition, and he packed the boxes with whatever he felt like, now and then pausing to ask me what sort of thing Patrick wanted. I couldn't remember, of course. I know that he had no iodine, but when I said so Pavloff threw his hands up, crying, "What does he do with all the iodine I send him? Bathe in it?"

Incredible! When I think of how we worked on that requisition, taking careful stock of what remained and then counting up how much would be needed – and all Pavloff did with it was to pack it away in his papers. I squeaked with rage when I spoke of it, and everyone said, "But that's what always happens in Africa. You'll get used to it."

Then there was no way to send the boxes. The only transportation canoe had gone upstream the day before and would stay there for some weeks. Pavloff was willing to wait for it to come back, and I was too tired of arguing to do any more about it until I had an idea and said to Vandevelde, "Can't you send the stuff up the new road? At the end of the road send it over to Ketshui's by porters – it's only three hours – and Patrick will come down in his canoe and get it there. The whole business would take only one day."

He shook his head. "Too expensive sending by truck like that. The canoe transportation is much cheaper."

"It ought to be," I said bitterly. "At least five days to make the trip, with all these portages."

Another idea, then. Let Pavloff take the cases on his next trip to the road-head, in his own car. "Cheaper than the canoe," I explained, "because the whole expense will be the porters."

Pavloff's face beamed and he promised to do it on Wednesday. I wonder.

At last then, on Sunday morning, we packed all my things on top of Smet's, and with a swarm of hunters piled on top of that, we rode out of Avakubi.

It was almost noon and very hot and bright when the road climbed a high hill, and at the top we followed a branch to a house sitting on a crest, looking out over the whole Ituri Valley, it seemed. There were blue mountains in the distance. Have you ever stayed in a valley by a riverside for six months, surrounded by high trees? There is nothing like it for making you want mountains.

It was mostly *barza*, that house, with evidences of great wealth in the bunches of bananas that hung all around it, and a glittering new gramophone on a table, with a deep box of records sitting next it. My eyes were glued to the gramophone, and I paid almost no attention to Smet when he said, "You are going to meet my cousin."

The cousin was a small young man; he was named Smet, too, and probably wasn't a cousin at all. But they were good friends, because they said "*tu*" to each other, and the small Smet didn't stare at me in the peculiar way that most strangers do here. I didn't talk much, but made for the gramophone and started to work. The boys who came up to look at us and to talk to our people were all Bobudu, and the Smetses discussed guns and game, and I played music and was happy.

Someone brought news that one of Smet's (the big one's) boys had shot a fairish-sized elephant near the road we were going to take, and everything was good.

So we came yesterday to this little Babili village in the forest, where all the people are gone to cut up the dead elephant, and I reign alone in the little shelter, shielded on three sides by banana leaves. A river runs nearby where I can go and take a bath when it gets too hot – as it does about noon – and in the very clean clearing the boys are playing a game that calls for much screaming and jumping about by Matope. Just now, news has been brought that two big elephants are ravaging a *shamba*[1] nearby and Smet is getting ready to go and commit more murder. It is a nice place, and when this job is finished, he says, we will go to a nicer place farther on. No one says anything about going back either to Avakubi or to Penge. The only thing we could want to make it perfect, we agreed yesterday, was a horse apiece.

---

1 A plot of ground, also a farm or plantation, from the French *le champ*.

163

Friday, August 21

One of the boys killed another elephant, and yesterday we went to look at it, crossing the big *shamba* across the road and then leading through forest where the pygmies who came with us cut a way with their machetes. Twice we ran into swarming colonies of red ants. A two-hour walk brought us to the corpse, but not until we had waded through swamps full of elephant tracks, and crossed greasy red-clay stretches where Smet slipped and sat down very heavily. I make more noise walking, Smet said, than a whole herd of elephants. Well, I can't help it if I can't bear to go without shoes, as he does.

Just a few rods along the riverbed the other day, when we went down to take a bath, almost killed me, and as for plunging ahead in the forest – no thanks! Therefore, I donned my heavy boots, and with a great crashing and slashing and snapping of twigs, got there – but not until every shootable thing in hearing distance had covered ten miles of escape. That is hard on the pygmies, who were probably at much trouble to conceal their disgust.

The elephant was lying on his side, having broken a few trees in his fall, and one tusk was plunged deep into the red earth. He was red too, deeply covered with the dust of the iron clay that reddens everything here. His huge head looked as if he might wake at any minute, and his legs were bent clumsily as if he were ready to spring to his feet, but his little eye no bigger than my own was open, and he was looking at nothing in particular. At his trunk and his tail, where the end had been cut off so Smet could prove his ownership, there were little pools of very red blood, and yet there was a smell that made me think of circuses or of the zoo at Regent's Park [in London], a fresh, almost cow-like smell of chopped grass. He didn't make me think of circuses.

One pygmy leaped up to the top of the gigantic swelled side and began to cut with his knife, a neat slice in the hairless wrinkled skin. "Tut, tut," said Boniface, "Wait till Kolongo gets back. ..." for Smet had gone again to see if I had by any lucky chance refrained from frightening a bit of game. All the men turned to building themselves a house to live in until they should have finished cutting and smoking the meat, and Boniface made me a bench of woven bark and bits of small trees, covered with leaves.

Because it was fresh, we had a piece of the meat cut off to eat, and carried it back to camp wrapped in leaves and tied with bark. It tastes like beefsteak, but is larger-grained and tougher.

Walking along the path the other evening, while the sky was still blue and the moon was white, waiting an hour before it turned yellow, I suddenly sniffed something and called to Smet to throw away his cigarette and help me smell it. That smell, too, was like a zoo. We waited until it was gone – it had only been a whiff – and then walked on, but I looked behind me very often, because it had been a leopard.

From Smet's babbling, I pick up bits of information for hunting, such as: When an elephant is standing still, listening, you must not move. But when he shakes his head and his ears flap, you may make all the noise you want because his head is so full of the sound of his own ears, and then it is best to advance in little rushes, ready to freeze again when he stops.

An elephant is right-handed like a man, and usually his right tusk is bigger. Also, when he is turning around, if he makes a right turn he goes fast and you must look out, but if he turns to the left he is more awkward, like a man dancing, and he takes a bigger sweep, and then is a good chance to shoot.

When he is in full flight, galloping, he makes a terrific noise and somehow it does not occur to him that he is being followed. So if you run close after him, be ready to shoot when he stops, because he is over-confident that he has left you behind.

Matope ate some of the meat yesterday, but Sabani didn't. "If I eat elephant meat, I will die right away," he said. "Kolongo's cook is the same. Matope can eat it, though. ... Madame, are we really going to Wamba?"

"I don't know," I said for the thousandth time. "It's for Kolongo to say. I think, though, that we will, because I've broken a tooth and I think maybe the doctor there can fix it." Sabini looked worried and suddenly blurted out, "The white man is men there at the mine told me to look out for the people at Wamba. The Basenge and the Bobudu are bad men. They take you in your sleep, and you don't wake up; they take you down to the water and rub you with juice of banana leaves, here and here on the legs, and they say, 'Sleep for two days and then you will die.' And that is bad medicine, so when they carry you back you know nothing about it, but you die after two days, just as they say. Then they eat you."

"Yes," said François, "it's true. The bushmen do it."

"But Agalanga's a Bobudu," I protested. "He's all right."

"No matter. He's bad," said Matope flatly. "All Bobudu are bad. You look out. There is an Administrator ..."

"Yes," broke in Sabani, "there is an Administrator at Wamba who went to a Bobudu village to collect the tax and they ate him. Not so long ago. You look out."

"I'll look out," I said heartily, and I meant it. "And mind you lock your doors at night when we sleep there. So will I. Lock all the windows and everything."

"Yes, Madame. You're awfully silly to leave your windows open the way you did at Avakubi. They're bad people."

"I guess if we go to Wamba, we'll only stay one night," I reflected.

"Good. Abanzima says it's a bad place, too. Lots of medicine. She doesn't like it any more than we do, because she's a Mangbetu."

When Smet came back I said, "Isn't your wife a Mobudu?"

"Yes. Why?"

"Does she talk about how they eat people there?"

"*Comment donc!*" ["How so!"] Her grandfather ate lots of men in his time, and used to tell her about it. They got a missionary there once and an Administrator. Another missionary told me not long ago how he heard about one family that was in the act of eating someone, so he went to their house to argue, and he saw the meat there on the fire, a big piece, and suddenly decided not to say anything about it. He passed the time of day and went home."

SMET WENT TO BED BEFORE SUNSET as his fever had arrived in force, and as soon as the moon – almost full – had come up, I went to bed, too, not having anywhere to walk. I could hear Smet breathing as if he were asleep, and I began to think about all my past life, and I was marveling at how much had happened to me in a relatively short space of time, and the moon had come up quite high and was shining on my stomach, when I heard something on the other side of the tent as if Smet were snapping his teeth. So I said, "Are you snapping your teeth?" and he said, "Yes," and I said, "Why, if it isn't rude of me to ask?" and he said, "I haven't anything else to do and I'm tired of lying in bed. I am all wet with perspiration, and this bed is too hard and my head doesn't hurt any more, so I'm snapping my teeth." I said, "Well, let's talk. I'm not sleepy either. Have you ever been to Florence?" and he said, "No, why?" and I said, "It's cold there in the winter. I didn't have warm feet all winter there; not once," and he said very excitedly, "That's exactly what my mother says about Florence. She used hot-water bottles all the time, though," and I said, "Funny, I never thought of using hot-water bottles. That was stupid of me, wasn't it?"

He was just about to answer when François came to the tent flap and said, "A Mongenya has just come and says that there are elephants in the plantation up the road." Smet said, "Where is my hunter with the good gun?" and François said, "You sent him across the river today."

Smet said, "Then I'd better go myself," and I said, "I'll come, too, but you oughtn't to get up when you have a fever. It is just like elephants not to let you have a comfortable fever of an evening." He said, "You'd better not come," and I said, "Why?" and he said, "All right, come along if you want." So I put some clothes on and went outside to wait for him.

It was light, with a green brightness, and all of the Negroes in the neighborhood were awake except for Matope, who had gone to bed by the fire. One of the women, a fat one with empty breasts, said,

"Greetings, Madame," and I said, "Greetings, Mama. I'm going to kill an elephant." And every one laughed, which is not very flattering.

As it turned out, we didn't kill an elephant. The Mongenya walked with us up the road, saying, "He crashed some wood right at the edge of the road and said 'Hrrrumph,' and then walked away in that direction. He stole one banana tree." We came to the plantation, but didn't see anything. All of a sudden, Smet said, "I'm hungry. I'm dying of hunger. I am going back to get something to eat, or I will faint of hunger."

The Mongenya looked surprised, and so, no doubt, did I. Smet handed the Mongenya the gun and said, "You wait here and if you hear him coming, call me. I'm starving to death. Come on, Mickey."

We went back to the village, and Smet called, "François, cook me some dinner." François was surprised, too, but he did his best, and Smet gobbled half a dozen sweet potatoes and a roasted banana he had swiped from a Negro's pot on the way back, and four eggs, and half a loaf of bread, and three cupfuls of coffee, and I said, "You are shaking all over. I think you'd better go back to bed." But he said no, first he'd better shoot the elephant. So we went back to the plantation, but the elephant hadn't reappeared, and suddenly Smet was almost asleep, and everyone went to bed. I have no idea what time of night it was. The queer thing is, he's all right today.

Azivali went to Avakubi on Sunday and came back Monday saying that Patrick had been there! He had come and stayed at Smet's house for two days. I suppose he followed my advice in my last letter, for once in his life, and came to see in person about the medicine.

Friday, August 28

Wamba, and when I remember that I thought it was just a little post I marvel at my stupidity. It is a big city; the biggest city, I think, that I have ever seen. There are actually streets there and districts. I saw the houses of at least seven white men, and so many white people that they actually don't all know one another.[2]

Incidentally, we found that our trip and two hundred francs' worth of gasoline had gone for naught. The Greek who has a rifle to sell was not in town, and the doctor couldn't fix my broken tooth. Nearly all the shops were closed for no particular reason except that nobody is interested enough to keep them open, and the proprietors are all traveling or just tired of life. We did find two places open, though, and I made a strange and significant and staggering purchase.

There it was with a dozen sisters of the same complexion – a cream-colored box, not too smudged, with embossed green leaves on it and a picture of a lady with powdered hair, and a few tiny pink roses around her, and a legend, *"Mes Délices, Houbigant."* ["My pleasure, Houbignant]."

I picked it up reverently and looked at it a long time. What thoughts came to me in that moment no one, not even myself, will ever understand. First, I remembered that never in my life have I bought or used perfume. I thought of an excursion boat on the Hudson [River] on a Sunday, with thousands of young people all crowded together, sweating and exuding a discouraged scent of Woolworth's greenest and strongest perfume. I looked at the street before the shop; Wamba's principal street, with banana palms all about and a hard green color triumphing over even the dusty red soil, waving vulgarly over the house of the carpenter across the street, trying to disguise the trim red brick of the doctor's house down at the corner and flourishing unchecked along the road just outside of town. Next to that, the

---

2 It was at this point in her narrative that Hahn, in response to moral and legal threats from Patrick Putnam's parents, introduced a fictional Englishman who related a version of the incident that would prompt Hahn to leave Penge, telling it as if it were his story and not Putnam's. The full text is included at the end of the book as Appendix I. Hahn's original version of what happened is related in chapter 16, where it has been included in this restored version of her narrative.

timid little daintiness of the green on the box looked pallid and frightened. A cream-colored box, only faintly smudged. I remembered how my mother had always told me that the French had invented perfume to save themselves the trouble of washing.

The box looked like a tiny coffin, or an old-fashioned packet for a portion of wedding cake. No, it was not an excess of whimsicality that made me buy that box; it was a sudden fierce hatred of too much Nature.

Now, back in the bush with only a camp chair between me and that same Nature, I wonder what possessed me. The glass stopper won't come out, but I didn't really mean to use it, after all. I think of perfumes and powders, beauty parlors on Dover Street and Madison Avenue, long aisles of wardrobes full of evening frocks in Fifth Avenue shops, buses and cocktail parties and restaurants where you go to look at people, a milliner in Chicago who used to make me buy hats that never again looked as well as they did in the shop – and why shouldn't I grow old here, where it is no effort to be beautiful, and people don't even notice when you are not? One little face and figure: Who cares? Not I.

I shall avoid the cities hereafter, and subscribe to a Book-of-the-Week club. And Matope may have old lady Houbigant to wear as a hat or to sail as a boat in the Ituri, for all I care.

Saturday, September 12

Back in Penge. Kherkhoff, the Territorial Agent, who was here, grew very regal last night and ordered a dance to be performed by the women, then sent word to Patrick and me to come to the bare space in front of the old prison with chairs, a table and something to drink. It sounded very Roman and dissipated. We looked Roman, too. I was almost ashamed. We settled down behind a noble array of bottles, lounging among our women – that is, all except me. The girl that Kherkhoff has brought here (Saidi's one-time favorite, discarded for

The women dance

infidelity) ran like a rather plump butterfly from the dance to her new boss and back again, crying out to all her friends and tossing down glasses of port and being very gay and nightclubish. It looked like a movie idea of a nightclub; we, the big capitalists, looking over the girls. I think she enjoyed showing off before Saidi, who pretended not to notice her.

The women sang well, but the dance as always was rather monotonous until our merry blade Saidi's girl took a hand in it and started to dance ahead of the others, leading them in a snaky circle all the way around several times, and Asumini danced, too. It grew late and merry. We saw a real beauty among the onlookers, a stunning girl, and Kherkhoff immediately invited her to sit with us. He's a funny little man. When at last the women were tired, the men started to dance. They danced better, and Patrick and I settled down to watch them, but the other gentlemen lost interest the minute the women stopped, and called a halt.

I very nearly protested that now it was my turn for a little recreation, but I didn't dare. We all went home then.

CHAPTER 13

ADMINISTRATION
AND AMPUTATION

Wednesday, September 16, 1931

IN THIS DISTRICT, THE CHIEF PROBLEM IS the new road, and in relation to the building of this road you can get some idea of the Administration of the Congo. I don't know if we are typical, but I suppose that in a general way we are. Colonial policy, large and shadowy as the term is, must impose a certain big pattern on all these small posts and their works.

As all the petty officials will tell you, it is the petty official who counts with the Native. Certainly he has considerable power; he judges all cases that are not settled in the native tribunal. Important cases may be carried to higher authorities, but the Man in the Forest depends heavily upon the Territorial Agent and Administrator, and he knows it. The Administrator's boss, the District Commissioner, comes along once in a while, but he is too busy for anything but large, impersonal problems.

The head of our post is the Administrator. He spends most of his time writing reports; one morning of each week, he sits in judgment. He interviews the chiefs and sub-chiefs, and in our neighborhood he sees to it that the natives supply food to the workers on the road, and also he must make them supply men for the work. He is faced with a bad problem here, for in the first place the Congo is not heavily inhabited, and in the second place the road workers are a heavy drain on the land. Taken themselves from the villages, they leave behind their plantations, and yet they must depend on these plantations for food. The Administrator is therefore in constant friction with the chiefs and *capitas*, who protest that they have neither sufficient food nor sufficient people to carry it to the road.

His personality has a lot to do with his work, naturally. He is a first-termer with ideas about the native – he is what is called a "Negrophile," in a mild way. That is, he hasn't yet come to look upon the Negro as an inefficient machine that must be employed for lack of a better machine, to develop the Congo. However, he is not really interested in his work; he hates his job and waits eagerly for the day he will be finished. Therefore, his vague idea of "justice" and sympathy seldom reach much beyond the realm of ideas. He hasn't the time nor the impulse to be practically courageous. His ideas are not really convictions, and to save himself the discomfort of thinking, he usually follows in the footsteps of his predecessors, except for small matters that cost him nothing to decide in his own manner.

The Agent Territorial is an old-timer and conscientious after the best administrative tradition. His convictions have not much chance to govern his decisions, for he allows himself very little latitude. He adheres whenever possible to the letter of the law. Naturally, where there are gaps in the law book he must fill in according to his own ideas. In general, however, he is a good hard worker, an excellent soldier. A body of petty officials like the Agent, under one leader, could work wonders.

Two men are working on the road itself; they are subservient to the Administrator in rank. However, since the road and only the road is their business, and the Administrator has so many things to do, he really fills the role of purveyor only. Of the two men, one is an old trooper who understands how to build a road and does not take it too hard. He curses the Administrator in a half-hearted and traditional way, and smokes his pipe. The other is an eager young man and conscientious. He wants to build his road well, and with that in mind, he is willing to forget all other problems. He needs food for his men. Very well, he gets it. That he is scouring the countryside and spreading mild famine does not worry him. He is building a good road and any *capita* who says he hasn't enough bananas to fill the weekly demand is a scoundrel and a liar.

If, on the other hand, he had the job of conserving the plantations and increasing the food supply of the Congo, he would curse all roads and do his best to skimp the worker. However, at the moment, he vents what spleen he can spare on the Administrator, whom, he says, is not hard enough with the Negroes. For instance, he is having a bad time with deserters. Two or three men manage to desert almost every night. This, he says, is because the Administrator has not replaced the men whose terms are up. He keeps them on; therefore, they desert. It is the Administrator's fault for not insisting that the *capitas* supply more men.

There is an alternative that no one admits. That is, to send the men home and tell the Government that the road cannot be built on the Congo's own resources. It is impossible to do this, not only because no one wants to, but because too much money has been spent already. In the first place, who said that the Congo could build this road? Someone has blundered slightly, unless such a program of half-starvation is the usual thing in Africa when a road is built. It is a general inspector, perhaps, who traveled through the district in an auto and spent a night in each of the bigger posts, talking to the Administrators. At present, the men are too hungry to work well. The *capitas* are angry. The villages are gutted of men and food, but the road goes on. If it ends well, we will forget all the rest of it.

Well, what do you expect? You can't find a group of supermen to govern a colony. Look at the big business houses in America, where the office work muddles along somehow in spite of dumb business managers and half-witted executives. Ask any intelligent stenographer. I dare say that every one of those offices has a House Policy, too. How far does that policy extend beyond the inner office where it was conceived? You lose track of it going through the masses of sub-managers and office martinets.

Remember how furious you always are with the clerk who grants your passport in the States? Then reflect that he and millions like him are really the backbone of the Law.

Sunday, September 27

Last night we had a pitched battle with a whole army, navy, and marine corps of driver ants. I had noticed that the ground just outside the light from the *barza* seemed to be moving, and when I investigated, I found what it was – all the cleared space in sight was a carpet of ants, moving on the house from what looked like all directions. I shrieked for help and we got to work, burning straw and cardboard and wood and scattering the embers among the forerunners of the army that were just beginning to pour in. It wasn't just the red ants.

There were millions of the tiny black, harmless sugar ants, moving in great clots and swarming streams over the posts and pillars. Were they fighting the red ones? I think so, though they would never have a chance. I don't know where they all came from. I don't know where they went, either, though they disappeared fast enough when we threw the sparks at them. We made a circle of glowing embers all around the house, and the few streamers of red ones that had penetrated to my room and the bureau were quickly routed.

For a while, we were busy moving all the monkeys and things to safer places, too. At last they turned tail and ran toward the river; very quickly there were almost none left, except a few small ones running around wildly looking for the main body. I think there must have been many caravans. Next morning, their trails were all over the ground and a few lines were still going, while Sada sat in the tree where he had perched all night and chattered.

Thursday, October 8

"Mickey, please come over. I want to cut off this fellow's leg, and I need an etherizer," said Patrick.

It was a boy who was brought in three days ago with a badly cut leg, and Patrick had been worried about the blood, which he couldn't seem to stop. I hadn't thought it was bad enough to cut, though; it wasn't very wide but might be awfully deep. When I got there, I found Patrick in a high state of indecision. He made me feel the leg, and the minute I touched it I saw he was right. It was dead, cold, giving at the touch with a nasty feeling of fluid under it, blistered and rotten.

"It's just been like that today. If I'd sent him to Wamba he'd have died on the road. It would have been two days with the best of luck – one day to Avakubi and if there'd been a truck going by, one to Wamba. I must cut. Look at him. He's in pretty good condition otherwise."

He did seem to be, strong and cheerful and demanding cigarettes without ceasing except to smoke them when they were handed over.

"I must cut. I think I can do it all right; I've seen it done and they say that some people cut their own legs off. If only he doesn't die of blood-poisoning afterward."

"What does his family say?"

"All that have felt the leg seem to agree. He, himself, is willing."

Patrick was walking up and down trying to plan it. "Count how much ether we have." There were only three ampoules. He shook his head. "I don't know. If I were a good surgeon, it wouldn't have to take long at all, but as it is I must go carefully and tie up as I cut. I don't think that's much ether. Well, get it ready."

While he was finishing up the other patients – it was an Injection Day – I studied the book about etherizing, and one part said that if he had an overdose to give him adrenalin. We have none. There was another stimulant, a caffeine compound, that I got ready though, and the home-made mask we had fixed up, and then Patrick made me inject morphine and told the boy to stop smoking. Then he sent for his noon porridge and the *infirmiers* got busy scrubbing the high table out under the eaves, where it was to be done.

All of a sudden, the boy's father arrived – he hadn't been before – and raised hell. He wanted to take the boy home. "If you cut off his leg, he'll die," he said, and wept.

Patrick said, "You want to bury him? Then take him home. He'll die day after tomorrow if you take him home. If I cut off his leg, he has a chance. It's God's affair. I don't know, but I do know one thing: if you take him home, he'll certainly die."

The old man said, "I'll call the Sultan," and Patrick said, "All right," and told me to look for the gut for sewing up.

The Sultan – it was Abedi – came in a minute and Patrick told him the same. He made them both feel the leg. All the boy's family, little girls and young boys, were crying loudly outdoors; one was frantically beating the air and saying, "Don't let him kill him – don't, Father!"

I got scared and said, "If they don't really want you to, you've no right." Patrick didn't answer and I said, "In America if the family objects, what does the doctor do?"

"It depends on the family. If they're strong and influential, he's got to obey, otherwise …" He finished his porridge and went on giving directions, which I obeyed but I was still scared.

"He will likely die anyway, and no one will come to hospital any more," I said, voicing the same argument that must occur to thousands of doctors at a time like this – and a damned silly argument too, which I blush to remember.

Patrick didn't even answer. He did a better thing: he talked to the father and said, "Have you never seen men before who have lost their legs and still live? You're an old man, you must have been in the wars with Tippoo Tib."[1]

"Yes, that's true."

"The boy might die if I cut his leg, but it's better to try. He's a strong boy. If I don't cut, he *will* die."

Then the old man consented and said he would go home; he didn't want to see it happen to his son, and Patrick said, more gently, "Good, Papa. Take the children with you."

So we got to work, and as usual the ether gave trouble. It evaporates so quickly, and Patrick gets nervous and thinks it has been hours when it's only ten minutes. He had everything else washed and ready and waiting, and still I kept trying and trying.

Once the boy did go under, but he started to vomit and we were trying to keep him from swallowing his tongue. We had no tongue clip or anything; the few tools there were needed by Patrick! The boy came out again and it was all to do over. But at last he did sleep and didn't cry out when he was cut, and for an hour I kept him under well, not too much and not too little; and I could even see what was happening. Patrick wanted to cut all around the bone. I don't know if that's the right procedure, but it seems proper – only that took longer than you would think, tying up the blood vessels as he went. Thousands of flies came, attracted by the smell of the leg. We had a few men holding him in case he should begin to fight, which he didn't yet. Patrick was almost finished cutting round when the ether gave out. So I ran back to the house and called all the men and they stood ready

1 Tippoo Tib (1837–1905), also known as Muhammed Bin Hamid, was an Arab trader who dealt in slaves and controlled the lucrative market in ivory in Central and East Africa in the latter decades of the nineteenth century. By 1870, he and his private army controlled much of the Congo basin, and this inevitably brought him into conflict with Belgian's King Leopold II. After a series of bloody clashes, in 1887 Tib agreed to cooperate with Leopold and was appointed governor of a large portion of the Congo. However, he soon realized his new position was untenable, for he was caught between the interests of Belgium and those of his Arab trader allies. In 1890, he abandoned his interests and fled the Congo.

to hold him when he woke, but luckily for another time he didn't wake and Patrick worked as fast as he could. Only it was awful. Patrick had to be sparing with the gut because there was only one ampoule, and his knives were too small and few and dull, and he had no curved needle, only two straight ones. But when the worst seemed to be over and I could go into hospital for a minute to get over the sun and the ether, which were making me sick, he woke up. He didn't cry much, only when Patrick had to go near the skin. Cutting inside close to the bone didn't hurt much, at least I don't know. He was a brave boy and hardly cried at all, and when he did cry, Patrick would say, "There, child, you're being a man, and it will be over soon and you can have food and tobacco and even wine if you want it ..." working fast and sweating and not seeming at all tired, though it took incredibly long and he must have been suffering from his own fever. It took horribly long. I thought it would never finish, but it was coming well. It looked right. The bleeding had been stopped and it was quite a straight cut, and now Patrick was sewing it up, which was terribly difficult with those needles.

I had gone in again and Patrick yelled, "Fix that salt solution for injection. He's acting funny." I started to do it, and he called again, "First give him a shot of camphorated oil. I'm afraid." Then I heard the boy talking cheerfully, asking for tobacco again and if he could urinate, and then he stopped and Patrick said, "Drop that and come on out with the caffeine, quick. He's dying."

He spoke very softly, but I heard him and gave the needle quickly and then ran back for the salt solution, and Patrick said, "Isn't it ready yet, damn it?" and of course it wasn't – it should boil for fifteen minutes – and he said, "Bring it hot or cold and a hot brick. He's a goner." The hot brick revived him, but he died before Patrick could give him much of the solution.

We couldn't believe it. The operation had been finished, and he had been all right. I saw that it was almost six. He didn't hear me when I tried to make him sit down. He tried to clean it all up, and put the leg under a sheet, and the body under a blanket, and had the cloths and things thrown away, and called one of the men and said, "Go and tell his father," then sat down to wait.

Then he started to talk about what it might have been. "Either shock from the pain that lasted so long, or loss of blood. And yet he didn't lose much blood. Where I was wrong was in not having that salt solution ready and giving it before or during. ... There was a man Doctor Melius operated in Wamba, and he died the same way after it was all finished, but he had been so sick before, and this boy seemed strong. Pulse irregular today, and fever – I should have amputated yesterday. But it wasn't dead yesterday, and I was busy with the wound. The salt solution would have helped very much if it was loss of blood, and a little, if it was the shock. Still ... ." He looked at me as if I had said something. "That's a better death than slowly, from the leg. I think so. He died quietly. ... You never saw a quieter death."

Mautea kept saying, "Wash your hands. Wash your hands," and at last Patrick heard him and did, still talking about the salt solution. "Did you give him that injection properly?"

"You saw me."

"I saw you, but I wasn't thinking. Yes, I remember, you put the needle in right. I'll never know what it was. ... I wish his father would come."

But Lukamba reported that the minute he told the father, the old man turned around and walked away without saying anything. He went back to tell the others and at last Patrick went home, and while I was trying to eat supper I heard them carrying the body and crying. All the food smelled like the operation, and I couldn't get to sleep because of the smell that followed me into my room, and Matope said, "If I should have to sleep alone in a house I would see ... ." He said a word I couldn't understand until later; it means Fear.

Sabani said, "It was God who did it. The operation was finished, but he died anyway. It was God."

That is what everyone says. Which would be a much easier thing to believe. But Patrick was right; I know it now.

CHAPTER 14

KAYUMBA'S

Thursday, October 15, 1931

IT IS PRACTICALLY SETTLED NOW, and I can go when I want to. I've written Van Roon for information about the road to Mambasa, which must have changed a great deal. Patrick says he doesn't want me to go, but he knows that I'm really going this time, and I don't suppose it will be an irrevocable loss to him, poor kid. He must be relieved, really. As for me, I shall be overwhelmed with sadness at the last minute, as usual, and make many promises to myself to come back. Well, perhaps I shall. I'll want to, I know. But now I'm too excited. I feel as if I were being born again.

Patrick is worse, having been working and running around too much. He went to bed yesterday when everything was finished, feeling pretty gloomy, and then the impossible happened. Pavloff arrived, with no warning except that his porters got there a little ahead of him. It is perfectly typical of him not to write and shows only his usual neglect, but Patrick thinks it was a Machiavellian ruse, of course. We had time to get all ready. Patrick says he'll be damned if he is found in bed when he's really been keeping his work up so well, and so he insisted on rising and dressing and arranging things so that when Pavloff arrived he found us sitting peacefully on the *barza*, drinking a friendly glass and talking about books. I was sewing on something dragged out at the last minute and Patrick was smoking. Pavloff asked right away for food for his people, and cooking oil. Of course, we have no oil; it is his own affair. Patrick has been begging him to send some for six months. He said so, in no uncertain terms, and so Pavloff tried to make the Banguana bring some. Naturally, they simply won't. They haven't much; they never sell it. There is none in this neighborhood. Pavloff screamed and stamped and ran after one of them with a whip, but he didn't get any oil, and I saw Patrick grinning in a perfect ecstasy. I was pleased, myself. Pavloff came back muttering that the people were undisciplined; I know what he was saying to himself about Patrick for spoiling them. He said a few things, and Patrick replied easily, "Yes, they're pretty independent. It's a long way from the Post, Monsieur."

"In general, I find the people in the bush much more amenable," said Pavloff.

"Have you ever been in the bush before?" said Patrick politely, and of course Pavloff hasn't. He's never been away from an automobile road, but he said that the people on any motor road, miles and miles from town, were as wild as you could find anywhere. Which is ridiculous, and I changed the subject to keep myself from wrangling. It's no use arguing with an idiot.

Naturally, things were uncomfortable all evening, but I enjoyed it in a perverted way. I kept expecting a row. However, at about nine Patrick made his excuses and went to bed, and I played the Victrola and pretended to listen to Pavloff and smiled, and smiled, and smiled. When he had finished one bottle of whisky, though, I made no move to bring out another. I was too sleepy. I ought to have, because Pavloff is certainly generous with his own liquor. But I was too sleepy. So he went to bed. He more or less insisted on sleeping in our house instead of the *gîte*, so he's installed in the bureau, and today he and Patrick are probably having rows all over the landscape. I am out of the way, down at the *gîte*. Pavlov will leave tomorrow morning. We have no idea, or at least we didn't this morning, why he had come. My theory is that Patrick's last official letter must have a lot to do with it. Either he feels guilty and has come to have a grand clean-up before the investigation,

or has come to fire Patrick or something. I wonder. This suspense is
… why, yes, it is rather pleasant. But I wish Patrick could go to bed.
This is Thursday; usually the only day in the week that he has nothing vigorous to do; only consultations and the school for the *infirmiers*.

Friday, October 16

When I got back for lunch all was quiet, and Patrick didn't look
red and angry, and so I decided that my natural lurid hopes were
warping my judgment. Lunch was pleasant, and the two men seemed
on good terms. Afterward, though, we sent Pavloff off to bed and
Patrick gave me the high sign and we adjourned to his room, where
he reported a lot of things. Pavloff, he said, did not seem at all angry,
but … Melius complains that he hasn't been doing the work he
should have done. Patrick was sent here to make census reports and
not to have a dispensary or a hospital or anything; that work is to
be distinctly subsidiary. When the census is finished here he is to
be sent somewhere else to do the same thing, and so on. So good-by
to all his ideas of having a homestead, etc. Patrick didn't seem much
annoyed at this, but only said that why the devil hadn't they told
him? No one had, and he's been doing the wrong thing for eight
months with no objections from headquarters. Well, he said, he'd
start right off being a good boy and he'd practically close the hospital, though it seems a pity. Next, his expenses are too high. He is
to have only three *infirmiers* and three workers. He says no; that can't
be done. He needs two workers only for wood and water and three
more. In Avakubi, it's different; they have the prisoners to get their
wood and water, but here he has no prisoners. Very well, that must
be arranged later. So. All serene.

Patrick sent me away then because he wanted to sleep, and I went
back to Pavloff who was through with his siesta and getting thirsty.
While getting him the whisky I saw an unopened letter on the table,
and picked it up hoping it was for me. No, it was for Patrick, and it

had a Red Cross seal. Soho, thought I, what is this? Pavloff saw me do it and said, "Oh, by the way, that's something I forgot to give Putnam when I came. They handed it to me when I left; Vandevelde forgot to send it by the last *planton*."

We proceeded with our drinks and talked about other things, but the letter remained on my mind. When Patrick joined us, just before five o'clock, he got the letter and read it while putting a friendly word now and then into our conversation. Later, he managed to get me alone and said, "Look here, I've had a son-of-a-bitch of a letter from Melius. It's a blood boiler." He seemed calm and rather amused, which I couldn't understand when I read the letter. It *was* a blood boiler. Melius started out by saying – I must paraphrase: "Monsieur, I have conducted an exhaustive inquiry into your work. We are distinctly dissatisfied with it ..."

He went on to complain about the census, or rather to give Patrick hell about it, and dove into the subject of reports. "I may add that it is not necessary to be so lavish with your paper, as for instance in the matter of your report about Penge. The history of the Congo and ethnological questions may be very interesting to you; they are not to us. ..."

Here I really lost my temper. Patrick added fuel to the flame by reminding me that the whole report was written on my paper, anyway. Of course, his not sending the reports because of lack of paper was really a protest against having been ignored for so long; if it had been only a subject of paper, he'd have managed. Which is easy to understand. I feel like sending a bill to the Red Cross myself for all the paper I've contributed. To continue: that was a damned good report he sent in and absolutely what they had asked for, for their records. And to scold him for making it too elaborate! But more followed.

"Mr. Pavloff is to do the work on the *chantier*. [a workyard or constuction site].

When I want you to take it over, I shall inform you." But Patrick has one of the very few official letters from Pavloff telling him to take the *chantier*! And also, "I must remind you that you came to Avakubi without permission, deserting your post." That was the time he went down to get medicine. And Pavloff wrote him and asked him to come! Well, where he has documents to prove it, he's all right. It's the business about the report that annoys me.

"It looks like the parting of the ways, doesn't it?" he asked. I nodded. "But I shan't quit," he said. "Let them fire me. Now, what sort of letter must I write? I don't want to fly off the handle."

"What a pity," I said. "I certainly wouldn't go to the *chantier* tomorrow, though."

This because Pavloff has just asked him to do it as a favor to himself, because he's too busy investigating a chicken-pox epidemic. Patrick had promised. Well, he thought that was a good idea if a nasty trick, but at last he did something else. He wrote a draft of an official letter asking Pavloff for an official order to go to the road this week, explaining in the letter that he had had orders from headquarters, etc., etc. I typed it in the privacy of my boudoir, all on official paper and so forth, and we hid it in the wardrobe until it should be time to present it. Then Patrick, growing rapidly worse with an attack of fever, went to bed and I bathed and dressed and went out to be lovely to Pavloff.

We took a walk and cut some pineapples for him to take home and talked about what a fine chap Patrick was and what a pity it was he was ill on top of all his other troubles. We talked, too, about what a fine chap Pavloff was. We dined alone and Pavloff, almost weeping for pity of Patrick, played the Victrola with all the gayest records he could find to cheer the suffering invalid. After a while, he forgot the suffering invalid and took to the bottle in dead earnest. I wanted to find out what he really thought about Patrick and this business, and why he was here. When the bottle was about half-empty, he began to talk, absolutely unprompted. It was extraordinary luck. I had to sit up until almost morning talking and listening, mostly listening, but it was worth it. I didn't even lie or pretend. I told him just what I thought of him and he admitted a great deal of it, but as I talked, I began to stop being so mad. He said he'd had a terrible scolding from Melius for not having sent things and for never having even visited Patrick. I was glad of that and said so. He said that he envied Patrick, having such a beautiful post and such tranquility, and I said, "Yes, it's lovely. I'd like to see what you would say, though, if you had to struggle along with no answers to your letters and requisitions, and no word at all from headquarters. You wouldn't like it at all. But of course I understand, Monsieur, that you have too much to do. It's really the fault of Melius."

"Absolutely," he said. "I have too much to do."

"It's a shame," I said warmly. "And you so interested in the scientific aspects of your work." Which may be true, for all I know. Anyway, he agreed and enlarged on that idea. He drank more and almost cried about the scolding he had from Melius. We agreed that Melius was a fine old chap really, but it was necessary to *know* him. (I have met him exactly twice and know absolutely nothing about him.) We had a sudden happy thought that he had just forgotten to give orders to Patrick in the first place about taking census and had forgotten that he had forgotten. Just a great big misunderstanding all around. But a fine old chap, really. ... Then Pavlov told me how hard it was to have to cut his own number of *infirmiers* to eight, and how they always wanted him to do wonders with absolutely no money. ... But Melius was a fine old chap; it was necessary to know him; that was all. At the end, I said I was sure it would be a good idea to get all three of them together and talk it over. I said that sometimes men made me so mad; they were such babies, really. Regard, I said, the three of them all sulking and saying things they didn't really mean. Wasn't it a pity ? (Just then, far off on the river there was a roll of thunder and a lightning flash, and I was scared. But nothing more happened.)

The bottle was ending, and I was glad. Pavloff had a way of filling his glass so that I didn't even see him do it. I would look at the glass and say to myself, "Four more gulps and he'll be finished," and then the next time I looked the glass would be full again. There was nothing for it but to wait till he'd finished the bottle, and after all why not? It was getting cool at last, and one can always sleep.

I reported it all this morning before breakfast and so Patrick was more friendly, and handed over the official letter almost apologetically, explaining firmly, however, that he wouldn't dare go again to the *chantier* without a written order. Pavloff smiled, shrugged, and said well then, there was nothing to be done because he didn't dare give it. So Patrick tore up the letter, and this week nobody will give the men on the road their injections. That seems an important factor to me, but not to anyone else evidently, though I dare say Patrick will worry a bit. Just the same, I'm glad he can rest this weekend. He's quite ill, and not getting better in the time he should.

Pavloff left with the pineapples and we said farewell almost affectionately after having agreed at breakfast that the Congo is a nasty backbiting place and that we were no better than anybody and would undoubtedly say awful things about each other at the first opportunity. And now what is going to happen? Patrick is writing a letter to Melius now.

I've read *Jameson's Diary*[1] about the story of the Second Column, and I wonder that it's not better known. People who read Stanley certainly ought to read it too. I'm inclined to side with Jameson myself; he wasn't rewriting for publication. Besides, I just naturally don't like Stanley. He talks too much about ideals and God, and too little about other things. He's slippery. Jameson suffered more and exploited less. I don't know that I blame Stanley for leaving the Second Column – he couldn't foresee what was going to happen but he might have been decent enough to say the truth, which was that it was all very regrettable, and not try to blame somebody right away.

---

1 Scottish-born physician Leander S. Jameson was a close associate of British Empire builder Cecil Rhodes. Jameson is remembered for leading British settlers on an 1895 raid into the Boer-controlled Transvaal region of South Africa that was one of the causes of the Boer War (1899–1902). Afterward, Jameson sat as a member of the Cape Colony legislature and served as prime minister from 1904 to 1908.

Thursday, October 22

The news arrived next morning that Vandevelde was coming – and going. His projected visit was to be only overnight, and downriver next day to meet some Governor who was coming through.

As if someone with a perverted sense of humor were planning these things, we got word that day that Smet was at Kayumba's and coming up as soon as he had had a look around. I hastily wrote that Vandevelde was here and he should come in a hurry if he wanted to see him. That isn't exactly what I meant, but he understood and didn't come till the next day. They passed in midstream and were awfully polite to each other, I believe. Vandevelde told him he'd be back in three days, as there were lots of things he still had to do when he was interrupted by the Governor.

I probably shan't see him again, as he's going on a long trip to Bomili, and I refuse to wait till he can come back to escort me to the Ehulu. If I thought he'd really be back in five weeks I'd wait, but he always lags a fortnight or so in hopes of culling another ten-thousand-franc elephant. Each of us thinks the other most unreasonable. I'm grateful to him, though, for helping me out – he's cashed a check and given me all the money Patrick owes me in return for Patrick's I.O.U., and so I can go now any time I get my stuff together. I can't sleep at night for thinking of it. Another two weeks or so to get debts paid off and things arranged, and then the road again.

Meantime, Vandevelde came back last night bringing a load of stuff Patrick had ordered. He will wait here two more days, he says, and wants me to come back to Avakubi with him for one more visit. Not much! Not much!

Also, he has begun a house for me, in utter disregard of my protestations that I am going. Patrick will be furious; it cuts off the best view from his porch, but when he has company it'll be nice to have it. He's well enough today, I think, to finish his letter to Melius in answer to that awful one.

That leopard got Moké and Kisangane. The leopard left Kisangane's headless body on the ground. Suppose it had been Angélique! We are going to put another trap near the goat house, but that doesn't help the two poor monkeys that are dead. I hope they were killed quickly: they have such pitiful faces when they're scared. Last night, even the big apes were brought into the house for safety; Sada was chained but got away almost immediately, and Chimp was left free to raid the larder.

Tuesday, October 27

I'm helping Vandevelde foil Kherkhoff. He's hidden away here in the forest a long way from his mail and any possible message to come back quick. He's determined to have one day's hunting undisturbed, though I begin to have less respect for hunters now that I see how he does it. We left Penge two days ago and went via *tipoye* to Kayumba's. I honestly didn't want the darned *tipoye*; the road to Kayumba's is excellent and not too long, but Vandevelde was horrified at the idea of going without. As it was, he wasted a day waiting for a canoe to take us there and it never turned up, as it's still at Avakubi, where he took it on his last trip. We were late starting because he had a last-minute *barza* at the hospital to settle Patrick's various disputes with the chiefs: Patrick dragged himself from bed to come and refute any lies that would surely be told, and it is shocking how thin and tall he looks. It was all because the Banguana are trying to avoid having a census taken, as it's too much trouble, and they complained that Patrick makes their wives undress before everyone and refuses to let a woman examine them. This is a lie, and Vandevelde was shown the examining room and the records, which proved that there has always been a woman nurse for the ladies. In the presence of Patrick, whom they had thought was safely tucked away in bed, they faltered and admitted that they'd lied.

Then as to the case of the *capita* Halafu, much was said but nothing done. He took two syphilitic wives away with him while they were in a very contagious state and had had only two injections; it was he, himself, who had brought them to hospital requesting that they be cured. Patrick wanted to have him punished for doing such a bad thing. It's so hard to convince them that two needles aren't enough, as it's then that the outward symptoms begin to go away.

They had stayed away two months and Halafu never even answered his letter about it. All this is decidedly punishable by law, but Halafu has found a weak spot in Vandevelde and flattered him into exaggerating his usual good nature and extending a protecting hand. Vandevelde kept telling us that after all it was only a first offense, etc., etc.

"It's the principle," Patrick tried to explain. "If a *capita* can get away with it, all the others will do it. There are too many people running away already. I don't say he ought to go to jail, but he certainly should be fined."

Well, Vandevelde couldn't see it. Like all the governing people, he thinks privately that doctors are an awful nuisance. He spent a pleasant day watching a dance in the village and Halafu obligingly translated all the songs for him, probably making them dirtier than they really are – Vandvede likes smut – and telling him interesting details of life in the harem, till he was overflowing with the milk of human kindness. Ordinarily I'm glad to have him like that about the Negroes, but this is a really bad case.

"It's not as if Patrick were always sending you people to flog, as Pavloff does," I said. "It's the first time he's asked to have anyone punished."

"Well ... I'll give him a good scolding," he said at last. "I don't like to punish too much."

Well, it's none of my business after all, but I was rather peeved. Especially as I saw Halafu, after the barza, almost rolling on the ground with laughter behind the hospital, when he had been scolded. He was interrupted by Vandevelde calling him about some small matter, and he hastily readjusted his expression to a respectful solemnity

A men's dance in progress

before going back. Of course, he didn't know that I saw him. We were at Kayumba's before I told Vandevelde about it, and his reaction was most interesting. He straightened up and glared. "He made fun of me?"

I left it at that. Later in the day he said out of a silence, "He was laughing, you say? *I'll* get him. The very next thing he does, into jail he goes! The idea of laughing at the Government. These Banguana are getting too smart."

Vandevelde is getting enormously fat and expresses much perturbation about it. Yet he rode every step of the way to Kayumba's. Now, a *tipoye* is to be used only when you're tired of walking, and to ride like that on a cool day and a good road betokens a certain amount of depravity, I think. And I am one of the world's laziest mortals. I teased him about it, and the day after, on the way here at Sadalla's, he did walk for about a quarter of a mile. For the rest of the way, though, he rode, and it's a double march of nine hours and he had little porters to carry him. "For hunting, I walk," he said, "but for the road, it's too much trouble."

Matope stayed behind at Kayumba's, under the Sultan's special protection, because he was tired after the first day, and I got tired of it. Which is just as well, for the last day was really long and even Sabani protested.

When Vandevelde suggested that I go to his special waterhole and help him hunt, I refused with thanks. I thought I'd be too much in the way; Smet says I am. Vandevelde was hurt at that though, so I went today. If that's all the walking he does, he's going to swell up and burst. It's a beautiful place and only an hour's walk from this village; he'd had people go a few days ahead to clear the path and build him a little shed to sit in and wait for the beasts to come, and he went heavily fortified with sandwiches and coffee and coats. I admit, however, that he went on his own two legs and kept cautioning me to go more softly. Himself, he made a great noise. I looked around and then bade him good hunting and came home, at his suggestion. He reappeared a half-hour after I got here, saying the flies were too bad, but he'd go back tonight. Just now a pygmy has come in with news that he's found a buffalo track, and he's gone again to follow it.

That waterhole is really lovely. It's a hollow at the foot of a staircase of slate that gaps up one end of the valley, and all about the hole are paths through the forest made by the animals, radiating in all directions. Out of the middle of the pile of slate comes the spring, and all about the mud is trampled with a million tracks – elephant, buffalo, and pig. The birds are deafening.

The people here belong to Kayumba. Vandevelde says we are the first white people ever to come here, which is ridiculous. It's right on the old road to Opienge, and it's a regular caravan route and entrance to Avakubi. Of course, we move to paeans of praise, since he is the Government, and the people can't bring us enough to eat. I shall always think of Vandevelde after this when I hear the expression "The fat of the land."

One mental picture, for instance, is of him sitting at ease on the barza of the rest-house at Kayumba's, discussing hunting with the chief. Kayumba is crazy about hunting and had just killed an elephant.

Vandevelde turned to me, his chin creasing a bit above his collar as it has a habit of doing, and said, "He has a passion for the chase. Myself, I think a man who does not like hunting has no right to call himself a man."

☙

OUR TALLEST AND BEST WORKER was taken prisoner for being out of his own district, and he's with us now, carrying Vandevelde's bathtub with another prisoner. They're chained together. He's to work for seven days and then go back to Wamba. Maliamungu is in the same fix, but I don't care about him as he's been fired twice and is a liar and a bad chap anyway. But for the tall boy, it's a pity. If Patrick had been up and about, it wouldn't have happened; I'm sure he doesn't know. I've asked Vandevelde please to let me hire him over again when the week is up, and I guess he will. Meantime, the man grins at me cheerfully when I pass him in the caravan and wipes his neck under the chain. Maliamungu won't even look at me.

They must have written permission to leave their own districts so that they can be kept on the records for their tax. These boys have paid the tax, though. If Vandevelde makes trouble I must tease him again about his cook. He's very sensitive about that. The cook was caught red-handed carrying on a brisk commerce in banki, and he hasn't been punished at all, because he is a good cook and Vandevelde doesn't want to send him to jail. When I want to annoy him I have only to mention banki.

Thursday, October 29

Vandevelde came back without anything, and his face was a choice ruddy color. He had followed the buffalo for five hours without stopping and was, he said, almost dead but intended to go back to the waterhole that night just the same. Or what did I think? I said I

193

thought it was his own business. He hemmed and hawed and ate his lunch and finally decided that he really must hurry back to duty, therefore he was reluctantly compelled to give up the waterhole idea. We would start home the next day ... or what did I think? I said again that it was for him to say. So he decided against the waterhole and stayed home that evening. A soldier came in puffing with rage, to exhibit a chicken tied up in a basket. ... "And that's why they have no eggs for you," he said. "All these heathen tie their chickens up when you come."

"I know they do," said Vandevelde calmly, "so that my soldiers won't steal them. If they want to tie up their chickens that's their affair. They know that as for me, I eat only one or two chickens a day."

Then two more soldiers came in with a man they'd caught out in the plantation, running away because he hadn't paid his impot tax. The chief excused him by saying he was only a child. "Look," said one soldier, jerking the boy's arm up. "What's that? That's hair. Child? You're crazy." The man was thereupon hustled off to be taken to Avakubi, and the soldiers were overcome with pride and joy.

We came back to Kayumba's yesterday, then, and met Kayumba himself halfway to Sadalla's, waiting to meet us and escort us back. He was all dressed up and had a *tipoye*, and told me that Matope was playing contentedly with his children and had been a good boy. He had had the road even more cleared – it's going to be an auto road one day – and for Vandevelde's special benefit there was an antelope trap set near the road, and, farther on, an elephant trap. It was a long thick log with a spear fixed to the end, hoisted way up between two big trees – at least twenty feet, I think – and a rope stretched between which if you pulled released the whole affair. We were got out of the way and Kayumba himself set it off. Down came the tree with a splendid crash, driving the spear more than a foot into the ground.

We reached here just at sunset as a storm burst and as Patrick climbed wearily out of his canoe down at the dock. What possessed him to come on Wednesday, or to come at all when he's sick, I don't know. I guess it was his conscience. Anyway he's much better. It was very gay and adventurous, all of us meeting like that away from home, and though he decided to live at the hospital so as not to have to walk, we all dined together. Kayumba called afterward, sitting at the table with us and talking. Patrick told Kayumba that he didn't know whether or not to believe him when Kayumba said his father had given Stanley[2] food and help when he came by. Stanley never mentions anyone giving him anything but arrows on this road. But Kayumba insisted, and we decided at last that it was Stanley who had lied.

Patrick is to stay till Sunday, doing census work, and says indignantly that of course I must stay, too. Vandevelde stays for two days for tribunal and then moves on, Saturday morning, for another tribunal downriver.

I set out with him this morning to listen-in on the tribunal, and was caught on the way by Asumini, hustling along all in a hurry. "Madame," she gasped, "Doctor Putnam has kicked me out."

"You're joking," I said, while Vandevelde paused curiously and looked delighted.

"No, I'm not. Come here and listen," she said.

So I sighed and while Vandevelde went on to his work, I plodded behind her to a house where her whole huge family was sitting, looking at me like a litter of whipped puppies. Someone brought a chair, and I settled down to listen.

"He kicked me out for nothing, Madame. That is, this sister and this one" – she showed me one old, cynical-looking lady, and one young, amused one – "were going to sleep with Sabani and Mokwanzanza, and the doctor got mad and said he didn't want any of us around his house anymore. So I'm asking you please to see if he means it."

2 The Welsh-born explorer Henry Morton Stanley (1841–1904) traveled extensively in the Equatorial Africa in the latter decades of the 19th century and worked in the employ of Belgium's King Leopold II staking the king's claim to the vast area that became known as the Belgian Congo. For more on Stanley's role in this, see American journalist Adam Hochschild's 1998 book *King Leopold's Ghost: A Story of Greed, Terror, and Heroism in Colonial Africa* (New York: Houghton Mifflin).

"Why is he angry? Did you sleep with anyone?"

"No, not me. My sisters. I don't know why he's angry. You go along with the Government, Madame; I don't want to bother you. But when the *barza* is finished, you'll talk to him?"

I promised and hurried on to the tribunal. There were about seven cases to hear before lunch. The *barza* is like most of them, a big barn with a raised platform on which sits the judging body, and me, if I happen in. There are benches on the lower level for anyone who wants to listen, and the involved people stand in line waiting to be called. Kayumba sat in his high chair behind a tall table, before a Belgian flag on the wall, the same eternal pictures of the King and Queen, and a big poster advertising cigarettes in Dutch, with large portrayals of two Javanese on it. I don't know why Javanese; probably they're thought to be Arabs there.

On each side of Kayumba was a chair with a smaller headman in it, and Vandevelde was in the corner listening and now and then writing something in a notebook or asking a question or getting something translated for him. Kayumba was wearing a tuxedo. He is very dignified, and while people were talking, he kept reading and answering letters that arrived by messenger, changing his spectacles – both pairs of which are plain glass – and looking meaningfully at one or the other of the headmen. I don't mean to make fun of him really, because he is honestly dignified and capable or he would never hold this job of being a big chief – as Patrick is never tired of explaining, the people in this part of the Congo never did have big chiefs. They had systems of tribunal and they were practically republicans. It's only the Government's all-embracing theories that have set Kayumba where he is, and he keeps his seat well, if probably unscrupulously.

I heard seven or eight palavers, all but one of which were about women being stolen, or women running away, or women refusing their husbands. Some of the time, the woman wasn't even called in; when she did testify she spoke in Kindaka, for most of the women have little use for a trade language like Kingwana. They were, to a woman, naked and hopeless looking, except for one small fifteen-year-old who simply looked snooty while her husband, a doddering old man, told graphically how she had stayed with him on the nuptial couch only two nights and had then gone and slept on the floor. And when he had said, "Ha!" very indignantly, "Why do you refuse me, who have bought and paid for you?" she simply made no answer, but ran away shortly afterward to another man. Whereupon he demanded her back again or her equivalent in cash. He got her, because the other man couldn't pay. The lady was led out, still looking snooty. I'm ready to bet there will be another palaver at the first opportunity.

The one that wasn't about women was about somebody stealing seven bunches of plantains out of another's *shamba*. It was proved to Kayumba's satisfaction that he had stolen them, I mean the culprit, and the plaintiff then was asked to give the value of the stolen plantains. I was amazed when he calmly said, "One was worth ten francs, two worth six, two worth seven, and two five." The state price for one regime is two francs. His evaluation was accepted without question, for had not the other man stolen?

Well, I repaired afterward to Patrick, to find what about Asumini. I found him resting on his bed after a full morning. "Yes, I thought she'd appeal to you," he said. "I'll probably take her back, though you mustn't tell her. I want her to have a good scare."

"But why? It was her sisters, it wasn't her."

"Exactly, her sisters. What kind of family is that? If they haven't been raised any better than that, what can I expect of her? I dare say I'm very narrow-minded, but I won't have them whoring on my front porch. D'you think the girls of any decent African family would act like that?"

"I think any woman here would. I've just come from the *barza* and it was all about women, and I don't blame any woman for acting like a sheep or a cow or a bitch if she's treated like one."

"These girls aren't married yet. Why, they simply picked these boys up! I've kicked Mokwanzanza out."

"Then I guess I'll have to kick Sabani out?"

"I don't say that. He's your boy. I only say I won't be delighted to see him around the house anymore."

We argued a long time, but Patrick was inflexible. I left him at last, wondering what stand to take about Sabani. I couldn't quite understand Patrick. Was he sincere about there being well-brought-up young women in the Congo? I don't think there are: not by his standards. If most women here are whores, it's simply because men treat them like whores, especially white men. Patrick was perhaps right in being furious with the men, but would the black men consider a thing like that an insult – that is, to a white man?

CHAPTER 15

COME TO JUDGMENT

Sunday, November 1, 1931

I'M AT KETSHU'S NOW, in spite of all my protestations that I wouldn't come that far downriver. I decided at the last minute because Vandevelde and I had a fight that was mostly my fault, and I didn't like to refuse any invitation. We had just time to pile my things into my box and climb into the canoe with him; Matope remained behind because he didn't like the idea of walking back, but Angélique is with me, and a new boy that I hired from Kayumba. He was one of my *tipoye* carriers and wanted a job. I don't need anyone, but I like his looks, and, of course, I *could* use a private *planton*. He's a little chap with a pointed beard and a hooked nose and no clothes but a bit of bark cloth, but it was his teeth that fascinated me most of all – they're so beautifully filed. He asked me please to ask Kayumba, because Kayumba would surely refuse him if he asked, but wouldn't dare turn me down. Which is just how it turned out.

The quarrel was a beautiful affair. It was about Patrick, of course, and started with the woman with the bad ear. I went to the hospital and found Patrick in deep conversation (by means of his *infirmier* Joachim) with a woman who speaks Kindaka. She was handsome in the way the boy is handsome, with a strong neck and shoulders, and there was a button neatly inserted on her upper lip. I was surprised to know she has two grown children. The troubles was, a soldier had slapped her on the ear, always a bad place to slap anyone, and the ear has been running for three weeks and Patrick was annoyed and wanted her to complain of the soldier – it was a soldier of Kayumba's, she said. She went on to explain that she had been the wife of a brother of Kayumba, and when the man died, she was passed on with his other worldly goods to another brother that she didn't like. She was always running away, and much preferred Abedi, a *capita* across the river. But her father refused to pay back her purchase price, so she had to stay with this new husband whom she didn't like. Undeterred by the fact that this was the affair of Kayumba's own family, Patrick looked it up in his law book and discovered a little-known item to the effect that an inherited wife need not stay with her inherited husband if she does-n't want to, and her father must pay him if she goes away.

❧

VANDEVELDE CAME IN JUST TO SAY good morning on his way to the tribunal, and Patrick put the affair up to him. Vandevelde looked very hesitant, indeed, especially as Kayumba came in, too, and seemed to be annoyed to see the woman there. At last Vandevelde said, "Well, it's an affair for the tribunal. Send her along this morning. She says it's a soldier of Kayumba? What's his name?"

The woman gave his name: Ngalla. Then Kayumba and Vande-velde went off and Patrick asked me how much it cost a person to have a case heard, and I said, "Three francs a case." So he gave her six francs, three for the soldier affair and three for the husband affair, and told her not to be afraid but to speak up in tribunal. After she'd gone I said, "Do you think she'll go through with it? I've never yet seen a woman unsupported by several dozen male relatives in an affair like this."

"I don't think she will, as a matter of fact," he answered, "but one can always try."

Pretty soon she came back with her six francs and said that they hadn't allowed her to speak. So Patrick was angry, and so was I, and we worked all morning on his reports while waiting for Vandevelde to come back and explain. He didn't come, though he sent word by his boy that lunch was ready, so I went home alone.

In the middle of lunch, I began the trouble. I said, "Why didn't you let that woman with the ear present her case?"

v.: "Why, I *did*. She presented it, and I sent her away because I had found out the truth. She lied, that woman did. The soldier was a soldier of Avakubi, after all."

m.: "Who said so?"

v.: "She did, when Kayumba asked her."

m.: "Did you hear her?"

v.: "No, because she spoke Kindaka. He translated. She didn't even know the soldier's name."

m.: "But she did. She told you at the hospital. Don't you remember?"

v.: "No, I don't."

m. (exasperated): "Don't you see she was just afraid of Kayumba? You've thrown her case out of court without hearing it properly. And the other thing, the business about the husband?"

v.: "Oh, that. I can't do anything about that, against the custom of the country."

m.: "But it's *not* against the custom of the country. You didn't listen properly and you threw the case out, because she didn't even have to pay to have it heard. You're not telling the truth."

v.: "You call me a liar? Very well, young lady. Putnam would do well to remember that he mustn't meddle with politics."

m.: "What do you mean?"

v.: "Just that. It makes the chiefs angry. Kayumba says he's always doing it."

m.: "You mean if someone comes in with an ear badly treated, he … ."

v.: "He must dress the ear, and that's all. A doctor must not show that he has any power, or anyone with a grievance will be coming to him."

M.: "But what if they have a grievance and it's the only way?"

V.: You are only a little woman; you don't understand. A doctor must not show that he has influence. He must not meddle with politics."

M.: "Oh, now I begin to understand. The tribunal doesn't really mean anything; the soldiers can go on wounding people. …"

V.: "What can Kayumba do? It was a soldier of Avakubi."

M.: "It was *not*! Don't you understand yet? She was afraid to say."

V.: "I can't go against the customs of the country."

M.: "But you go against the customs of the country when you appoint Kayumba chief. He wouldn't be chief if the Government wasn't behind him."

V.: "Well, of course, anything within reason. But it isn't for Putnam, no, nor the missions, either, to stir up trouble."

M.: "How is he stirring up trouble? He's pointing out the law, that's all."

V.: "He must not have any power. …"

M.: "I suggest you give him twelve strokes in the middle of town, just to show that he has no power."

V.: "You're ridiculous."

M.: "Yes, that was silly, but. …"

V.: "I've done plenty for Putnam before. Has he any reason to say I don't uphold him?"

M.: "Yes; the Halafu case."

V.: "What! He's not satisfied with that?"

M.: "Oh, you know perfectly well that he's not. You ask him to send people who need punishment, and when he does, you won't punish them."

V.: "It was for him. I do not like to punish too much. I told Putnam, and he agreed with me."

M.: "He did not!"

V.: "He did. Very well, let him go his own way. I should be glad to see what will happen. A man with ideas like that … He can write to Stanleyville if he's dissatisfied, and. …"

M.: "You know perfectly well what would happen. Your successor would make life miserable for him. Why do you use big meaningless phrases like 'meddle with politics'? Why don't you tell the truth and be done with it?"

V.: "What truth?"

M.: "How do I know? I don't understand you at all. Tell the truth; say either, 'I'm doing my job with the least trouble possible so that I can get paid and go home,' or, 'The Government is afraid of Kayumba,' or, 'I'm too damned lazy to investigate my cases thoroughly,' but don't say, 'You, mustn't meddle with politics." It's Patrick's business to see that people don't get knocked around any more than is necessary; he's a sanitary agent, and it's not good for people to be slapped hard on the ear so that it runs for three weeks. It's his job."

V.: "I'm sick of Putnam. I've done my best for him, and now I'm sick of it. *Je m'en fous. Je m'en fous." Je m'en fous*" ["I don't care"].

M.: "Exactly." (Whereupon I left the table and went into my room and locked the door.)

I stayed there for two hours; once Vandevelde called to ask if I wanted coffee, and I answered very politely that I didn't. When I came out at last, it was because I thought he'd gone long ago to the tribunal, but he was there, and he asked me if I was still mad, and I said no, and he said he wasn't either, and we both apologized for everything, and he said he'd interview the woman alone if I wanted him to. That does not uphold the dignity of Government very much, but since none of it was my business to begin with, I felt very much chastened. Then he went to the tribunal, only an hour late, and I reported it all to Patrick, who laughed but said that he would certainly go on making trouble when it came within his jurisdiction to do so.

There was a dance given in Vandevelde's honour, and he sent for me to see it. It was much better than the monotonous Banguana dance. Everyone sang in a queer recurring little tune, like a helix, intertwined and intertwined, and yet always coming back where it started. Everyone went round and round the drums at first, while a very small and very old woman danced by herself, sometimes before us – Kayumba and Vandevelde and me – and sometimes before the drums and sometimes before the four old men who led the dance. Her step was an imitation of making love. Then they changed the tune of the dance and all of them – women with babies and men with straw chicken-feathered headdresses – made gestures like spearing the elephant, and then they scattered bits of leaves to show how the elephant tore up the forest in his flight, and that was all. They waited then while the drums played another tune, and now and then just one young man or girl would run to the center and do a Charleston step and run back again, until they got worked up to a fine pitch and started a whirling dance again, so wild that they almost knocked our chairs over. It looked splendid; they were all so naked and excited. At last, it was too dark and rainy to see any more, and so we went home.

Vandevelde and I went to hospital first, though, and visited Patrick a while. Patrick said after a half hour, "Mademoiselle tells me you had a fight, and from what she reports it sounds as if you both said rather foolish things. Among other things, though, I believe you said I mustn't meddle with politics?"

"Oh!" Vandevelde laughed, and told him everything frankly, apologizing for losing his temper, but as he said, "When a young lady calls you a liar … ."

"She gets excited," said Patrick indulgently. "*C'est un avocat.*" ["It's a lawyer," or, colloquially, "She's a lawyer."]

I simpered and drew pictures on the floor with my foot, and then the two gentlemen began to talk seriously, leaving me out of it as was proper. They settled the affair of the woman first, Patrick admitting that if she hadn't enough sense to tell the truth she deserved to suffer ("As a matter of fact, she can really talk Kingwana, I happen to know," he said to me) and Vandevelde admitting that perhaps Kayumba might have been prejudiced in his brother's favor, and that certainly it was part of Patrick's job to investigate bad beatings. "Now, Mademoiselle says you're not happy about the Halafu business," said Vandevelde. "Is that so?"

"Oh, I'm happy enough," said Patrick. "Halafu's nothing to me. But I admit I was rather astonished that you didn't even fine him, as an example."

"I never punish for a first offence."

"That's right. But it was a second offence."

"Oh, really? I didn't know."

"But I told you."

This died out in polite murmurings. At the end, of course, nothing was done about the woman, and perhaps as Patrick says she deserved it for lying either to him or to Vandevelde.

"They try to stir up trouble between the whites, you know," Vandevelde reminded us. As for the husband business, this Abedi man is always seducing Kayumba's women and there are three affairs on trial now, so Vandevelde doesn't want to add another.

Ketshui's village is almost completely deserted; everyone is over at the road building the new place. It's a great pity; he had a splendid new village here, but the Government changed their minds about running a road over, and, of course, he must go. He was worried about the new place, which he says gives no room for all his plantations, and the agronome man has told him that the forest must all be preserved and the Negroes can't go hunting anymore, or even walking in it. Which is nonsense; it is only that certain plots of big trees mustn't be cut any more. Vandevelde explained and they seemed relieved – and, of course, happy that a white man was put in the wrong.

Ketshui is almost as splendid as Kayumba but not quite, for he has only one pair of spectacles instead of two. He wears a real dress suit, though, with satin lapels and a waistcoat and a white helmet. There is trouble now with the chief, Isumi, from way over on the Wamba road. He has refused to come to this tribunal, as he claims to be the rightful chief of the Bandaka and won't admit Ketshui as master. When he comes to Avakubi he scorns to imitate the whites, like the other chiefs; he wears the barkcloth *molumba*[1] and a leopard-skin for

1 a loincloth

his shoulder, and a belt of iron, and leopard teeth as a fringe for his head, under the feather headdress. And he will have no one inferior in rank within ten feet of him; he sits alone and proud. Kherkhoff hates him for it and would like to humiliate him, but Vandevelde likes him and won't punish him severely. I don't know what he will have to do, though, about this tribunal.

Most of the white men hate a man like that for being reactionary, and yet on the other hand they hate Kayumba for being so like a white man. They have excellent reasons for both attitudes, which they will give you on almost no provocation. ... Though if they think Kayumba is really like a white man, for all his spectacles and hunting clothes, they're wrong. You've only to watch his eyes if someone displeases him, to see what I mean.

Here at Ketshui's I stopped the tribunal without meaning to, after one of the eternal woman-affairs had been heard. It was like a thousand others. A doddering old man came up on the platform and planked three francs down on the table, and then cleared his throat and began. "My plea is this. Is it a good thing when a woman who is my woman runs away and becomes the property of another man? I ask to know.

"I bought this woman" – he gestured toward her, a mahogany-colored girl with firm thighs and upstanding breasts – "years ago from her father. Her father put her hand into mine and said, 'My child is your woman now.' Last year, she ran away and lived with Asumani. (Asumani was called up. A tall handsome man with a firm jaw.) I brought the affair to court and Asumani was told to send her back. She came back, but later went back to him and there was another case in court. Now it has happened again."

Asumani spoke and said, "I say it is a lie."

Ketshui, a little alert man who is a born lawyer, leaned forward and said, "Asumani, I am tired of this affair. You have denied the tribunal long enough. I sentence you – but it is for you to decide," he remembered abruptly, turning to the *capita* of the man.

"Asumani," this man ruled, "must – but first, Suleiman (which was the name of the old chap), what do you want? Money or the woman?"

"I want my woman," said Suleiman, and the girl hung her head and looked miserable, though no one even bothered to look.

"Well, then, Asumani is to have a month in jail with the chain at his neck."

"And I say," said the other *capita*, "seventeen days in jail with the chain for the woman, and afterward back to Suleiman for her."

"Another time, Asumani," said Ketshui, "you will be flogged."

Asumani saluted and marched out, disregarding the *planton* that scuttled behind him, and the girl was hustled out after him. She began to wail after they had passed the door.

Now, it is such a typical case that anyone who knows the Congo will be too bored even to listen to it. I murmured, as I always do, "Poor woman," but Vandevelde heard me and took it as a criticism or something like it. Quickly he protested, "Oh, but it's not so hope-less. That unhappy girl can appeal on her account, you know; she can prove that her husband's too old to sleep with her, and she'll be free."

Now, this is a blatant lie. There has never been any such custom in Africa, at least in this part of it, and I was so shocked at his igno-rance that I protested. He thereupon turned to Ketshui and demanded if that was not the truth. I was awfully embarrassed for him. The whole courtroom was shocked, and Ketshui started to answer, hesitated in the face of such a monstrous suggestion, and at last let a *capita* say: "Why, Bwana, a woman – a woman – Look here. If I buy a field and then I grow old, has the field any right to say, 'You are too old to have me, I shall now go to another, a young one?' Why should a man lose his wealth simply because he grows old? All men grow old. Must they grow poor because of it?"

I added hastily in a whisper, "You see? Why, someone has to pay for that woman, of course. Who will pay for her if she simply decides to walk out?" I almost squealed, I was so shocked, and as for the Negroes, they were pale.

"Why, Bwana," said Ketshui, who had found tongue at last, "if that sort of thing were started, all women would run away."

"It's the law in Belgium," Vandevelde answered me in French defiantly.

"What the devil has that got to do with the Congo?"

He shrugged – he, who is always the first to excuse an injustice between Negroes by saying you mustn't interfere with Custom, as though he could tell what Custom is. If it comes to that, is it Custom to be managed by a white Administrator? But he tried again with Ketshui.

"If a man already old, Ketshui, buys a young girl – a child – it will always turn out badly. Therefore, the Government has said that a man must not buy a girl so much younger than he is. You know that the Government has said that. A man cannot buy a girl who is still a child."

"I know, Commanda," said Ketshui.

"Very well. This man says he bought the girl years ago when she was still a child. Was that since the Government made its law, or before?"

All the *capitas* looked at one another uncomfortably, and at last they decided to do the most obvious thing.

"She wasn't a child, Bwana. You didn't understand very well. She was a grown woman, with breasts."

"Oh! All right then. Go on," he said and sat back. Everyone drew a deep breath, and my blush began to fade, and the next witness was a brother of Ketshui's who has, to my certain knowledge, just lately sold his very young daughter to a syphilitic man, but whose case was an entirely different matter.

"You see," Vandevelde explained to me kindly at lunch afterward, "it was all right, after all. The woman simply changed her mind after taking a husband. That sort of thing can't go on, you know. One does well to follow the custom of the people." He smiled. "Poor tender-hearted little woman that you are. You are really angry about her, aren't you?"

"Not particularly. I'm used to it."

The woman passed just then in file with the other prisoners, carrying water, but Vandevelde didn't see her because he had just noticed that there was no dessert, and he was very angry.

CHAPTER 16

WHITE HOT MAD

Tuesday, November 3, 1931

PENGE. I LEFT VANDEVELDE AT KETSHUI's yesterday still wrestling with pink and green cards, which show if a man has or has not paid his tax. He found cards of people who've been dead for years; no one thought of throwing them away. Vandevelde was damned tired and fed up with the idea of more work of the same sort in Avakubi, whither he was going in the afternoon. I'm sorry for him for having a job he doesn't like, but he does not work as hard as he pretends, and I begin to be annoyed when he talks about it too much. It's always just when he has neglected something, I notice.

He sent me with eleven of his own porters, whom he has taken in the first place from the work on the road and kept with him for ten days, mostly I think because he doesn't want to anger the *capitas* by snatching more men from the villages. That's all right, but now why must all the porters walk the two days' journey (three from here) to Avakubi to get their pay? Because he didn't want to bother counting up the pay at Ketshui's and he hopes to hand the job over to the clerk at the office at home. This loses six days out of twenty-five men's programs, though I dare say they welcome the comparative vacation. They kept telling me they didn't have enough to eat. I don't know how true that is. One of my *tipoye* men was reported missing, after we'd gone through Sembo's village (on foot, which gave him his chance) and when I asked for his name and village he miraculously reappeared, so we said no more about it. I must say the roadmen on this side of the forest look better nourished than the village dwellers. As for Van Roon's show, *plantons* report that things are much better now that camp has been moved to the Ehulu.

Halafu came this morning to sit a while and to talk some more about life and nature. We talked about medicines, and he shook his head sadly at the Doctor's refusing to admit the efficacy of cicatrization. Then he said, "To have a baby is easy. I wanted children for a long time and couldn't have them, and then I read all about it in the Koran. If you just wait until your wife's stomach is making a noise and then lie with her, she'll conceive. That noise means that she's opening. White men don't know that. If even that doesn't work, there's a sort of drink you make with beans and water and all sorts of things; you drink half of it and give your wife the other half and you'll have a child all right. The Koran knows all about those things.

"These bushmen know nothing. This business of not being able to lie with your wife while she's suckling her baby is nonsense. Women made that rule up so they could have lovers and wouldn't have to sleep with their husbands when they didn't want to. These people suckle their babies too long, too. Nine or ten months is enough. To suckle a child for two years is bad for it and for the mother."

Just then Abdulla came in and they greeted each other affectionately and sat down side by side to look at pictures in *The Curse of Central Africa*[1] that I've been reading. Abdulla wanted to see a picture of Dhanis, but I couldn't find it. He saw him once when he, Abdulla, was a small child, and he remembered him. Shortly after that Halafu decided to go away, and they shook hands warmly and made a date for the near future. The minute we were alone, Abdulla leaned forward and said, his eyes narrow and his voice discreetly lowered, "What did

---

1 By Guy Burrows (London: Everett and Co, 1903). When Burrows, a former British army officer who had worked for King Leopold II's company in the Congo, wrote about his experiences, the book sparked international outrage over the extent of the brutality that was occurring there.

he want? I think you ought to know these people are bad, Madame. Halafu killed a white man here a long time ago, and no one knows it but me. Beware! What did he want?"

I started to answer, but he called his bodyguard and said, "I think I hear someone moving out there. Go and see who it is." The boy came back and reported no one, and then I said, "Whatever he wanted, Abdulla, he hadn't said when you arrived. You know that his spirit is full of guile; he comes to look and to listen, and he says nothing."

"I see. Now, Madame, about our moving – I wish you'd put in a good word with Libadu. I want to move to the land near the Ysai River, far away from these people. I wonder if you wouldn't ask him for me."

"I'll do what I can. It's none of my business, but I think the Commandant thinks it'll be all right. He said so anyway."

"Good. I'm having an ivory trumpet made for you, if you'd like it."

"I would, very much."

Abdulla leaned back and glanced around. "Where's Sabani?"

"He's sick today."

"And you sit here all alone, with no one to watch you? That's bad." He called his aide-de-camp and stationed him on the *barza* for the day, to protect me.

Thursday, November 5

There was a tattooing bee yesterday. Asumini is so heavily covered already that I hardly noticed the additional line of small scratches running around her chin from ear to ear, and Abanzima, after searching for a clear place, at last had to be satisfied with adding two lines to the already existing arrow that divides her eyebrows. Nambedru and Matope each received an arrow on the forehead, running down from the hairline to the nose, and a small series of triangles on their forearms. Kiussa got the same. Matope in addition got a couple of semicircles at the outer corner of each eye. I approve of tattooing as long as they leave me out of it, but when they all came to see me with dripping needles in their outstretched hands, I declined with thanks. It looks too bloody. They do it with knives and needles, cutting the design in little scratches and then rubbing something black and greasy over it. When the blood stops running and the black stuff dries they wash it off and the only place it stays is in the scratches. A day or so later when the swelling and irritation goes down – why it does go down instead of developing tetanus is more than I can understand – they cut afresh and do it all over again. They were awfully keen to do me – the black would show up so nicely on my skin, they said, and they wanted to see if I could stand it without crying.

Saturday, November 7[2]

I sat on my veranda this afternoon feeling hungry and wondering why the dinner bell hadn't rung. Usually Nambedru rang it, running around the house and calling "Food! Food!", but today I had heard nothing, though the sun was setting and it was past dinnertime. At last, I walked over to the other side of the house and found a group of women – Abanzima, Sissy, and a couple of friends – gathered around Nambedru, who was crouching on a stool and sniffling. Her head was freshly bald. The other girls were plainly furious. I asked what the matter was, and Abanzima replied bitterly that it was Patrick's fault.

I went in search of him. He was working quietly in his office. When I asked what was going on, he answered impatiently, like a man with more important things than women on his mind. "I shaved Nambedru's head," he said. "Her hair was getting too long. That is, I clipped it. There was some row with Sissy over plaiting it, so I put an end to that."

2 Hahn's original account of the incident that prompted her to leave Penge was cut from the original edition of *Congo Solo*. Hahn related the actual events that transpired in an October 22, 1966, *New Yorker* article titled "Stewart," which she reprinted in her 1970 book *Times and Places*.

Shock took away my breath for a moment, and then I said, "She's crying out there, Patrick. You told me they didn't mind having their heads shaved, but ..."

"Well, it seems I was mistaken," said Patrick, bored, and then he shouted for dinner.

Though I was hungry, I hoped the girls wouldn't come. I wanted the girls to rebel. But dinner did come, almost immediately, and Nambedru carried her tray in with the others, though her brow, under her naked head, was wrinkled with resentment and grief.

Sunday, November 8

Last night, in bed, I expanded much indignant thought on the subject [of Nambedru's head shaving] and lost a good deal of sleep over it, so it was not as gratifying as it should have been when, this morning, Nambedru appeared in her normal happy mood, laughing and chattering with the other girls just as if there had been no crisis at all. Once again, I reflected, I had let emotion outrun reason. I had applied my American prejudices and principles to a culture wholly different from my own. Even so, my feelings toward Patrick had changed. This afternoon, when the whole house went swimming and divided as he ordered, women in one bend in the river and himself and the boatmen in another, I heard him expounding something, and the sound of his voice, heavily authoritative, made the skin on the back of my neck prickle unpleasantly.

It was a relief when one of our Belgian acquaintances arrived a little while later on a tour. He was planning to hunt elephants a day's journey from Penge, and when he suggested that I go along, I leaped at the invitation. Patrick, surprised, pointed out that I had often expressed abhorrence for big-game shooting, and I had to say, lamely that everybody ought to do a thing at least once before condemning it.

So I went hunting. The official habitually travelled by *tipoye*, the native chair carried by four men. I had always been opposed to *tipoye*s because Patrick was, and I often quoted him to the effect that anyone not crippled ought to walk in the forest, especially on a hunting safari. But the official, naturally, objected to riding while I walked and as he also objected to walking, I had to ride. It was a bumpy business. Clearly, *tipoye* riding was not only wrong in principle, but uncomfortable. By the time Monsieur, aided by a local chief and a number of trackers, had got his elephant, I was heartily sorry I had ever gone along. The thought of Penge seemed good once more, and my liverish dislike of Patrick was sweated out. I left the Belgian official before the next leg of his trip and went home to Penge by *pirogue*.

Saturday, November 14

The landing was deserted when I arrived at Penge. Nobody was in sight, even at the top of the bluff, and as I climbed, I wondered why. At the top, I saw some sort of activity near the house, but I couldn't make it out until I had got there and stepped up on the porch. "Hi!" I called.

Chimp answered from somewhere with a burst of coughing, but there was no glad rush to embrace me, not even a jingle of chains, so I presumed she was tied up. I walked around the veranda, where I stopped short. Under the branches of a large tree in the middle of the lawn stood Abanzima, her head hanging. She lifted it and glanced at me, and then it drooped again. A collar like Chimp's was padlocked around her neck, and a chain tethered her to the tree's trunk. The male cook was squatting close by, chopping something in a bowl. He gave me a furtive look and said, "Salaam, Madamu," and bent again to his work. Around the corner came Sissy, who stopped when she saw me and rapidly reversed, disappearing. I went to the office and found Patrick working as usual at his papers.

A "wicked baboon" that Patrick Putnam kept as a pet. Note the collar and lock, which were sometimes used to chain the animal. Putnam put a similar, larger collar on his "wives" as punishment for what he regarded as disrespectful behavior.

I fell into a chair opposite him and said, "Now what?"

"What drives me crazy is the way Abanzima lied to me," said Patrick. "I've often told her that I understand sometimes a person isn't satisfied with one other person. I myself am not satisfied only with her. Why, I've been thinking of taking a Bandaka girl, myself. I've told her that if ever she wanted a vacation, to tell me and I'd send her home or somewhere till she felt like coming back. I wouldn't like it, but – I wanted to know. Well, this started when I went away to see about supplies.

"Two days after I got back, Abanzima told me I was neglecting Nambedru. It seemed natural that she should; wives often do try to keep things peaceful in the harem. Of course, now I know it was because she wanted to be free for her own man in Kongolo. So that night I spent with Nambedru, down in the *gîte* by the river, and about midnight we were awakened up by a drive of red ants. You've never had that happen, so I'd better tell you first what it feels like. You don't know when you wake up what it is; you feel as if little fires are burning all over your face. Then, if you have nowhere else to go, you light a fire and scatter charcoal around the floor: that gets rid of them. But since I had a perfectly good house to go to, I just said to Nambedru, 'Come along; we'll go home.' I shall never understand why she didn't try to stop me. She must have known. She didn't, though; she just followed me without saying a word.

"I came up on the porch without making much noise, naturally, and threw the door open; as I did, I saw someone jumping out the window. Even then I didn't think. I thought it was Abanzima being frightened; she told me there had been a leopard-man in the vicinity. So I called loudly, 'Don't be frightened, it's only us. There are ants in the *gîte*. I can't even remember what I felt like when I heard her answer from the bed, 'Is it you, Bwana?' "

He stopped for a minute. All the time, his voice had been perfectly calm. It was calm now as he continued, carefully calm. He told me lots of details as if he wanted to get everything exact, even the tiniest things.

"I said to her, 'Who was the man with you?' and she wouldn't say. She refused to admit that there had been a man with her. I took her by the throat, and she said, 'Kongolo.' Why do you suppose she told me the truth right away? Frightened, I guess. I meant business. I made her get up and walk with me because I wanted to have her alone. She wouldn't tell me a thing. I strangled her over and over again – she has marks on her throat – and at last she said that it was the first time it had ever happened and that they hadn't even made love; Kongolo was only sleeping there. I lost hope of making her tell anything but lies that night, so I brought her back and tied her to a tree. Nambedru had been lying in her bed, waiting, I guess, until I came back and wondering what was going to happen. All the while, perfectly calm and quiet. I shall never understand her; nor Abanzima, nor any of Them. I thought I did understand Them, and now … well, to go on. I was going to leave out my feelings until afterward, but I forget as I talk.

"I took Nambedru in the other direction, so as to keep them separated. I told her that Abanzima had admitted everything, and asked her what about herself. Yes, she said after a minute, she had a lover, too – Yusufu. I asked her when it had all began with Abanzima, and she told a silly story she never knew about it except for one night she had an idea someone had been in the room, and when she asked Abanzima about it next day, Abanzima said yes, that was Kongolo, and why didn't she take Yusufu? So she did."

Patrick looked at me hard. "Do you know, I believe even that. It would be a good stroke of policy on Abanzima's part to get her little cousin to keep quiet, too. Wouldn't it? I'll never know. I wanted to be perfectly calm and reasonable, and that night I was. I sent for Kongolo, who had been sleeping in his own bed, probably thinking he got out before I saw him, and I got Yusufu, too, and told them that if they had been my own men on my own payroll, I would beat them or shoot them, but since they weren't, we would all go on just as if nothing had happened, so long as they did their work. Perfectly reasonable, you see."

"Oh, yes," I said, "perfectly reasonable. And then?"

"Then I told the women that I was through with them and what they did was their own business; they could go to the men's houses if they wanted. So they did. It was almost morning. I had to go out next day, it being Monday. I thought and thought about it, and at last, just about noon, I called Abanzima again. I had come to a decision. I said to her, 'You have three things to do: you must make your choice. You may marry Kongolo and live with him anywhere you want – here or at Wamba.' No, she said, she didn't want to, even though I told her that she could have her own things. Then I said, 'You may go home to your own village and take all your clothes with you. Only I shan't let you have the kid because you have been giving her a bad example. I shall keep her, and when I go back to America, which will be soon now, I'll take her home myself to your village and give her to her grandmother.' She cried at that because it is a disgrace, I fancy. I don't know. But then I said – because I'd been thinking that I wanted her anyway; I like her – I said, 'Or you can come back to me. But you must take twelve strokes of the *fimbu*, and shave your hair, and sleep in another bed till I call you back, and for six months I will buy you no more clothes, and we will rub out the blood pact we once made because it seems to do no good – you lie anyway – and you must take a bath and throw the water into the river, and I will burn this bed.'

"You understand that really the bed business meant nothing to me; it was to impress her. And she said, 'Well, I want to come back to you, and I accept all of the punishments.'

"So I gave her twelve strokes, which she took bravely, though they were as hard as I could make them. I told her to stay in 'jail' in the room until the other things were settled. And then, I started to think about things, and as long as it had been – I don't really understand, not yet. So I took Kongolo out of the roll-call and told all the men what I was going to do, and I had *him* beaten, twelve strokes."

"Poor Kongolo, did he cry?"

"No. Once he said to the man who was doing it, 'Can't you count?' because he was afraid of getting thirteen strokes instead of twelve. Then I tied Abanzima's bed to him and made him walk naked through the village. I don't know if that really shamed him or not; I suppose it shamed the others, the ones who saw him, more. Then I said to him, 'If I see you or your brother again, when I get back, I'll shoot you. I don't care where you go, but if I see you here again I'll kill you.'

"Well, I came back next day as usual, and found that the houseboy had done something on his own account. The men had come back while I was gone, to get their clothes. They asked the boy for them, and to please me, I guess he did something I shall always be sorry for.

He said, 'Wait here a minute,' and went and instead of getting clothes he called the chief, and the chief sent soldiers and arrested the boys. He did it for me, but now that I think of it, I wish he hadn't. I was calm by this time. I asked the chief to send them back to me so that I could really see them off this time, and I was angry, but I didn't mean any harm. The chief promised to send them at noon, though he demurred and asked me if I was going to kill them, in which case it would be his responsibility with the Government, you see. Well, they didn't come at noon, and I boiled over again. I meant business.

"I took my gun and went to the jail and called the chief, and he still said no, so I came back and called eight of my men and told them I would be responsible if there were any trouble, and we went back and it was perfectly simple; the jailer didn't resist and the boys weren't even tied up. They were sleeping. I had them both beaten again for coming back after I told them to go away, though I was perfectly reasonable. I explained that I knew it was not their fault that they had gone to jail."

"Quite, quite reasonable."

"I wanted the chief to walk with me to the river, the Locoya, and really see them off with an impressive escort. He had gone back into his house. I went up and called; he wouldn't answer. I boiled over again, and to frighten all of them I fired three times. I had no intention of him. Then I tried to open the door but I could feel someone pushing on the other side.

"I waited a minute and rushed it with my shoulder, and this time it opened with a bang and the chief, stark naked, fell on the ground, and one of his wives ran out the back way. So I had him dress – oh, I forgot to say that he snatched the gun away from me, and I was too surprised to take it back for a minute, but of course I did when he dressed. He came along then, with everyone else, and his mother started to yell. She likes him, I suppose. She almost ran up and scratched my eyes out, and she kept yelling, 'My child! He's going to kill my child!' I got mad and handed the gun to her and said, 'There, protect your damn child, if you want. I tell you, I'm not going to hurt him.' The chief still objected, and I slapped him."

"Hard?"

"Not hard enough to knock him down. I boxed his ear. He said, 'I can't come now; my ear hurts,' and I said, 'This, then, to balance the other,' and boxed him on the other ear. His mother was almost crazy. Now that she had the gun, though, he ran away, so I had to abandon my idea. I was tired if it by that time, anyway, so I let the boys go without any more ceremony.

"Kongolo said, 'What about my clothes?'

"I told him he could have his clothes, but that he must send a friend to get them. Both boys must go away. They went off then without any more about it."

"And the chief?"

"I was really sore at him. I came back and took a shotgun and went toward his house again, but then I came to my senses and cooled off and remembered that I wasn't really quarreling with him. I went home. That's all."

"You didn't slap any of the chief's women?"

"Of course not. Why should I?"

"Well," I said after a slight pause, "I just wondered."

"It was dark now, and I thought he was becoming a little more vague in his speech, but I was still interested.

"Now about my feelings. I still don't know what to do. It never occurred to me to spy on Abanzima. Thank God for the driver ants – why, I might never have found out! Never! I still don't know. I had planned to stay forever, settle down with her, but why should I? She's lied to me. She says now that the blood pact isn't the right thing to do between man and wife. I should have taken a crocodile tooth and said a charm, so that if she lied to me after that the tooth would wound her all over her body, under the skin, and I'd know. Or if she had a child, she said it would not have happened because women who lie always die in childbirth. What do you think?"

"I think that sounds fishy," I said.

"So do I. Now I've figured out something else. I've begun to think that perhaps this is the first and only time it's happened because Abanzima told me about the two men she'd lived with while I was back in America for a year. Why should she tell me about that, which I thought was all right, and not about this? I think this way. I took her out of the bush and I brought her to town, and she met all the town girls and listened to them, and Satuma, who is purely a towny, helped give her ideas, and probably Kongolo was bothering her all the time and so ... ."

"If it makes you feel any better," I said, "I think that it sounds reasonable enough. If it comes to that, I'm willing to believe that it's the first time she's done it."

"All that isn't so important as the way she lied and went on lying. Even now, I can't believe her. She says everything in that honest way that I used to love so much. And yet, damn it, what am I going to do?"

He stopped and looked at me as if he were actually asking my advice. "Yes," he said, "I want you to tell me. I'm not saying I'll take your advice, but I want you to tell me what you really think. Should I give up my whole plan of life and go back home? Or should I stay here?"

I thought fast. I knew I had no business trying to advise him. On the other hand, he had asked for my opinion. My honest opinion.

"Well, then, though you won't do it – I think you *should* go home. You're probably homesick. I honestly don't think the 'epic' is very important, unless you get put in jail. Yes, it would be good for you if they actually jailed you, which they probably won't do, however."

"Thank you. Of course I don't want to be jailed," he said.

Tuesday, November 17

Nothing is static, and little by little the house grew noisy again after the incident between Patrick and Abanzima. Chimpo stole food from the kitchen; Abanzima shouted curses at her, and we all laughed. The great silence was over. There was a lot of work at the clinic. A band of pygmies arrived and set up their little leaf houses at the village outskirts, where they would stay for a few weeks before moving on. I did a lot of thinking about Patrick during the long afternoons, sitting on my porch, looking at the river. Once again, I wondered if I shouldn't have taken a firm stand. But Abanzima's punishment had been none of my affair. She had submitted, hadn't she? I was no anthropologist to know what was and wasn't correct in African lives. I had to admit to myself that I hadn't the slightest idea what went on in the girls' minds and hearts. Oh, I got on all right with them; we laughed and talked together and gave each other little presents, but that was all – and probably that was all that was possible. And it was obvious that Patrick and Abanzima were on good terms again. I was very glad.

Wednesday, November 18

I was brushing my hair before dinner when I noticed that it was getting very long. I liked to keep it almost as short as a boy's, and I had been cutting it whenever I could, getting Nambedru to snip it off in back. Patrick or one of the other girls would have to do it now, I thought, and so I took a pair of scissors with me to the big house, where Patrick was sitting out-of-doors with his before-dinner drink. Sissy and Abanzima stood beside his chair, one on each side, like a couple of guards. Genially, he asked, "What are you doing with those shears?"

"I explained and asked, "So will you cut the back for me?" and pulled up a chair of my own, ready for a drink.

Patrick said, "No."

"No, what?"

"I mean I won't help you with your hair," he said. "It's silly to fuss around with it the way you women are always doing. Why don't you let it grow?"

I said, "Because it's much too hot here for long hair."

I was smiling, but Patrick wasn't. His eyes were shining coldly. "All right then, cut it all off," he said. "I'll use the clippers on you if you'll do that."

"Oh, don't be such an idiot. Sissy or Abanzima can trim me if you won't."

"No, they won't," said Patrick. "No member of my family is going to use halfway measures on her head anymore. And that goes for you, as well as the *other* girls." He repeated the order to Abanzima and Sissy in Swahihi and they nodded solenly. Abanzima making little clucking noises in her throat to confirm the agreement. Bewildered, I looked from one dark face to the other. They looked back with identical expressions – sympathetic, wary, warning. Solemn and inflexible, Patrick sat on his throne. No member of his family ... . "clippers or nothing," he said.

I decided to leave Penge forever, as soon as possible.

Thursday, November 19[3]

My own plans are changing about the trip. Asumani first suggested that I chuck the idea of cutting straight to the new road, as I did before, and take the old caravan trail to Lubero, which is some fourteen days south of here. From that town I can get a lift of some sort to the main road below Beni, and it will save a large amount of money in the way of automobile fare, which is enormously expensive here. The only flaw in that scheme is the fact that the country around here is swept so clean of food that I must carry enough rice for my porters for three or four days – seventy-five kilograms.

Can I get it in Penge? I doubt it. Everyone is poor, and Bwana Donga is actually sending his children to Yuma's, where there is more

---

3 At this point, Hahn resumed her narrative as she had recorded events in her journal.

to eat. To be sure, Abdulla has promised me a couple of baskets, for he owes me a hundred francs and can't possibly pay it. But I don't know if he can produce them. Halafu brought news that might be true: all the camps on the road are abandoned by order of the Government, and only Morot's station will be left to carry on. This is practically abandoning the road, or at least putting off its completion for a great many more months. I hope, nevertheless, that it's true – it would be a lifesaver for the Basenge. One chief, Yowly, must send out a contingent every week of people to carry bananas seven days to Van Roon's camp and then return. As Kayumba said some time ago, it's worse now than in the notorious days of the rubber regime, as it is in all the other African colonies that I know. All those atrocities are not true that I've been reading about – they don't cut off hands any more, nor throw children into the river, nor give people to cannibals to eat, but certainly they are still impressing all the labor they can to the extent of chaining them in gangs; surely the women continue to do the hardest work of carrying; surely a high food tax is still levied, for the price paid by the Government for food is practically nothing.

We've just had a white man through here, the agronome, who is very pleasant and jolly, but he makes his porters do the work for nothing, openly, and takes prisoners on his way just to do the carrying. The reward for native produce goes down farther and farther, and the tax goes up and up. Trade conditions are much better, but the Negroes are too poor to buy.

Halafu has now suggested that I take another road that will bring me out at a mine in a town neither Patrick nor I have ever heard of, where I can easily get an auto to Lubero and thence to the main road, he says. But of course he really knows little about it, whether it is far or near on that auto road, and I'm trying without much success to discover more from other people. This broad band of uncultivated forest scares most of them into staying at home and peddling back and forth on the more populous trails. I begin to feel rather like an explorer, and I'm glad Asumani had that bright idea of missing all the bigger posts. I've no desire to go through the cities if it isn't necessary. So I've written a letter to Smet, who is at Akoa's village near Morot's cutting up two elephants he has just killed. If he has ever hunted over the river, he ought to know something.

I've fired Sabani. He was sick a long time, or pretending, and repeatedly refused to go to the hospital for it. At last he did, but turned down the medicine they offered him (Epsom salts, which he hates), and sent word next day that he was too sick to come to hospital. Following an old rule, we promptly forwarded a litter to carry him to the hospital where he was to be installed for the period of his illness. He objected. I can't have my own servants acting like that about Patrick's hospital, so I said, "If you refuse to be cured, I'll fire you."

"All right," he said stoutly.

"All right," I answered, and started to train Msaba. Sabani came yesterday to plead with me, but I wouldn't take him back, nor will I. I don't think he was really sick at all. He certainly wasn't yesterday.

Abdulla was in again today. He says he has ordered a hundred kilos of rice to be brought in from his *shamba* and I'll get it tomorrow. This will pay off his debt and then some, but it sounds too good to be true. I'm willing to bet dollars to doughnuts it isn't true. I'll be much surprised if I get enough food to make this trip. Besides that, he says he has a framework bed, light enough for one man to carry, and he will sell it to me. This transaction, too, must be in the past before I believe it. All my mats piled up together make a pretty good mattress.

Friday, November 20

What a row, and what business! People here all day saying goodbye, begging for tips, rushing up with letters and food and sympathy, etc. Matope in the last stages of excitement – I think he will be sick if this goes on. Trip scheduled for day after tomorrow – probably a trifle optimistic, that. It began with another row with Patrick, and this time it's up to him to make advances for peace. If he doesn't I shall leave without saying goodbye, and I shan't visit his friends in Urundi, and I'll leave him to his conscience.

I asked Patrick to tell me how much he wanted for the bed that he told me long ago I could buy when I left. I found out that he wouldn't sell the mattress. Since the bed itself is large, heavy, broken and expensive, I naturally objected and said it was off if I couldn't have the mattress. I grew angry and said that he could keep his bed, but that I hereby refused to cash a check he's been wanting the money for.

Yesterday Yuma's fortnightly shipment of eggs came in, and they were welcome. Patrick said, though, "I'm awfully ashamed. I hate to take advantage of them this way, and yet it's the only way to get food so long as the white men on the road keep snatching it. But you won't let me have any money."

"No, I won't," I said promptly. "You won't let me have a mattress."

"Then you can't have any eggs. Not one egg will I give you."

"They're not *your* eggs," I pointed out. "Vandevelde has them send fifteen each a week; fifteen for you, fifteen for me."

"You shan't have one egg," he repeated.

"All right," I said. "If you mean it ..."

"I mean it."

"I shall go to Morot's and wait there for the rice, and I'll tell him why, too. I shan't eat anything here again."

"Good. Then I'll be saving butter and sugar and lots of things."

White hot mad, I wrote Saidi for ten porters for next day (it was too late to get them yesterday) and went back to my house and packed. Msaba and Koto's brother, who has just asked for work – his name is Ambena; I'm always glad to have a Mobudu – helped me, and it was a terrific job to collect everything after eight months of spreading it about. I didn't say anything to anyone, but Patrick seems to have told the cook in a loud voice that I wasn't to eat there any more, and a moment later lots of his people came down to see what was afoot. The Zamu was worried; he had guessed something was afoot. "What is it, Madame? Why are you going?"

"Nothing. Just that I'm mad at the Doctor and he's mad at me."

He shook his head and spoke with tears in his voice, an old man's voice. ... "It's bad to get angry. Don't get angry. It's better to laugh, to laugh." He wandered off muttering, "To laugh, Madame; that's better."

But I didn't want to laugh. I wanted to cry, though I didn't. Too many people were watching. Everything was packed by one o'clock, and I was tired and hungry. There was, of course, nothing to eat. It's all at Patrick's. Msaba managed to buy a bowl of rice and cooked me some. Two of Patrick's men came and offered to sell chickens, in the nicest way. I bought them both. I'll need at least four for the road.

I had given up hope of Abdulla's rice which he had promised, but he came again to say that it was arriving at his house, one hundred kilograms, and he'd send it up – also he would be responsible for my porters if Saidi made trouble. (Aha! Politics!) All of Patrick's bush boys came back to stand around and look sad. I planned to buy the necessaries, such as cooking oil of some sort and kerosene, from Morot, but now that the rice had actually arrived, I decided to go straight to Lubero as soon as Smet's letter with information should arrive, sending a man to Morot's.

Abdulla waked me this morning at some impossibly early hour with seventy-eight kilos of rice. Good rice, too. I could hardly believe my luck, or rather his honesty. It's enough for all my people for four days in the poverty-stricken forest, and I can go now, so far as the porters are concerned. He promises another twenty, but even if it doesn't come I don't care now. I've enough. Then a couple of Patrick's men came to ask me to take them with me. They were florid and obvious, saying that they were afraid to stay here without me. I laughed at them and said that I knew why they wanted to work for me; because I was a woman and a fool and wouldn't make them work hard. They laughed too and went away. One of them, though, sold me two eggs. I've just bought a huge fish and a bowl of salt, at the regular market price, too. They're becoming remarkably decent. Sombe or some other sort of spinach is always easy to get. I shan't starve!

A *planton* suddenly appeared with a letter from Vandevelde. I started to read it, most interesting news it was, when I heard a noise and looked up to see a skinny naked man writhing on the ground, coughing up spittle. "What's that?" I asked. The *planton* said, "It's a man who wanted to kill me on the road. His chest is sick. Look what he did to my shirt; he wouldn't sell me food. I had to hit him, and so he's followed me."

I called my men quickly and took him to hospital. Patrick fixed him up and scolded the *planton* – not severely, because it's a Government affair and he mustn't make politics – but to me he had nothing to say, so I came back and read the letter. Vandevelde is coming today to Kayumba's to do old court cases over again, those that were badly judged in the last year (a man can always appeal a judgment) and though he can't afford the time to come here, he wants me to come if at all possible to say good-by. Well, I don't want to because there's too much to do here. But I sent Ambena with an emergency call for what I need in the way of flour, kerosene, and oil, and asked him please to get all the information he could of the road, etc., and to tell me where I could get relay porters. If he has no supplies with himself, to send my boy on to Morot. I explained all the rest by saying that he well knew my bad temper, and that I was quarreling with Patrick about things. I didn't take advantage of his offer of a soldier to go along with me; I don't want one. He would only knock everybody about and cause trouble.

☉

LATER ... AMBENA HAS JUST COME IN with a wonderful load of loot. A tin of butter, a tin of lard, tea, a bottle of kerosene, four candles, a bottle of honey, a whole tin of flour, and three tins of milk, two liquid and one powdered. Oh, and lots more matches. I can face the world with this. Behind him came a man carrying a native bed with Kayumba's compliments, and immediately behind him another native bed sent in a great hurry by Abdulla as soon as he saw the first one pass his house, I suppose. Abdulla's was more elegant, but Kayumba's came from farther off, and I sent back Abdulla's with my most polite compliments. Ambena had a letter, a nice one from Vandevelde apologizing for not sending more (oh, and there is a pan too, for eggs – I have two pots besides, one with a cover) and saying that he knew nothing of the road, but that of course it would be all right if I only took plenty of quinine.

CHAPTER 17

WHERE MY CARAVAN ....

Monday, November 23, 1931

SALUMA'S VILLAGE ON THE GREAT EXODUS TRIP, first night out. The war is finished. My proud spirit softened after all those things to eat arrived; when I saw I was independent of Patrick, I wasn't mad at him any more. I had sent a note – "Doctor, the hospital. Dear Sir: Since I don't need anything any more, I should be pleased if you would let me cash your check. Sincerely, etc."

An answer came promptly: "Madame, before accepting your kind offer, I must beg for time to reconsider my financial position. I should be greatly pleased to have your company at whatever meal I share with the approaching white man. Believe, etc."

I had heard nothing of a white man. When he arrived, however, he turned out to be the director of the mines near Wamba; I had lunch at his house once. So we all ate together in amity, and I planned to start out yesterday at the same time he did, though he went another way. Of course, I didn't. Patrick had to review all my porters, sixteen, to give them medical certificates, and while he was doing it, an awful rain started up and lasted all day, so I put it off with a great deal of relief. This morning, however, all went quite smoothly. We crossed the Ituri in Patrick's boat, making three trips of it, while he, himself, showed off to the assembled multitude by going out in a tiny rotten *pirogue*, with a spear as a paddle. Everyone was most admiring at his daring, especially when he crossed the river like that. But on the other side, just as we had embarked on our last trip, he got involved in a bush and a bit of rapid water and was swept downstream a little. We had to follow him and give up one of our paddles, and then we were swept downstream, and altogether we were quite late in getting started.

Of course, if Patrick hadn't done something like that boat trick at the last moment, it wouldn't have been Patrick. Therefore, I curbed my temper and devoted my energies to controlling my tears when I said good-by to everyone. Patrick made a nice speech that I was too embarrassed to listen to, something about how he had never seen anyone with so many natives about to say good-by, and how I would be long remembered and my going would leave a void, etc., etc. So I said I would come back just as soon as I had enough money, which is a doubtful period, and off we went.[1]

The first day of a trip is always pretty straggly, I guess, and we've made no attempt to reach Pumba's, which is the regular first march. We're a little more than half way, having stopped here at the village of one of Kayumba's men. I think we'll be able to get bananas here, as they're brothers of Msaba and not terribly poverty stricken. I had to chase all the porters out of all the villages, Banguana villages, that we passed; not that they were deserting, but they feel as if they'll be gone for years and must say good-by to everyone for hours and hours. I hope we can get bananas, thus saving the rice for one more day in the future.

No one knows anything at all about the road except that people do go to Lubero. I've given up the other shorter road idea; if it is a

---

[1] The usual pattern of safari travel in Equatorial Africa was dictated by the reality that it was too hot to walk comfortably in the mid-day sun ("Mad dogs and Englishmen go out in the noon-day sun." as the Noel Coward song points out.) It was customary for travelers to set out an hour or two before sunrise and to walk until about 11 a.m., when everyone stopped for lunch and a rest period that lasted until mid-afternoon. At that point, the journey would continue until late afternoon. The sun and heat were less of a concern in the shade of the Ituri Forest, through which Hahn was trekking; however, she and her bearers followed the usual practices out of habit.

mining town, that means restricted land and a lot of red tape. We'll go slowly and pleasantly, I hope – so far all is well – and see what we shall see. Everybody here ran away the minute they heard us coming, but they're come back now, and I'm installed in a tiny *barza* with a mud wall. They speak Kindaka; tomorrow we'll hear Kiballi, they tell me.

The thing I regret most is that I left just as Patrick had acquired a pygmy for himself. I think it's his all right, for I asked the other day, "Whose pygmy is that?" and Andekai said, "Oh, that's the Doctor's." He came to hospital, very feeble and thin, and said that his brothers had deserted him on the road but that his wife had stayed by him and told him to come to the Doctor, who knew all medicine. He said that he was finished with his brothers, absolutely. Patrick has installed him in the old cookhouse with his child, a little boy, and is hoping that his wife will come to see him and decide to stay too. It would be wonderful to have one. If he lives, I think he'll stay. The child stood in odd corners, and stared at me, running away if I look at him, so I don't. Yesterday, though, he came up and talked to me and looked at pictures in my book and smiled. They talk like most of the pygmies that I know, with an unmistakable pygmy brogue. As Patrick says, you could tell it was a pygmy talking with your eyes closed. They talk slowly, painfully, with a drawl. I think if a dog should suddenly find speech, it would talk like that. But then Kingwana is a foreign language for most of them; they speak other languages – Kibuddu or Kiballi or whatever language is used by the towns where they hang out and beg for bananas. I feel very sad and lonely. I'm glad Matope is with me, and that it isn't raining this first day of the last great adventure.

Tuesday, November 24

Pumba's village in a heavy rain. How they hate to walk in it! They would rather sit and starve than get wet. If it's raining tomorrow morning I shall have to speak roughly to the *capita* of the porters, who is, of course, the laziest and least powerful of the lot. He carries nothing, having just enough authority to palm off the lantern, which has been allotted to him, on someone else who is already loaded. However, the women go on walking and working just the same, I've noticed.

We got enough bananas yesterday, and two legs of a deer that were turned up at the last-minute after they had sworn there was no meat in the village; the porters wanted me to let them loose to hunt for it, but I've no right to do a thing like that. Bananas, yes, but meat's another thing. It's no use, as I told the *capita* afterward, to pretend that these men are in the habit of eating meat every day. Anyway, the old chap in charge was bribed by a tip, and the meat arrived. All the people came back and went about their business, and when I went walking that evening, no children ran shrieking from my path. Msaba scolded me for paying too much and maybe he's right, but his own suggestions are ridiculous. We must strike a medium.

This is a Babili village, like that one of Njoka's on the way to Mambasa, and they send posho to the Mambasa road. In fact, I met a couple of old friends. This must be a big chief (of course he's not at home) for it is a big, clean, rich-looking village in spite of the fact that they are dying of hunger when I delicately broach the question of food. There is, he practically admitted, plenty of corn, which I hope will turn up. Some of the houses are painted in red and blue stripes and designs; on one of them I see a very handsome horse. Horses? There are none here, I believe. I have the house of one of the chief's brothers, a place more comfortable than most rest houses I've slept in. The courtyard is enclosed like a Mexican's place, and there is a window in the inner room. Also, I can walk quite four steps without stooping, which is nice as after a little while in the usual huts I begin to feel hunchbacked.

It's a big difference between this place and the villages I've passed through near the big roads. I hope I see more of them. We will have a long walk tomorrow to the next place, without even a homestead in between. That's fine in case we have any rain, for the minute my people see a roof, they huddle under it and almost refuse to come out. In fact, it's no good giving them orders altogether. If you say, "Porters, run along," no one moves. You must look at the first one and say, "You, take your pack and go," and he runs like a rabbit. After the first one has broken the spell, they are easier to budge. One of my men has acted sick ever since we first started, though Patrick pronounced him whole and strong. I insist on having them all in front of me, but I almost step on his heels. Maybe Patrick was wrong? The other men, of course, say it's only laziness. If it is, he'll be all right after tomorrow, because he'll be a long way from home and anxious to finish his job.

Last night, I discovered that my *kalagba*[2] is more comfortable than my bed was and for some mysterious reason, it seems bigger. Matope shared it with me and I didn't even notice. There was such a throng of cooking women, chattering children, and gossiping people about that I felt as if I were sleeping in a farmyard, but it all calmed down in time. I carefully asked if the circumcision ceremonies were over for the time being, because if they aren't it is very bad luck to blow an ivory horn, and that's what I have to signal the porters in the morning. They were just over, so we could go ahead. A high pole stood in the village square, topped with a straw effigy of a foreskin; this was a remnant of the last ceremony. Here at Pumba's they don't circumcise, so we're all right. Hope to get some real rest tonight.

Wednesday, November 25

Durunga's village, where the *capita* is not, for some odd reason, Durunga, but his brother Isumi. Durunga came out to meet me on a road sloppier than anything I have seen in Africa, always excepting that historic march to Mambasa. I greeted him with great dignity and set off again with my head in the air, suddenly slipped and sprawled full-length in a mud-puddle. He didn't even laugh at me. The road

---

2 This word does not appear in the *Oxford English Dictionary* or any of the generally available French, Portuguese, or Swahili dictionaries. It appears to be a local word – possibly Kingwana, a Swahili dialect that is a spoken language of the Congo – for a kind of bed that was carried from place to place.

was met half-way by another one leading to Kayumba's, and it's the *posho* carriers who have cut it up so. I had hardly arrived and got sat down on the *barza* of a splendid big house with carved doors when news came that Yowly himself, the chief whose village I will visit tomorrow, was close on my heels on his way back from Kayumba's gathering. I was glad to see him and almost had an attack of inferiority complex, owing to the fact that he was riding in a *tipoye* and was not nearly so muddy as I was.

It is Yowly's subvillage here, and Yowly's house. He was a perfect host for the short time he was here, and the way he ordered everyone around was a revelation to me. He got the house opened, swept, and garnished and decorated with at least three regimes of bananas before he bowed his way from my august, if spotty, presence, leaving behind him orders for five more regimes and a whispered word in my ear that there are really no eggs to be had. Also, we are going to stay there two days to rest the porters' weary bones, and then he will send food for the next day along with us, as it's a small village of his own in the forest where we will have to stop. Beyond there, he says cheerfully, he knows absolutely nothing. This is better than the woman who filled the porters' ears last night with bad news of the road until they begged me to try to get more men at a central village.

We had to eke out with rice again last night; that finishes one basket and encroaches on another. Just now, I see six good regimes here, and I have some hope. The small flies have followed us here, but the village is nothing like as sad and dirty as last night's stand.

We had a bad time this morning getting off when one of the biggest porters with one of the lightest loads refused to carry my chickens, on the grounds that I've bought two more since the expedition started. For the moment, the *capita* swallowed his pride and carried them, but the three of us – he and Msaba and I – conferred on the road, and this afternoon in Yowly's presence, mainly because he wouldn't go away, I made a short speech to this effect: that the *capita's* word was my word ("Applesauce!" said the audience silently) and that he was with me to save me the trouble of settling squabbles. Therefore, they must obey him unless he became too outrageous, in which case there I was to settle things. All of this still seems audacious to me; I can't get it through my head that a large lumbering crew of males are really so cowed that I can get bossy with impunity. It wouldn't surprise me a bit if something happened. But of course it won't. They're really that way. They might run away but that's as far as it could go. I added that the man who had refused to carry my chickens would be fined, and hereafter anyone who refused would also be fined. A second offense would be reported to Headquarters (I don't know just where, but that's all right). A third one, I said to myself but not aloud, would mean a whipping, but it won't come to that. The one who had refused almost burst into tears and said he would be good if I would revoke the fine, and when the *capita* said it would be all right, I did. But, I said in a schoolmistressy way, he must certainly carry them tomorrow without a murmur.

Everyone promised to do his work silently and efficaciously hereafter, and I pretended to believe it, and that was that.

Excellent news from Yowly. He confirms the rumor that they're closing down on all the camps except the one near Adinotta's, and lots of men have already returned to their villages. Six months' respite, Vandevelde says, to grow more bananas. As for Yowly, he has even more respite, because after this he can make banana flour at home and send it on instead of gutting his village every week for carriers of the raw bananas. Even farther back, he says, they've been taxed – so far that the bananas rotted on the road. Himself he's been sending fifty-five people every week, and it's a five days' trip to the camp, another five back. So he sends a hundred and ten altogether, almost always on the road. That's just for carrying; that doesn't include the people who work the plantations or the heavy toll of his own men who work on the road itself.

Thursday, November 26

Sadalla's village. This is *not* the same Sadalla that we visited on that hunting trip on October 27; it's a village of Banguana, who stayed behind when the rest traveled to Penge by this road, years ago. Of course, there are not many people about; the road shows how little traffic goes on between the two places. We were lost in a sea of leaves most of the time, or stumbling through clear spaces floored with broken trees, traces of elephants. Not even the vestige of a deserted village all the way – and a long way, too. We crossed two considerable-sized rivers. The second was so high it had washed away the tree that spanned it, and we crossed by wading, with a rope to hold on to held out by a few hardy souls who went on ahead. I took off my boots to do it, but caught myself in a swamp later on that soaked them just the same. It was muddy underfoot, but we had no rain.

If it hadn't been orthodox forest, I'd have minded the heat, but as it was, the only drawback was the swarm of flies that accompanied us from the second river; I was covered with little blood spots in a few minutes, and in a very bad temper. To cap it, when we did reach the Lenda and shouted for a boat, the people on the other side ignored us. They didn't believe a white person was there at all; it was a trick, they thought, of a few Basenge who wanted a quick crossing. Therefore, they went about their business for more than an hour, while I crouched over a smoking fire trying to get rid of the flies. The water was high and strong and I doubted that they would come at all. At last, two men arrived, fighting for every inch of the way, in a big boat that nevertheless made three trips to carry us over, with the crew augmented by Msaba, who knows the water extraordinarily well. A good boy to have in a pinch. I didn't know what was a good boy, before I got him. Of course he can't make a bed yet, and his cooking is nothing extra, but he can paddle and fight for food and talk to most of the people in their own language, and he holds his own with the Banguana. I heard him replying to their taunts about Basenge: "Look here; for two nights we've slept in the towns of my brothers, and you've had food

– haven't you? We'll see if any food arrived at this Banguana place tonight, and if it does you can tease me tomorrow." So say I.

Three venerable gentlemen carrying salt arrived last night and said they were Abdulla's men, going with me to Lubero to buy sheep for him. The *capita* here is an old patient of Patrick's, and seeing as they're all brothers together, they ought to get along as to food. I had to give out half a kilo of rice to each man last night, the banana supply was so small. However, we draw near the end of the dangerous section, and so far they've even had meat with their stuff.

Friday, November 27

Yowly's village and house. I wish the *capitas* weren't so terribly polite; I should like a few moments now and then, when I could relax and be impolite all by myself. However, he does very well by me and I should-n't complain. We had too many bananas yesterday, actually, just because he had ordered it thus – thirteen régimes, and we need only eight good ones. Today we have plenty again, and meat. I myself will have filet of dwarf antelope! However, I'm not ashamed here; he has a well-fed town and lots of pygmies. I've just given him a big cup of flour, and since we're staying tomorrow I'll give him a necktie too.

It was a beautiful road today, with hills and near here a big water-hole full of buffalo tracks. Isumi yesterday complained that he would soon have to move his village to get away from the elephants, which were a pest in the plantations.

I have very stupidly scratched my leg and developed a small ulcer again near the ankle. Hope I can stop it with iodoform and potassium permanganate. I've nothing stronger.

Angélique acted like a devil last night, and I nearly killed her with the *chicotte*, with no effect. I tied her to one of my boxes and she man-aged to open it and ravaged the medicine supply, ending by biting a large hole in my one tube of toothpaste. I whipped her and locked the box, whereupon as soon as the lamp was extinguished she tried to open it, with a great rattling of tin. I got up and whipped her again, very hard, and she wept dolefully and settled down to sleep. As soon as the lamp was out, she started again. When I yelled at her, she barked and was quiet a while, but soon she began all over, and I had to get up and practically bounce her all over the floor, until we were both tired out and went to sleep.

She is learning, though, to walk on the ground without having to be pried off my leg every other step – a most irritating proceeding. She runs along ahead of me or just behind, in little dashes and hopeful stops, like a dog. If we come to a trail of driver ants, she stands not on ceremony, but leaps upon me, usually carrying a half-dozen with her.

They say now that I may be able to get fresh porters at Kanyama's, four marches from here. I think, though, that we'll be so near Lubero by that time – five marches, I believe, though no one can tell me – that the boys will decide to go along and call for Patrick's potatoes at the Mission there. The march after next, Msaba says gloomily, is nothing but a pygmy path, and he expects I will die of fatigue. Maybe so. But no one really knows anything. We still have almost three baskets of rice in case there's no food in the forest, but I'm beginning to be sanguine about the posho question. After this next march, we will be in Kanyama's territory, Babili people. Clothes washing tomorrow, and bread baking and all sorts of things. I was distinctly glad to get sweet bananas today; I didn't know how tired I was of just chicken and rice. I've been eating more or less as a duty. But that was true of the last few months of Penge. To think that we used to eat just for fun in America!

Sunday, November 29

At Masenge's, the other side, of what? Of the Forest, the real article and of a high hill. We slept the night after Yowly's at a little one-man stand in the forest, a tiny two-house clearing. Here we encountered a Government clerk, a black one, in a very sad state. He had come from Lubero on his way to Avakubi, and his porters had run away the other side, leaving pygmies to get him through. But they, too, dumped his loads at this place and escaped. I am surprised they saw him that far. He was in a fix, all right – six heavy loads and two very young squalling little girls, in the charge of his sister, a big fat woman with no ideas of cleanliness. Yowly had refused to send porters – no one loves a clerk – but the men who accompanied us with the day's food took his stuff back with them, and Yowly will have to give him porters once he's on the land. He said he was dying of hunger, but they had an enormous hamper of chickens, so I didn't take it too seriously. I asked for news of the road and all he could say was that there was mud up to the waist and the road through the forest was only elephant tracks. He dramatically pulled out a pair of old papery shoes to show me how they had worn out. "I threw away two more pairs like that," he said.

"Well, why don't you go barefoot?" I asked.

"A little more, and I will."

It took a long time to get his mind off the last day's walk, but at last I did and he admitted that back of the Forest it was good going. To Lubero from Kanyama's he said was sixteen days. In my astonishment, I called him a liar. However, it seems that another white man's town, Motokolia, is the one all the Banguana call Lubero on our side, and that's about six days from Kanyama's, which tallies with the other reports. About twenty white people he said, and lots of automobiles of the mining company there. Meantime, his sister had finished and they were ready to go. He asked for quinine "for dysentery" but he had to be satisfied with Epsom salts and the assurance that he would find a hospital at Kayumba's. The lady presented me with a chicken and begged for a hat for one of the children. She was satisfied with salt. What would I be doing with a child's hat?

I grabbed a man from this place – the only one there except for Yowly's doddering uncle – to go ahead of us and cut creepers next day. He was a huge idiotic-looking, but pleasant, Mondaka who had lately been released from the road and gone completely back to Nature and the bark cloth. His name was Alubé, but he had probably started out as Albert. Meantime, the porter and I had a long fireside conversation about the wicked Babili who would desert a man in the forest, as the clerk's porters had done. They all protested their love and fidelity for me – mostly, they said, because they'd been so well fed. This burst of good feeling on the eve of the real long pull made me suspicious; I fully expected to find an empty camp in the morning, but no. We started out full strong.

It was a hell of a day. The clerk was right; there was no road. There was a maze of elephant tracks, and only Alubé kept us from getting lost too often. We went deeper and deeper; after we crossed one big river we got into the deepest forest of all. We skirted two big *idos* – waterholes – with tracks of every sort. I was so interested in it all that I forgot I was getting tired, until rain threatened and I began to think it was getting toward evening. Once Ambena and I got lost completely; intercepting a battlefield of red ants, we forgot to watch the tracks of the others and found ourselves up a blind alley. We had to go back through the ants. Toward the end of the forest trail, we crossed a huge, perfectly round plot of ground where the trees were very tall and there was no underbrush on the hard leaf-covered ground. It was very quiet. They said it was a dancing ground of the animals, where they all met.

We came out at last in a deserted plantation, and we crossed a clearing where once there had been houses. Then we fetched up in another one, and Alubé said that he was lost. He hadn't been through the forest for three years and the first clearing had been a village then; he had never been farther. I was so weary and so sorry for the porters that I was willing to camp there, but they weren't. One of them hunted around in back of us till he found the right path, and we went on, wearily stumbling over innumerable roots and creepers and fallen trees.

Then it rained! In torrents and floods and waterfalls. We hit a sandy place and followed the riverbed that we found there for a long way, and everyone was cold and scared for fear we should have to sleep in the open. I said to myself a dozen times, "We must stop somewhere. People. Don't go on walking forever."

Suddenly the path changed. It was so abrupt that it was almost like finding a warm inn and·sitting down. Someone had cleared it several feet on either side, and there were no more fallen logs except once in a great while. Even then, they were fixed with branches to cross over, and even handrails of a sort. There must have been men there recently; someone besides pygmies. We walked faster in the rain.

Even this went on for what seemed like hours, but all of a sudden, going down a hill, we found ourselves there in the village, with a surprised *capita* staring at us and the women and children scuttling for cover. It was ecstasy to sit down; even more to drink hot tea and relax. It was a dirty little place, but it seemed beautiful then. The *capita* seemed a weak sort of person; I asked for water and he ordered several people to bring it before he got it himself. I didn't bother about food, though; I ladled out rice to everyone, much to their satisfaction.

Wednesday, December 2

The country is changed. We're in hills now – crossed a big one today – and the soil is red laterite. Yesterday, I would have stepped square on a red snake (I don't know what color he was originally) if Msaba hadn't jerked me back and chopped off his head with a spear.

This village is on a hill, and the air is fresh, and I can see for a long way around, which state of things has its usual effect of making me light-headed with joy. This *capita* wouldn't believe a man who went ahead to say I was coming, and when he did actually see me his mouth dropped open.

Friday, December 4

Kanyama's, which is a sort of disappointment. It's a dead village. All the houses are decaying, and the few young people remaining are in seclusion for circumcision. The sultan is away in Lubero, and his house, which I ought to be sleeping in, is closed up until the spirit of the dead Kanyama shall depart, so I am in the tribunal shed, which is flimsy, but anyway airy. What has happened is that the village proper is moved off the main road, and very sensible of them too, except that of course in time that will become the main road and this path will be left to the forest. There is still food – bananas and rice, as yet unpounded, but the porters are willing to do that for themselves. They did very well yesterday, going into the woods and trapping themselves a small antelope. Then Faki went down to the river and caught an enormous fish. I bought some of it for my people, feeling somewhat annoyed that it arrived just too late for me to find room to eat it myself. For the hunting and the fishing, of course, they had to pay the village, and stiff prices too, I thought. But that's the custom and none of my affair anyway. They seem to be more superstitious in this part of the country than in mine. I can hardly take a step without bumping into some prejudice.

We came a rather short way, over two very high hills, or maybe there were more. We're slowly climbing, I think, for the air is decidedly fresher. This place is really clear of big trees and if we hadn't had clouds the last hour would have been more trying. I did a dumb stunt this morning anyway – woke up feeling seedy and suddenly remembered that I've forgotten quinine for four days! So I took a man-sized dose at breakfast and on the road my eyes went all fuzzy and my legs felt rubbery and my head hurt. My own silly fault, which was small comfort at the time. I'm almost recovered now. It will get more and more hilly from now on.

A great tribunal of the porters has just taken place, to the intense delight of the town people. I sent back the man with the sore this morning, with Ambena. The others have decided to go to Motokolia with no more fuss, since we're only five or six days off. But we've finished two baskets of rice and that leaves one porter theoretically to carry Matope. The porter who ought to do it is a healthy specimen and for two days when Ambena did the Matope job, he carried nothing but a camp chair. I noticed it vaguely, but didn't register it. The reason is, he's a brother-in-law of the captain, and Omali, who has had to take up the burden of the kitchen box (or one half of it) was enraged at this favoritism; I think with reason. However, he shouldn't have done what he did this morning, to wait till I was gone and then indignantly spurn those damned chickens again. So I held court just now to settle it all.

I noticed that the poor old man who carries the bed is getting weak, but since he is nobody's friend and probably someone's slave, he says little about it, coming in hours behind everyone. Now, the bed is the lightest load of the lot, but in the forest it was awfully hard to carry in the leaves and underbrush, and he asked for medicine for his back every day, though naturally I have nothing. So I had the bright idea of giving the captain's brother the bed and letting the old man carry Matope; that work grows less and less as Matope is beginning to get strong and to walk far. Well, the captain's brother started to raise hell, and he refused. So I said to go back to Penge without pay. All right, he said, all RIGHT. But I knew it was bluff. Then for the stubborn Omali, we started in and things began to happen.

I paid each man who accompanied us from the last village, one with the rice, one with the chickens – I paid them each a franc and said I would cut two from his pay. He exclaimed and rowed and said that his spirit had done wrong because of Alifani – that's the captain's brother. Alifani started to yell at him; the captain joined in and everyone took sides. I shrieked "Order!" to no avail. At last, I gave the high sign to several bystanders and the two sides were pulled apart. I laid the longest chicotte across my knees and conducted the rest of the court in more or less order, though I had hard work to keep from laughing.

Final result: Omali is fined not two, but one franc (because, I said, the captain had indeed showed favoritism and I understood how his spirit would rebel). The captain is admonished and takes it cheerfully, though protesting that it's all a mistake. Alifani, who persisted in refusing to save his face, was taken outdoors by his big brother and talked to. He will carry the bed, he said later, *sotto voce*. The only really satisfied person is the original bed porter, but the rest are at least halfway settled down. Then I shooed them all out and took a bath. What worries me for the future is that day after tomorrow we will probably eat up another basket of rice, and oh, dear, what shall I do with that porter? If he goes empty, there will be trouble. If he is sent home, the other rice men, now carrying new loads, will raise hell. Besides, he'll refuse to go home all alone and unaccompanied in a strange land. If I give him those chickens? I might even pack up a good heavy rock and hand it over, just to keep the balance. Still, it'll be only three days more and my ears may last it out.

Saturday, December 5

Azazi's *tongo*, abandoned village, where we are sleeping two nights. We decided yesterday to do it when we saw that there is food here and that the men lagged on the road, but we would have done it anyway at sight of the weather today: rainy and cold. I dreamed about snow last night, and my feet were icy. What the men really wanted was to stay yesterday at Kanyama's, liking it exceedingly for some reason, but I was very cruel and said that four days on the road didn't merit a rest. Msaba was on their side, but I insisted on at least five days' travel at a time, if the marches weren't any longer than they have been. What really worries the boys is this hilly country; they've never encountered anything like it and they're stiff; whereas I would rather tire myself out in half-an-hour on a hill than attain the same fatigue in a day of swamp. Moreover, I was selfishly dissatisfied with the shed, which was cold and noisy, owing to the goats which began before dawn to eat the banana leaves they had used to close the worst gaps in the wall. So we started.

A *capita* from a village farther along the road had done a very surprising thing when he heard of my arrival; he had hastily gathered six regimes of bananas and hurried to meet us at Kanyama's, with four good eggs besides. He was full of apologies for not having been there, but then I hadn't sent word, he said aggrievedly. I didn't need the bananas, but we stopped at his place for a while yesterday and looked around. At Kanyama's I saw for the first time a type of house that grows more and more common; it looks almost exactly like a Navajo Hogan, but is better made, with no hole in the peaked roof. The entrance to the place is the same. That is, the shape of the affair is the same, but the Navajos use logs, and these are made of leaves and withes. It must be awfully smoky inside. There were several at this man's village, and lots of imperturbably naked people weaving fish-traps and mats.

It was still a long way; much longer than they had said. Three hills to cross from this village, the woman said – little hills. They turned out to be good healthy ones, and seven of them. We wouldn't have arrived here much before twelve in good weather, and, as it was, a furious rain overtook us halfway. This made the downhill going very slippery and slow. Porters fell in all directions and slid down after their packs. On the hilltops, the wind was so strong that I had to put my head down and push against it; a branch fell dangerously near and farther back, a falling tree just missed a porter. I was drenched to the skin – no great affair, as I have never used the underwear I so care-fully bought in London – and we were all miserable when we pulled into this place.

A few young men were sitting around a fire in the *barza*, and sur-prised and annoyed to see us. Some religious affair was evidently going on, for they were painted up with yellow clay. These young people and their families were all that remained of the population in this *tonga*, this village. The others had gone on ahead to the village where we'll sleep tomorrow. But the plantations remain, full of food that can be had for the gathering. It grows more and more difficult to find a house with any room big enough to get my bed in, but we did find one. It has its drawbacks – we are on the peak of a hill; this house has a very slanting floor and I keep sliding down in my sleep – but in one tiny room the bed will just squeeze in, though I have to crawl in over its head, practically. It's awfully dirty, but I'm getting used to everything. My men say disgustedly that all the places are filthy and that these bushmen live like goats. But the roof is still watertight at any rate.

The boxes arrived very slowly, and the old man who has just been liberated from his load dragged in so sick and miserable that everyone – town boys, porters, and all – showed an unusual amount of concern and pity in making room by the fire and settling him down comfortably. I changed as soon as possible and found that my money belt, with all my worldly wealth in banknotes, was sopping wet. We tried to dry the notes one by one at the fire, but a couple almost burned up and we decided to wait till fair weather. That arrived at last.

At the same time, a house at the end of the row fell down with a great crash and a drum began to beat, and Matope came running in a frenzy of alarm to drag me indoors with several of the men, who closed the door tight and looked frightened. It was a magic dance on which women and children must not look, and my more sophisticated Banguana were equally reluctant to see it. Faki, who is more of a Mokumu than a Monguana anyway, refused to be impressed. He said they had the same thing among the Bakumu, and the language is almost the same. Matope is half-Mokumu, too, and speaks the language, I have discovered, but he is still uncircumcised and a child, and he was afraid. He cried out when Faki danced a few steps and sang. Outside the door, someone was walking or dancing up and down, beating a drum with a little woodeny sound and now and then singing. I crouched uncomfortably in the smoke from the cooking fire. Msaba whispered that if I saw any devils fleeing into the wood, I must tell him. I didn't, though.

When at last it was over, we opened the door and went out in time to see the young men running briskly down the hill with their hunting nets and a few big dogs barking joyfully at their heels. Life settled down again.

We spread out the money on mats in front of the house and it dried quickly, but not before everyone had come to stare at it and to make remarks about how rich the white men are. A contingent of people from another village came to visit, with a pygmy proudly carrying a fresh elephant tail. The hunting people came back at dusk without any game, and Angélique tried to fight with the dogs. Matope stayed up very late, sitting at the fire with the men and listening to their stories until he fell asleep and had to be sent home to me.

Monday, December 7

Roosa's place on the other side of the Lenda. It is a very small but neat village with almost no one in it, which somehow seems to make little difference, for one woman here is doing the work of any five men in the other places. She swept the house by herself, and it is a big one and needed a lot of sweeping. She went and brought the wood. She went back and got the water. When I asked for *sombé*, which has been refused me for the last three stops, she went and brought plenty and the manioc with it. Unasked, she brought two eggs – it's been so long since I had any eggs except in bread that I have forgotten the taste of them. Then she scoured the already-scoured plantation and got half a regime of bananas and a large supply of manioc, apologizing for the poor offering. Even my men have noticed, and are loud in her praises. No one else, they say, shall get any of their money. "Oh, I'll take it," she says cheerfully, and laughs till all her filed teeth show.

We were on the road a long time going to Azazi's new village, and found it indeed new. The roofs weren't yet on most of the houses. However, old Azazi lived up to the reputation his daughter had given him at the tongo farther back when she talked to me; he "knew the ways of white men," and talked to me far into the evening about how he had gone with one of the "white men of the Francs" (mining men) all over the countryside, long ago when there was still no impot tax to pay. Everyone rapturously greeted the salt-selling men and bought a lot of the stuff. I was given a brand new, perfectly square and diminutive house, which was nevertheless cut up into three divisions, and it was a struggle to get the bed in. There was a pointed roof to it like the roofs of the villages in fairy tales, but its quaintness didn't compensate for the cold, which gave me a miserable night. It gets colder and colder. We had stopped at a cleared hilltop on the way where one man and his family were making a plantation, and it was so clear that for the first time on the trip I could look around at where we had come. Far off to the west there was a row of hills, so far off they were blue. Between that series and one we were crossing was a sea of blue-green trees, and we had crossed it all on our own feet. I was very proud.

We left early next day, believing the old man when he said we'd arrive at Andea's at one o'clock, for this itself was not a very cheerful prophecy and we had no suspicions. I began to get tired when at eleven, without stopping, we were still deep in the forest which gave no sign of finishing. It rained a little, and the atmosphere cleared. We complained bitterly, however, of the hills, which never let up. True enough, at one o'clock we saw a village – those of us who were in front, for the trail straggled out for miles. With glad cries, we struggled up the last neck-breaking, clay-covered hill and fell into the *barza*, only to find that our village was still an hour ahead. This was evidently just a small shooting-box sort of place, with a few young men and pygmies to receive us. If we wanted to stay, they said, why, of course. ... But the next village had better housing.

A man who was wearing clothes and who had queer sleepy eyes spoke up and said that it was his town, and he'd lead us there, just to prove that it wasn't so far after all. For Omali, our professional crab, kept declaring that all bushmen were liars and that we would probably reach that near village after dark. "Look at the hill we've got to cross!" he cried tragically, and it did look pretty mean. But the man with the sleepy eyes laughed and picked up his spear and said to me, "I'm going. Are you?"

Now, I had been thinking and looking around. It was a miserable little two-house place and the short rest had heartened me. "I'm coming along," I said, and did, undeterred by Msaba's warning that the porters might stay behind. Another man with a spear, a man from Lubero, also came. The three of us headed up that hill, and I was almost breathless, but suddenly the path turned and ran along the side of it. We came out of the forest, and I could see that it was really a mountain, and that if I fell it was an extremely long way down. Once we stopped at a village that was hanging on by sheer force of friction, but this was just to pass the time of day standing up, and off went my guide again. Once, I refused to walk a skinny log spanning a small valley and we worked our way through the brush at the bottom of it. I was ashamed, but it was no use trying – simply looking at it gave me vertigo. I was glad to hear later that the porters had done the same thing.

When the hilltop had sunk almost to our level, toward the end of it, we climbed over and started down the other side. It was rocks and that meant jumping and working with the arms and rather abrupt descents, at least till we were on a lower place, and I thought very pityingly of my tired men. But we couldn't stop to see; the sun was too hot. A distant roar of water came to my ears. "The Lenda," said the sleepy-eyed man. "My village is at the beach where you cross." And then a short walk through fields, and there we were.

It was still on a hilltop, and every wind that blew tried to knock down the houses. Therefore, the *barza*, which is usually a roof and nothing else, was here a beehive like the houses I've described, only there were three doors to it instead of one, and inside was cozy and smoke-blackened and yet airy. There was an old man sitting there, and more pygmies and young men.

I sat there two hours listening and now and then saying something, and after a time Msaba came in and almost dropped to the floor, and then the porters, one by one at long intervals, very crabby at first but little by little growing cheerful again as they caught their breath.

The hills really torture them. Nowadays I am always ahead. Well, I should be. It's my sort of country; not theirs. I don't carry anything, and I feel stronger and stronger in the cold air, whereas they moan and huddle and talk fearfully of the nights they must spend outdoors, where the villages are small. Nevertheless, I felt proud when I heard them boasting to the village people about how I was so strong, and had walked all the way, and never seemed to tire, and they said, "She is like a man."

It was so cold in the morning that they were most reluctant to start, and they were still tired anyway. Some of them didn't arrive till four. Then we had to cross the Lenda on foot, for there is no boat. The two boys with spears came along, one of them carrying Matope on his shoulders in the water. It wasn't too deep considering its width – not quite up to the hips – but the current was so strong that I thought we would all be knocked over in the middle of the stream. It was a very wide river, so wide that two of my men absolutely balked and had to be led, while some of the others made two trips and carried their loads. The *capita* babbled, "Aren't we good, Madame, we follow you everywhere, and – we can't swim. Bushmen would have dumped your loads and run for it. Oh, the cold! Oh, the wet! Oh, the strength of the water!"

"Yes, it's stronger than I thought, today," said the sleepy guide, "but nothing to yammer about. What's the matter with you Banguana?"

All in all, none of us were in a mood to do another double march. So regardless of the fact that we should have gone much farther today and reached Motokolia tomorrow, I called a halt at about eleven o'clock or even before, at this place which is the last village before a long stretch of forest that would have broken a few hearts, I think. This puts off our arrival for another day, or even more if anything happens. Do I mind? Well, no. In fact, I hate to see the trip end. Even at my most tired, when I think about the end, I don't like it. Whitemen at Motokolia, and suddenly all my people, even Msaba, will begin to salute when I give an order and to say "Yes, Madame," and nothing else. No more careless conversation in my presence; no more loud arguments of a morning. Only "Yes" and "No" and "Master, I'm dying of hunger."

Meantime, my appetite is growing ferociously; I seem to think of nothing but mealtime. And supplies are almost exhausted. I am almost definitely unsatisfied with the daily ration of chicken and rice, and nothing else.

Friday, December 11

Motokolia. We got here yesterday after two days of slow going, slow because I lingered and didn't chase the boys properly. We spent the night after the first march at Lukambo's, where the village was tucked between two hills and the houses were at crazy angles, and we got enough food to make out with half a basket of rice. Lukambo asked me to write a letter for him to present to the Administrator somewhere, in regard to a pygmy he says is his, but who gives all the produce of his elephant hunting to another man. I wrote it (and hoped the worthy Administrator would never find out who did it) and then some one else asked me to write another one, about two goats that somebody had owed him for years. It was a very long process involving old men who couldn't talk Kingwana, but who insisted on telling me every-thing anyway, and Lukambo had a passion for retailing the family tree of each man who had had anything to do with the goat transaction, which has evidently been dragging out for ten years.

Just at the end, as the sun was setting, a man from the other side of the transaction came rushing into my house demanding to be heard, evidently under the impression that I was settling the affair. It was all very noisy. They were at last put out, the whole crowd of them, and I ate my supper and went to bed.

We came to a white man's camp about three o'clock, just across the Lenda. He was at work, and I didn't dare send him word, so we pushed on. His boy handed me a few bananas (do I look that hungry?) and they comforted me in the rain which now pelted down hard on us.

It was all a slough of mud up to Halafu's, the camp. Here I got *posho* with no trouble, and the sun came out for a few minutes before bidding us goodnight. I lay awake a long time after dark, watching the people dancing in the firelight and feeling sad that the trip was ending.

DIARIES NEVER END, but I think this is as good a place as any to call a halt. After that, it wasn't so much fun.

I took almost four more months to reach the coast, and sailed at last from Dar-es-Salaam in a very dirty Italian boat, not nearly so good as the West Coast one. There was an Italian policeman and a Parsee lady, but I was on my way home, and I didn't have so good a time because of that. I met a lot of people on the way across East Africa, but they were all white people, and the things that happen to white people among themselves can really happen anywhere, in other books.

There are a few loose ends to gather up. Patrick has another homestead, just like the one at Penge, probably. Matope and Angélique accompanied each other back to him and arrived safely after quite a lot of stops on the way. Lately, I saw a cowboy suit and sent it to Matope, hoping he'll like it as much as I did. There was a checked shirt and chaps and a pistol in a holster and a big hat. The chiefs write to me sometimes. I sent Abdulla three evening gowns with veils to match for his three chief wives.

Angélique is dead. A leopard climbed the zenana wall at night and got her. I always felt in my bones that that would happen to her if I went away. I shall never forgive myself. Lately in New York, I saw a large baboon in a pet show who looked rather like her. I went up close to look at him, and he took the veil off my hat and ate it.

☺ ☺ ☺

City Girl Feels Safer Alone in Gorilla Wilds

"A BIG CROCODILE WAS BATHING ON MY BEACH"

"THE ONLY NATIVE WHO SAID ANYTHING OUT OF THE WAY TO ME HAD BEEN TO EUROPE"

Miss EMILY HAHN

PST!

EEA! AUK! LE

"I UNDERSTAND MONKEY TALK"

"A SNAKE GOT IN MY BED AND STUCK ITS TONGUE OUT AT ME"

Emily Hahn, 27, graduate mining engineer, believes an American woman can go anywhere in the world alone without molestation, if she conducts herself properly. Miss Hahn is just back in New York from a long stay in the pygmy country in Africa, where she was the only white woman; and is now preparing to go to the wilds of Indo-China. Some of her African impressions are pictured.

A composite Emily Hahn cartoon that appeared in a New York newspaper,
August 14, 1933.
Courtesy Emily Hahn Estate

The cartoon that appeared in one of the New York newspapers shortly after Hahn's return home provides ample insight into the popular conception of Africa in the "civilized world" in the 1930s.

One of Emily Hahn's favourite photos of herself, taken in the
New Yorker office, circa 1975.

AFTERWORD

As mentioned in her narrative, it took Emily Hahn another four
months to finally reach the east coast of Africa. Many years later, she
published journal passages describing her experiences that she had not
included in the *Congo Solo* manuscript. She made use of this material
in articles that were published in *The New Yorker* magazine and that
later appeared as chapters in her 1970 memoir, *Times and Places*.[1] That
book was reissued in a 2000 softcover edition with the title *No Hurry
to Get Home*.[2]

1 Thomas Y. Crowell Company, 1970. See "Pawpaw Pie," 161–78; "Christmas
  with the Walkers," 179–92; and, "Dar," 193–203.
2 Berkeley: Seal Press, 2000.

GLOSSARY

banki: Indian hemp, which is smoked like marijuana

barza: a word that seems to have had a dual meaning as a public meeting place and also a public meeting

Bwana: the Swahili word for "sir"

capita: a variation of the Portuguese word *capitão*, which means captain, leader, or commandant

chantier: a work or construction site

chicotte: *see* fimbu

fimbu: a long wooden-handled whip of hippopotamus leather, common in the Congo and in former Portuguese colonies in East Africa. Also known as a *chicotte*

gîte: a lodging, resting place

kalagba: a bed that was carried from place to place

kanzua: a long white cotton or linen robe that men wear in many areas of East Africa

infirmier: a male nurse, hospital attendant

liane: a type of woody tropical vine

manioc: a kind of tapioca pudding made from the roots of a tropical plant called cassava

melikani: a type of unbleached calico cloth

ménagère: a household, especially as it relates to a man's multiple wives or mistresses

mokanda: a message

molumba: a loincloth

pirogue: a flat-bottomed canoe made from a hollowed-out tree trunk

planton: a personal servant or attendant

posho: rations – usually rice – given to soldiers, sailors, labourers, and safari porters in lieu of pay in East Africa

raffia: soft and very durable hemp twine made from the leaves of the raffia palm tree

shamba: a plot of ground, also a farm or plantation

sombé: a dish of manioc leaves and goat meat in a hot sauce, popular in Central and East Africa

tipoye: a sheltered seat hung between two poles and carried by native porters

tongo: an abandoned village

Grace Flandreau's Impression of Patrick Putnam (1928)

GRACE FLANDRAU (1889–1971), AN AMERICAN journalist who traveled to the Belgian Congo in 1928, published an account of her experiences. Flandrau's book, *Then I Saw the Congo* (London: George G. Harrap and Company, 1929), is written as a conventional travel narrative and as such stands as a revealing counterpoint to Emily Hahn's writing in *Congo Solo*, which is highly personal. Flandrau also provides us with revealing glimpses into Patrick Putnam's life before Hahn visited him at Penge.

Flandrau was in the town of Buta when she encountered Putnam and two companions, whom she described as being "members of a scientific mission sent out by an American university [Harvard] to measure Bantu skulls and test the blood of Pygmies" (120).

Flandrau, like Hahn, was intrigued by Putnam and goes on to describe him in more detail when she writes,

One of [our] visitors, a young man who had grown an immense, curly beard and was the most charming and cultivated person, I particularly remember because he had the curious habit of eating ants – ate them, in fact, before coming to Africa, where, of course, grilled ants are a favourite native dish. American ants, he assured us, were much the better, and he said that he ate the African varieties only in order to test their relative merits. Also, this young man was very scornful of the so-called dangers of the tropics – scoffed at sun-helmets, quinine, boiled water, and even at elephants, which, although armed with a very light gun, he was planning to shoot. We wondered how long he would beat a game that has never been beaten, and many months later we learned. He had had malaria, had been wounded by an elephant, his wounds had become infected, and he had contracted a parasitical disease of the intestines. Then all news of him had failed, and his father had sailed to Africa to look for him. (121)

Back in the United States, when Flandrau was writing her book she wanted some information on the Mangbetu people of the Congo region, and so she looked up "Mr. P. T. [*sic*] Putnam ... of the Peabody Museum on Archæology and Ethnology," who had finally returned from Africa. "I hastened to inquire whether his researches included the Mangbetus and whether he had any new light to throw upon their history and culture," Flandrau writes. "Mr. Putnam replied that, although he had spent a short time among them, his investigations on this occasion did not cover the Mangbetus. He is now, however, preparing to return to the Congo under the auspices of the Peabody Museum for the purpose of studying this people" (283).

Putnam was not being truthful – in fact, he had spent more than fourteen weeks recovering from the injuries he had suffered when he was attacked and gored in an elephant-hunting misadventure.

Fictionalised Account of Putnam's Rage from the 1933 Edition of *Congo Solo*

WHAT FOLLOWS IS THE "INVENTED TEXT" that Emily Hahn inserted in the censored 1933 edition of *Congo Solo* (pp. 208–17) She made Patrick Putnam an Englishman and changed place names and other details that might have enabled readers to identify him as the individual relating the story of his jealous rage and its aftermath. That story is revealing for what it says about the state of race, gender, and the realities of life in the Belgian Congo, where the country's white colonial masters and their agents acted with virtual impunity.

Occasionally they are mere passers-by, of course. We fell in with one, an Englishman from South Africa, who insisted in a nice half-ironical way on sticking around and talking to me. I think whisky had something to do with it, but not all. He hinted that it was trouble of some sort that was making him jittery. "Need apron strings to hold on to for the moment," he said. "White apron strings. Mind?"

"Of course not. I'm always glad to help. But what the devil is the matter?"

He hesitated, then just grinned and waved his hand.

"One of the great epics of Africa," he said. "Heartbreakin' drama, you know, only no matter. Let's get another drink."

I liked him. It was easy to see that he didn't intend to whine about whatever was worrying him. But I couldn't hang round with him all day, as I had plenty of errands to do. However, that evening he found us again, and by this time he'd apparently swallowed enough more liquor to affect his decision about the great epic. He wanted to talk. It was strange but the drinks hadn't addled his speech except that he'd blaze away without seeming to realize that the names of his people didn't mean much to me, and I'd no idea what any of them looked like.

"Shouldn't tell this," he declared. He stared at me with a drunken smile, half uncertain, half stubborn. "But I want to."

"Go ahead," I said. "Cut the apologies. I'm collecting epics of Africa."

"First, you ought to know what happened, and then I'll tell you how I felt. First thing of all, of course you know what drives me so crazy is the way she lied. I've often told her that I understand sometimes a person isn't satisfied with one other person. I myself am not satisfied with only her. Why, I've been thinking of taking a Bandaka girl, myself. I've told her that if ever she wanted a vacation, to tell me and I'd send her home or somewhere till she felt like coming back. I wouldn't like it, but – I wanted to know. Well, this started when I went away to see about supplies.

"Two days after I got back, Pantalo told me I was neglecting Satuma. It seemed natural that she should; wives often do try to keep things peaceful in the harem. Of course, now I know it was because she wanted to be free for her man Kongolo. So that night I spent with Satuma, down in the *gîte* by the river, and about midnight we were waked up by a drive of red ants. You've never had that happen, so I'd better tell you first what it feels like. You don't know when you first wake up what it is; you feel as if little fires were burning all over your face. Then, if you have nowhere else to go, you light a fire and scatter charcoal around the floor: That gets rid of them. But since I had a perfectly good house to go to, I just said to Satuma, "Come along; we'll go home." I shall never understand why she didn't try to stop me.

264

She must have known. She didn't though; she just followed me without saying a word. I came up on the porch without making much noise, naturally, and threw the door open; as I did I saw someone jumping out the window. Even then I didn't think. I thought it was Pantolo being frightened; she told me there had been a leopard-man in the vicinity. So I called loudly, 'Don't be frightened, it's only us. There are ants in the *gîte*.' I can't even remember what I felt like when I heard her answer from the bed, 'Is it you, Bwana?'"

He stopped for a minute. All the time, his voice had been perfectly calm. It was calm now as he continued: carefully calm. He told me lots of details as if he wanted to get everything exact, even the tiniest things.

"I said to her, 'Who was the man with you?', and she wouldn't say. She refused to admit that there had been a man with her. I took her by the throat, and she said, 'Kongolo.' Why do you suppose she told me the truth right away? Frightened, I guess. I meant business. I made her get up and walk with me because I wanted to have her alone. She wouldn't tell me a thing. I strangled her over and over again – she has marks on her throat – and at last she said that it was the first time it had ever happened and that they hadn't even made love; Kongolo was only sleeping there. I lost hope of making her tell anything but lies that night, so I brought her back and tied her to a tree. Satuma had been lying in her bed, waiting, I guess, until I came back and wondering what was going to happen. All the while, perfectly calm and quiet. I shall never understand her; nor Pantolo, nor any of Them. I thought I did understand Them, and now – well, to go on. I was going to leave out my feelings until afterward, but I forget as I talk.

"I took her in the other direction, so as to keep them separated. I told her that Pantolo had admitted everything, and asked her what about herself. Yes, she said after a minute, she had a lover, too – Yusufu. I asked her when it had all begun with

Pantolo and she told a silly story of how she never knew about it except for one night she had an idea some one had been in the room, and when she asked Pantolo about it next day, Pantolo said yes, that it was Kongolo, and why didn't she take Yusufu ? So she did."

He looked at me hard. "Do you know, I believe even that. It would be a good stroke of policy on Pantolo's part, to get her little sister to keep quiet, too. Wouldn't it? I'll never know. I wanted to be perfectly calm and reasonable, and that night I was. I sent for Kongolo, who had been sleeping in his own bed, probably thinking he got out before I saw him, and I got Yusufu, too, and told them that if they had been my own men on my own payroll I would beat them or shoot them, but since they weren't, we would all go on just as if nothing had happened, so long as they did their work. Perfectly reasonable, you see."

"Oh, yes," I said, "perfectly reasonable. And then?"

"Then I told the women that I was through with them and what they did was their own business; they could go to the men's house if they wanted. So they did. It was almost morning. I had to go out next day, it being Monday. I thought and thought about it and at last, just about noon, I called Pantolo again. I had come to a decision. I said to her, 'You have three things to do: you must take your choice. You may marry Kongolo and live with him anywhere you want – here or at Wamba.' No, she said, she didn't want to, even though I told her she could have her things. Then I said, 'You may go home to your own village and take all your clothes with you. Only I shan't let you have the kid, because you have been giving her a bad example. I shall keep her, and when I go back to England, which will be soon now, I'll take her home myself to your village and give her to her grandmother.' She cried at that, because it is a disgrace, I fancy. I don't know. But then I said – because I'd been thinking that I wanted her anyway; I like her – I said, 'Or you can come back to me. But you must take twelve strokes of the *fimbu*, and shave your hair, and sleep in another bed till I call you back, and for six months I will buy you no more clothes, and we will rub out the blood pact we once made – because it seems to do no good; you lie anyway – and you must take a bath and throw water into the river, and I will burn this bed.' You understand that really the bed business meant nothing to me; it was to impress her. And she said, 'Well, I want to come back to you, and so I accept all of the punishments.'

"So I gave her twelve strokes, which she took bravely, though they were as hard as I could make them. I told her to stay in 'jail' in the room until the other things were settled. And then, I started to think about things, and as long as it had been – I don't really understand, not yet – for good, they said – so I took Yusufu out of the roll call and told all the men what I was going to do, and I had him beaten, twelve strokes."

"Poor Yusufu, did he cry?"

"No. Once he said to the man who was doing it, 'Can't you count?' because he was afraid of getting thirteen strokes instead of twelve. Then I tied Satuma's bed to him and made him walk naked through the village. I don't know if that really shamed him or not; I suppose it shamed the others, the ones who saw him, more. Then I said to him, 'If I see you or your brother again, when I get back, I'll shoot you. I don't care where you go, but if I see you here again I'll kill you.'

"Well, I came back next day as usual, and found that the houseboy had done something on his own account. The men had come back while I was gone, to get their clothes. They asked the boy for them, and to please me I guess he did something I shall always be sorry for. He said, 'Wait here a minute,' and went and instead of getting clothes he called the chief, and the chief sent soldiers and arrested the boys. He did it for me, but now that, I think of it I wish he hadn't. I was calm by this time. I asked the chief to send them back to me so that I could really see them off this time, and I was angry, but I didn't mean any harm. The chief promised to send them at noon, though he demurred and asked me if I wasn't going to kill them – in which case it would be his responsibility with the Government, you see. Well, they didn't come at noon, and I boiled over again. I meant business. I took my gun and went to the jail and called the chief, and he still said no, so I came back and called eight of my own men and told them I would be responsible if there were any trouble, and we went back and it was perfectly simple; the jailer didn't resist and the boys weren't even tied up. They were sleeping. I had them both beaten again for coming back after I told them to go away – though I was perfectly reasonable; I explained that I knew it was not their fault they had gone to jail."

"Quite, quite reasonable."

"I wanted the chief to walk with me across the river, the Locoya, and really see them off with an impressive escort. He had gone on back into his house. I went up and called; he wouldn't answer. I boiled over again, and to frighten all of them I fired three times. Had no intention of hitting him. Then I tried to open the door, but I could feel someone pushing on the other side.

"I waited a minute and rushed it with my shoulder, and this time it opened with a bang and the chief, stark naked, fell on the ground, and one of his wives ran out the back way. So I had him dress – oh, I forgot to say he snatched the gun away from me and I was too surprised to take it back for a minute, but of course I did when he dressed. He came along then, with everyone else, and his mother started to yell. She likes him, I suppose. She almost ran up and scratched my eyes out, and she kept yelling, 'My child! He's going to kill my child!' I got mad and handed the gun to her and said, 'There, protect your damned child if you want. I tell you I'm not going to hurt him.' The chief still objected, and I slapped him."

"Hard?"

"Not hard enough to knock him down. I boxed his ear. He said, 'I can't come now; my ear hurts,' and I said, 'This, then, to balance the other,' and boxed him on the other ear. His mother was almost crazy. Now that she had the gun, though, he ran away, so I had to abandon my idea. I was tired of it by that time, anyway, so I let the boys go without any more ceremony.

"Yusufu said, 'What about my clothes?'

"I told him he could have his clothes, but that he must send a friend to get them. Both boys must go away. They went off then without any more about it."

"And the chief?"

"I was really sore at him. I came back and took a shotgun and went toward his house again, but then I came to my senses and cooled off and remembered that I wasn't really quarreling with him. I went home. That's all."

"You didn't slap any of the chief's women?"

"Of course not. Why should I?"

"Well," I said after a slight pause, "I just wondered."

It was dark now, and I thought he was becoming a little more vague in his speech, but still I was interested.

"Now about my feelings. I still don't know what to do. It never occurred to me to spy on her. Thank God for the driver ants – why, I might never have found out! Never! I still don't know. I had planned to stay forever, settle down with her, but now – why should I? She's lied to me. She says now that the blood pact isn't the right thing to do between man and wife. I should have taken a crocodile tooth and said a charm, so that if she lied to me after that the tooth would wound her all over her body, under her skin, and I'd know. Or if she had a child, she said, it would not have happened because women who lie always die in childbirth. What do you think?"

"I think that sounds fishy," I said.

"So do I. Now I've figured out something else. I've begun to think that perhaps this is the first and only time it's happened, because Pantolo told me about the two men she'd lived with while I was in Europe for a year. Why should she tell me about that, which I thought was all right, and not about this? I think this way. I took her out of the bush and brought her to town, she met all the town girls and listened to them, and Satuma, who is purely a towny, helped give her ideas, and probably Kongolo was bothering her all the time and so ..."

"If it makes you feel any better," I said, "I think that it sounds reasonable enough. If it comes to that, I'm willing to believe that it's the first time she's done it."

"All that isn't so important as the way she lied and went on lying. Even now I can't believe her. She says everything in that honest way that I used to love so much. And yet, damn it, what am I going to do?"

He stopped and looked at me as if he were actually asking my advice. "Yes," he said, "I want you to tell me. I'm not saying I'll take your advice, but I want you to tell me what you really think. Should I give up my whole plan of life and go back home? Or should I stay here?"

I thought fast. I knew I had no business trying to advise a perfect stranger on a matter so fantastic yet so real to him. On the other hand, he had asked for my opinion. My honest opinion.

"Well, then, though you won't do it – I think you should go home. You're probably homesick. I honestly don't think the 'epic' is very important, unless you get put in jail. Yes, it would be good for you if they actually jailed you, which they probably won't do, however."

"Thank you. Of course I don't want to be jailed."

That ended the story, for I was getting sleepy. He bade me good night in the solemn owlish fashion that goes with mixed drinks and autobiography, and I didn't see him again. Later, I heard he got off with a sizable fine, which wasn't so bad, considering that his crime included firing a gun, breaking and entering a native house, and worst of all, slapping a native chief ...

SELECTED BIBLIOGRAPHY

MANUSCRIPT COLLECTIONS

Lilly Library, Indiana University, Bloomington, IN, Emily Hahn
  papers
Peabody Museum Archives, Harvard University, Cambridge, MA,
  Patrick L. Putnam papers

SELECTED WRITINGS BY EMILY HAHN
Books

Congo Solo: Misadventures Two Degrees North. Indianapolis: Bobbs-
  Merrill, 1933.

With Naked Foot. Indianapolis: Bobbs-Merrill, 1934.
A novel written in 1933, partly in response to the changes Hahn had
been compelled to make in her *Congo Solo* manuscript and partly
because she aspired to be a novelist. The plot deals with the white
man's experiences in colonial Africa and many of the controversial
themes and issues that had concerned Hahn during her time in the
Belgian Congo – racism, colonialism, sexism, and miscegenation.
Writing in the publication *Books* (September 30, 1934, 3), reviewer
M.C. Hubbard commented, "There it is a tale that might offend if

it were not for the vitality and deftness of the writing." While the book earned some favourable reviews, because it was published in the depths of the Great Depression it suffered the same fate as *Congo Solo*, quickly disappearing from public view. Despite this, in later years Hahn stated that *With Naked Foot* was her favourite among the fifty-three books she had written, and furthermore, it was "the best thing" she had ever written.

Africa to Me. Garden City, NY: Doubleday and Company, 1964. Following her initial visit to Africa, Hahn returned home to New York via England before embarking in 1935 on an eight-year sojourn in China and Hong Kong. She returned to Africa briefly in 1943 when the refugee ship aboard which she was returning home from Japanese-occupied Hong Kong stopped at the port of Lourenço, Marques, in Portuguese East Africa and then again at Port Elizabeth, South Africa. It was not until 1955 that Hahn visited Africa again, this time of her own volition. She returned in 1960 to attend the Independence Day festivities in the formerly British colony of Nigeria and was back again in 1962 to visit with old friends in Kenya, Tanganyika, on the island of Zanzibar (now part of Tanzania), South Africa, the former Rhodesia (now Zimbabwe), and other areas of East Africa.

To say that Hahn's interests were wide-ranging is an understatement. Among the other books that she wrote, five touched on or grew out of aspects of her African experiences and her lifelong interest in the continent. Two of these titles dealt with the wealth of natural resources that drew the European colonial powers to Africa and that continue to be at once the Congo's greatest resource and its curse. *Diamond: The Spectacular Story of the Earth's Greatest Treasures and Man's Greatest Greed* (New York: Doubleday, 1956) was an informal look at man's fascination with and lust for the precious gems that are found in many areas of Africa, while *Love of Gold* (New York: Lippincott and Crowell, 1980) traced much the same story where that lustrous metal is concerned. Three of Hahn's other books dealt with apes and monkeys: *On the Side of the Apes: A New Look at the Primates, the Men Who Study Them and What They Have Learned* (New York: Thomas Y. Crowell Company, 1971), *Look Who's Talking!* (New York: Thomas Y. Crowell Company, 1978), and *Eve and the Apes* (New York: Weidenfeld and Nicolson, 1988). At various times in her life, Hahn kept primates as pets and was fascinated by the animals, wondering about the extent of their intelligence and latent abilities to communicate with humans.

Selected Articles

"Changeover in Tanganyika." *The New Yorker*, April 27, 1953.
"Though Tribe and Tongue May Differ." *The New Yorker*, December 10, 1960.
"Theresa." *The New Yorker*, April 13, 1963.
"Stewart." *The New Yorker*, October 22, 1966.
"Pawpaw Pie." *The New Yorker*, April 15, 1967.
"Christmas with the Walkers." *The New Yorker*, May 20, 1967.
"I Say This." *The New Yorker*, July 31, 1995.

SELECTED WRITINGS OF PATRICK PUTMAN

"A Mangbetu Game." *Man* 30 (April 1930).
"Report from the Field: Wamba, Vele-Nepoko, Belgian Congo." *The New Yorker*, February 28, 1931.
"Africa May Solve Nazi Food Wants in This War." *Los Angeles News*, July 1, 1940.
"Guide pratique pour l'identification et l'exploration des essences caoutch-outifieres." *Le Courier Agricole d'Afrique* 22 (1942).
"There Is Such an Animal [Okapi]." In *Through Hell and High Water* by Members of the Explorers Club, edited by Seward S. Cramer. New York: Robert M. McBride, 1941.
"The Pigmies [*sic*] of the Ituri Forest." In *A Reader in General*

Anthropology, edited by Carleton Coon. New York: Henry Holt, 1948.

"Our Camp on the Epulu in the Belgian Congo." Co-authored with Mary Farlow Linder Putnam. Privately printed, 1933.

SELECTED BOOKS AND ARTICLES ABOUT PATRICK
PUTNAM AND HIS CONGO EXPERIENCES

Chapin, James P. "Patrick Tracy Lowell Putnam" (Obituary). *Explorers Journal* 32 (1954).

Flandrau, Grace. *Then I Saw the Congo*. London: George G. Harrap, 1929.

Hilt, Frederick J. "Hotel in the Congo." *Travel* 94, no. 10 (1950).

Longnecker, Bill. "I Lived with the White King of the Pygmies." *Bluebook* 96 (April 1953).

Mark, Joan. *The King of the World in the Land of the Pygmies*. Lincoln and London: University of Nebraska Press, 1995.

Putnam, Anne Eisner, with Allan Keller. *Madami: My Eight Years of Adventure with the Congo Pygmies*. New York: Prentice-Hall, 1954; excerpted in *Reader's Digest* 65 (October 1954).